THE
WARRIOR
STATE

THE
WARRIOR
STATE

PAKISTAN IN THE
CONTEMPORARY WORLD

T. V. PAUL

OXFORD
UNIVERSITY PRESS

OXFORD
UNIVERSITY PRESS

Oxford University Press is a department of the University of Oxford.
It furthers the University's objective of excellence in research, scholarship,
and education by publishing worldwide.

Oxford   New York
Auckland   Cape Town   Dar es Salaam   Hong Kong   Karachi
Kuala Lumpur   Madrid   Melbourne   Mexico City   Nairobi
New Delhi   Shanghai   Taipei   Toronto

With offices in
Argentina   Austria   Brazil   Chile   Czech Republic   France   Greece
Guatemala   Hungary   Italy   Japan   Poland   Portugal   Singapore
South Korea   Switzerland   Thailand   Turkey   Ukraine   Vietnam

Oxford is a registered trade mark of Oxford University Press
in the UK and certain other countries.

Published in the United States of America by
Oxford University Press
198 Madison Avenue, New York, NY 10016

Library of Congress Cataloging-in-Publication Data
Paul, T. V., author.
The warrior state : Pakistan in the contemporary world / by T. V. Paul.
pages : maps ; cm
ISBN 978–0–19–932223–7 (hardback : alkaline paper)   1. Pakistan—Politics and government.
2. Geopolitics—Pakistan. 3. National security—Pakistan. 4. War—Economic aspects. 5. Economic
development—Pakistan. I. Title.
DS383.5.A2P385 2014
954.9105—dc23
2013022390

9780199322237

1   3   5   7   9   8   6   4   2

Printed in the United States of America
on acid-free paper

CONTENTS

——————

List of Tables and Maps   vi

Maps   vii

Acknowledgments   xi

1. War and Development   1

2. The Causes   17

3. A Turbulent History   34

4. The Garrison State   69

5. The Geostrategic Urge   94

6. Religion and Politics   127

7. Comparing Pakistan   150

8. The Warrior State Today   183

Notes   199

Index   241

LIST OF TABLES AND MAPS

Table

5.1. Material Power Capabilities: India and Pakistan (2011)   109

Maps

1. Pakistan: Administrative Divisions   vii
2. Kashmir   viii
3. Pre-partition Princely States   ix
4. Expanse of Mughal Empire in India   x

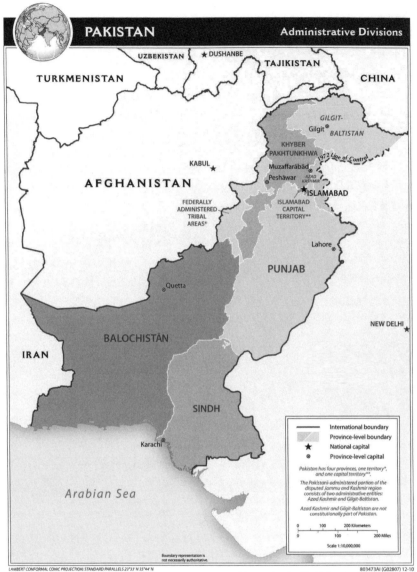

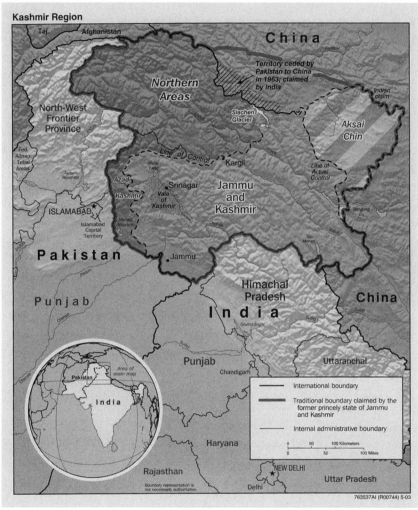

Kashmir Region

Courtesy of the University of Texas Libraries, The University of Texas at Austin

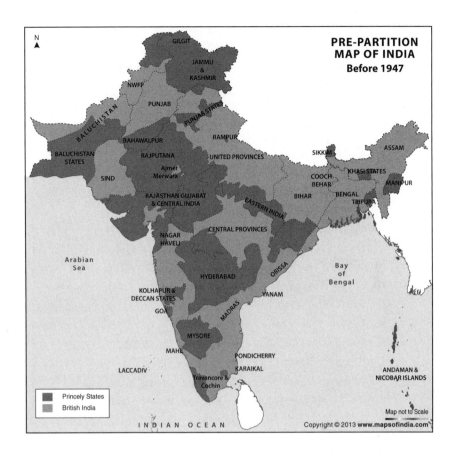

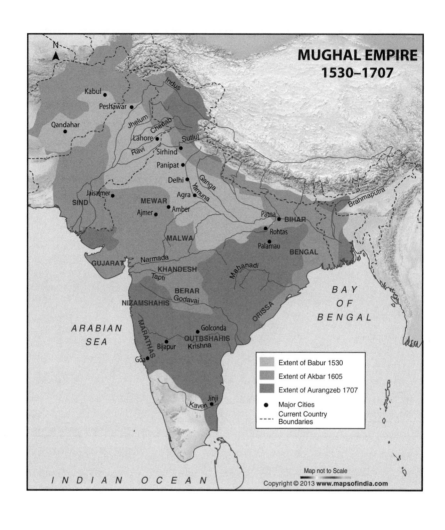

MUGHAL EMPIRE 1530–1707

N

Kabul
Peshawar
Qandahar
Indus
Jhelum
Chenab
Lahore
Ravi
Sutlul
Sirhind
Panipat
Delhi
Ganga
Yamuna
Agra
Jaisalmer
SIND
MEWAR
Ajmer
Amber
MALWA
GUJARAT
Narmada
KHANDESH
Tapti
BERAR
Godavai
NIZAMSHAHIS
MARATHAS
Bijapur
Goa
Golconda
QUTBSHAHIS
Krishna
Patna
BIHAR
Rohtas
Palamau
BENGAL
Mahanadi
ORISSA
Brahmaputra
Jinji
Kaven

ARABIAN SEA

BAY OF BENGAL

INDIAN OCEAN

Extent of Babur 1530
Extent of Akbar 1605
Extent of Aurangzeb 1707
● Major Cities
--- Current Country Boundaries

Map not to Scale

Copyright © 2013 www.mapsofindia.com

ACKNOWLEDGMENTS

THIS BOOK IS a continuation of my efforts to locate the causes and consequences of the intense internal and interstate conflicts in the South Asian region. My previous works identified sources of the India-Pakistan enduring rivalry and the weak state syndrome in the region. In this book, I make an effort to go deeper into the myriad of insecurities faced by Pakistan, a pivotal state in the region, the historically and sociologically rooted reasons for its inability to form a normal democracy, and the consequences of it persisting as a warrior state. I explain why the continued pursuit of war has not made Pakistan a cohesive strong state, unlike the developmental states of East Asia or historical states in Europe that became strong through war-making. I locate the fundamental source of the problem on the notion of a *geostrategic curse* that Pakistan is afflicted with, and the hyper realpolitik ideas that the country's elite hold in creating and maintaining a semifeudal society.

The book is the culmination of over seven years of work and during this period I benefitted immensely from exchanging ideas with many scholars and current and former policymakers from Pakistan, India, and the United States. The draft book manuscript was read by Rajesh Basrur, Maya Chadda, Stephen P. Cohen, John A. Hall, Kavita Khory, Matthew Lange, Baldev Raj Nayar, Philip Oxhorn, Norrin Ripsman, and Aseema Sinha and I owe them for many incisive comments. Seminar presentations at a joint series at MIT-Harvard-Brown, the University of Michigan, University of Hawaii, and George Washington University offered many insights, especially the comments by Robert Axelrod, John D. Ciorciari, Charles Glaser, Stephen Van Evera, Sankaran Krishna, Vipin Narang, and Philip Potter. The help of

Theodore McLauchlin and Mahesh Shankar was immense as they brought to my attention many a literature and helped shape my arguments in numerous ways. These two young scholars are models for high levels of intellectual acumen that any faculty supervisor can hope for. Over the years other graduate students Bahar Akman, Jean-François Bélanger, Mohamed Sesay, and Stéfanie von Hlatky helped me in the collection of data.

The Track-II meetings organized by Peter Jones of the University of Ottawa and Feroz Khan and James Wirtz of the Naval Postgraduate School, Monterey, enabled me to interact with several Pakistani, Indian, and American scholars and former key officials which opened up windows on how the elite in Pakistan thinks. The three anonymous readers of Oxford University Press offered useful suggestions. Don Fehr helped to navigate every step of the book submission and contracting process and David McBride has been the supportive editor at Oxford who realized the significance of this work. I also thank Tara Kennedy, publicist and Andrew Varhol, marketing manager of the press for their efforts. Research funding came from the Social Sciences and Humanities Council of Canada (SSHRC), the James McGill Chair at McGill University, and the Fonds québécois de recherche sur la société et la culture (FQRSC). The final manuscript was prepared while I was a visiting scholar at the East-West Center, Honolulu, in February 2013 and I thank the center's staff for their support. The constant support of my wife Rachel and daughters Kavya and Leah has been essential for my extensive travels and concentrated work.

Some sections of Chapter 5 are taken from my article: "Why Has the India-Pakistan Rivalry Been so Enduring? Power Asymmetry and an Intractable Conflict," *Security Studies* vol.15, no. 4 (October-December), 600–630 (author copyright from Taylor and Francis).

My aim in this book is to encourage the Pakistani elite and informed public to think hard on the nation's strategic and economic choices that were made during the past 65 years and the consequences that they have generated internally and externally. More fundamentally, I hope to open up the intellectual debate on war and state building and its relevance to the developing world in general and South Asia in particular.

T. V. Paul

Montreal, August 2013

1

War and Development

ON MAY 2, 2011, in a daring surprise military operation, 33 US Navy SEALs entered the compound of the residence of Osama bin Laden in the Pakistani garrison city of Abbottabad, shot and killed him. The US helicopters carrying the SEALs had evaded Pakistani radars when they penetrated the country's airspace. Bin Laden had reportedly been living in the compound for more than three years, just eight hundred yards from the elite Pakistan Military Academy. It is incredible to believe that elements of Pakistani intelligence and military did not know that the world's most wanted terrorist had been hiding in Pakistan for so long and so close to an important military facility. In the tumultuous aftermath of the bin Laden incident, civil-military relations in Pakistan deteriorated dramatically by fall 2011, although recovered somewhat by 2012 with the civilian government surviving the crisis. In recent years, Pakistan has approached economic collapse on several occasions, relying on life-saving support by external actors such as the United States, International Monetary Fund (IMF), the World Bank (WB), and Saudi Arabia. Natural disasters such as devastating floods have added to man-made miseries. The country is riven by a *mélange* of conflicts that pit competing ethnic and sectarian groups against each other. It is beset by violence between the state and terrorist networks, violence that inter-twines with the conflict over US-led NATO forces in Afghanistan. A continuing conflict between the elected civilian government and the judiciary added another challenge to the mix. Pakistan's condition poses major challenges to international and regional security, especially in the areas of transnational terrorism and nuclear proliferation. Pakistan is already the world's fifth largest nuclear weapons state, with about 110 nuclear weapons in its arsenal, and the prospects of these weapons falling into the wrong hands has generated a great deal of international concern.

Such developments raise some fundamental questions: Why has Pakistan become a theater of internecine violence? Why has its condition been so problematic for international security for so long? Why has it emerged as a "failing state," a state that cannot provide minimum law and order, control various competing societal forces, and survive economically without external support? Why does it remain a garrison or a heavily militarized warrior state, with an intense focus on narrowly defined national security concerns while several erstwhile military-ruled countries in Asia and Africa have become democratic and others reaped the benefits of increased global trade and investment? What sets Pakistan apart?

The story of Pakistan's checkered existence has ramifications that extend far beyond the Pakistani border. This book attempts to examine the role of war and war-making in the development of nation-states in the developing world, and the Pakistani case has much to tell us. Pakistan has devoted considerable energy into military security. Indeed, it is essentially a warrior state in many respects. But the outcome in the Pakistani case has been paradoxical. More than six decades of intense pursuit of military security has made Pakistan less secure and unified as a coherent political unit. Ironically, European history tends to show the opposite outcome: war-making was an engine for national development and consolidation. In Pakistan, however, it has not done so. The puzzle is why not. In this book, I compare Pakistan to historical and contemporary nations in order to examine the problems that war-making creates for state-building in our era. What the case shows is that excessive war-making efforts can have perverse effects on a developing country, as limited resources of the economy are siphoned off for military purposes with little, if any, long-term value for the larger society. Moreover, the public may not successfully demand economic and social reforms unlike in many war-making societies of historical Europe and contemporary East Asia.

In the post–World War II world, rapid development has come to states that engaged in deep economic interactions with the world market and transformed the competitiveness of their societies and economies by instituting universal education, health care, quality infrastructure, and land reforms. States that pursued extreme ideological or realpolitik goals have not fared well. Countries that received economic assistance from abroad for their strategic position as allies of the great powers benefited only if their leaders pursued a developmental state approach and undertook transformative policies internally. The contrasting experiences of several US allies—Japan, Israel, South Korea, and Taiwan versus Pakistan, Egypt, and the Philippines—attest to this.

For over six decades, the Pakistani elite pursued several geopolitically oriented policies at the expense of political and economic reform. The result has been domestic stagnation and even chaos. Pakistan's domestic instability, in turn, has worsened regional and global peace and security. Some of these policies looked successful from a short-term, tactical point of view, but in the long run they have only distorted the country's development and imperiled its national security (not to mention its unity). The policies of its great power patrons—the United States and China—have helped make Pakistan's development sluggish and make the state less secure. They have discouraged the Pakistani elite from undertaking the painful economic and social reforms necessary for rapid and equitable economic and political development. In fact, the elite's policies have resulted in the creation of a violent, insecure, and ideology-driven polity which is neither strong, nor prosperous, nor stably democratic, nor unified. The security they seek has been as elusive as ever. Why do elites pursue warrior state policies that do not produce long-term benefits to their society?

The answer I offer in this book, in a nutshell, is that Pakistan's elite has had both the motive and the opportunity to pursue such policies. The political elite's strategic ideas and ideological beliefs about statehood, development, and power are major factors in determining what kind of state strategy they will follow. If these ideas are based on hyper-realpolitik assumptions and deeply held ideological beliefs, devoid of prudence and pragmatism, they tend to produce unintended consequences that are often negative. Hyper-realpolitik assumptions prioritize narrow military security as an end in itself and above all other national goals, including economic welfare, irrespective of the consequences. An imbalance exists between means and ends in the security strategy and national goals that the country pursues as well. However, ideas alone are insufficient to explain national behavior over a period of time. For the elite to pursue its strategic ideas, it requires the right material and nonmaterial assets and the appropriate strategic circumstances. But provided those assets and circumstances, an ideological state with an intensely realpolitik approach to the world is free to act on it. The combination of ideas and circumstances, motive and opportunity, tells us why a country would pursue a warrior state strategy. The second important question is why that strategy does not produce desired outcomes, in contrast to the many strong, coherent, and prosperous states that emerged from war-making in historical Europe and postwar East Asia. Pakistan is the reverse image: an archetype of the perverse equation between war-making and state development today.

Since the very inception of the state in 1947, the Pakistani elite has held on to an ideologically oriented hyper-realpolitik worldview, as though chronically under siege. To be sure, over that time, Pakistanis have had a continuous debate about the best political system and institutions to achieve national security and developmental objectives. Despite this internal disagreement, dominant members of the elite have shared a particular worldview. As in Wilhelmine Germany between 1890 to 1914, this worldview has emphasized the need for a strong national security state based on military might. In addition, an Islamic religious and ideological framework served as the core of the country's nationhood and identity.[1] In this Hobbesian worldview, war is a natural state of affairs, only the fittest survive in an environment of endemic conflict, and the state should be able to advance its interests through coercive military means when necessary. From the vantage point of the Pakistani leadership, therefore, irredentist policies, that is, redeeming perceived lost territories from neighbors, has been absolutely essential for national security. Some members of the elite also developed an overly ambitious agenda due to a conception that as a state founded on the basis of Islam, Pakistan should be in the vanguard of promoting and defending Islamic values and interests on a global scale. The policies of the neighboring states, especially India, have contributed to this process, but the particular policy choice to respond militarily was largely Pakistan's own. Pakistan's leaders rarely considered nonrealpolitik strategies feasible or desirable in the context of South Asia, especially with regard to the country's relationship with its larger neighbor, India, and its smaller one, Afghanistan. What is notable is the absence of a modern developmental outlook alongside this preoccupation with military security.

Strategic circumstances have facilitated the perpetuation of this hyper–national security state approach. The rivalry with a more powerful and ideologically opposed India generated greater efforts on the part of Pakistan to compensate for its material weaknesses through a host of measures that offered a form of limited power symmetry in the military realm.[2] Pakistan has been somewhat successful in this balancing effort, but not enough to win the conflict. As the years advanced, Pakistan's difficulties in fully matching or winning its conflict with India incentivized the governing elite to look for additional coercive means relying on nonstate actors. Not surprisingly, this continuous search for strategic parity with its larger neighbor encouraged the elite to assign the utmost importance to war-making capacity. Often these efforts led to an overly ambitious agenda. It was beyond the capacity of a regional power like Pakistan to sustain this agenda without enlisting the collaboration of violent nonstate actors such as the Taliban and other militant groups.

The search for power symmetry with India has been facilitated by the geostrategic location of the country. Territorially, Pakistan is situated in the periphery of South Central Asia, a pivotal region where the interests of the great powers intersect. Geographically, it was quite close to the Soviet heartland during the Cold War. Pakistan was thus a clear choice as an ally for the United States. Pakistan's proximity to China offered it an opportunity to align with Beijing against India, taking advantage of the ongoing Sino-Indian rivalry since the early 1960s. No wonder it was called the "fulcrum of Asia." These strategic relationships brought considerable economic and military resources to Pakistan. But these were insufficient to make it a prosperous state.

Its strategic position has laid a "geostrategic curse" on Pakistan. This is similar to the idea of "resource curse." When a country is endowed with too much easily extracted natural resources and mineral assets like oil, it leaves political elites with little incentive to improve the state's economic resource base, reform its society, or develop a workforce with a variety of skills. Countries such as Saudi Arabia and Libya have been afflicted by this "resource curse," which allows them to buy off the population for a long period of time and resist instituting democratic reforms and equitable economic development policies.[3] Similarly, if a regime is well endowed in the geostrategic arena due to either its location or specific attributes regarded as valuable in great power contests, there is less of an impetus for it to prioritize internal economic development. The elite can use the rents received through strategic alignments to keep the state afloat. Pakistan, Egypt, and the Philippines under the Marcos regime attest to this pattern of development. Over the years, Pakistan's pivotal role in great power strategic contests also meant that it received vast amounts of foreign aid. Yet this has not resulted in substantial economic development. Nor has it produced much security. The United States has provided Pakistan billions of dollars in military and economic aid. Since 2001 alone, such aid has amounted to over $15 billion.[4] In Chapter 2, I expand on these themes further.

For us to understand the relationship between war and state building in the Pakistani context, a brief exploration of the European historical experience is worthwhile.

The European Experience

According to an influential school of thought, war and war preparation have been major factors in the formation of nation-states in Europe and in increasing their strength and cohesiveness over time.[5] European rulers, faced with powerful external enemies, engaged in economic, technological, and political modernization by penetrating society and centralizing the polity for the efficient extraction of resources. Another effect was winning the allegiance of their populations. The need for war preparation compelled many European states to reach deeper into the lives of their inhabitants through taxation, bureaucratization, and conscription.[6] This process had myriad consequences. The territories and populations of European countries coalesced, for example in German and Italian unification. Governmental control became centralized with coherent, bureaucratic administrations. Governments and their fiscal capacity grew; taxation ratcheted up for every successive war. War and preparing for it led to important social changes: integrating, socializing, and leveling societies.[7] The strengthening of the war-making state in Europe occurred through a multistage process that included (a) elimination of external rivals, (b) suppression or pacification of internal enemies of the state, and (c) extraction of sufficient resources for state activities from the larger population and the territories it controlled through increasing taxation.[8] Strengthening states made social pacts with powerful social groups that in turn conferred legitimacy on the state.[9] In addition, war preparation was most successful when it went along with economic development. States accumulated capital to use in areas they deemed important for the strengthening of their position vis-à-vis competing external and internal actors. They could only do so in conditions of relative economic prosperity; if an obsessive focus on security interfered with economic growth, the effect would be long-run military weakness given the reduction, over time, of its capacity to build effective armies.[10] Charles Tilly sums up this phenomenon neatly: "war made the state and the state made war."[11]

This does not mean that all European states that engaged in war-making succeeded in state building. Scholars do recognize that in some states war had a disintegrative or degenerative effect: some states were totally destroyed, while in others war catalyzed revolution, diminished state capacity, and brought about fiscal collapse.[12] The record is extensive in this regard. Several kingdoms and states vanished or transformed into different entities in Europe alone: Tolosa (418–507), Alt Clud (fifth to twelfth century), Burgundia (411–1795), Aragon (1137–1714), Litva (1253–1795), Byzantion (330–1453), Borussia (1230–1945), Sabaudia (1033–1946), Galicia (1773–1918), Etruria (1801–1814), Rosenau (1826–1918), Tsernagora (1010–1918), Rusyn (1939), Eire (1916), Austria-Hungary (1867–1918), and the Soviet Union (1924–1991).[13] Nor were all of these minor players: Austria-Hungary and the Soviet Union were, of course, great powers before they collapsed. Several others declined without disappearing, including Spain, Portugal, the Netherlands, and Sweden. Far from strengthening these states, war proved to be a catalyst for their decline. A notable example: World War I brutally exposed the weaknesses of Tsarist Russia and left it open to revolution in 1917.[14]

Thus, while war and war preparation spur development and cohesion, it could also bring about wholesale destruction and state collapse. The elimination of institutionally incoherent states that could not strengthen—Austria-Hungary again comes to mind—means that as we look back over European history, we tend to observe only those states that survived. There were plenty of weak states, but they are, by and large, no longer around to be noticed. But this very possibility of destruction was exactly how war ignited the development of those states that did adapt. It was the threat of becoming the next Byzantium or Burgundy that prompted reform in France and Germany. The demands of war in these cases encouraged states to create institutions and structures that offered legitimacy and monopoly rights to nation-states as the key protector and security provider. External threats also acted as catalysts for the deepening of nationalism and internal cohesiveness, as they reduced the viability of the "exit" option and suppressed "voice," thus leaving "loyalty" of the population to the central government as the only alternative.[15] The development of nationalism, based on a shared sense of identity, was a significant outcome of this process. Is this European experience unique?

A cursory look at the developing world suggests that war and war preparation have not produced similar instances of positive results among many of the newly emerging states as it did in the European context. In fact, war-making efforts have led many developing states to decay and failure.[16] Some studies suggest that states in the developing world have not strengthened because they have not repeated the European experience. While there has been no lack of war, the postcolonial developing world has been largely free of *conquest*, unlike Europe. Jeffrey Herbst argues that Africa never experienced the wars of conquest that occurred in Europe because of low population densities and abundant vacant land. The rulers focused all their attention on the capital cities and urban centers, leaving the hinterland underdeveloped.[17] Similarly, Miguel Centeno contends that the relative weakness of Latin American states has been due to their incapacity to wage big interstate wars. Because of their weak capabilities, they could not prevent recurring internal conflicts, civil wars, and political violence.[18] While these arguments sound plausible, there is a problem of circularity in them. They imply that original weakness did not allow the states to wage big wars, which in turn caused these countries to remain weak. Another problem is the assumed inevitability of a positive correlation between war and state strength without giving allowance to war's ruinous consequences, even for strong states. France exhausted itself in World War I, Britain in World War II—and they were the *winners*. The Soviet Union drove its economy into the ground to keep up its military preparations. Not all warrior states turn war-making into development. And not all survive. Hence the great unpredictability associated with war-making as a source of state strength and cohesion.

In the same way, it has hardly been from a *lack* of war preparation that Pakistan has stagnated as a state. We see from European history that external insecurity does not necessarily spur internal development. Rather, I argue that it was the kind of war preparation that Pakistan has engaged in that yielded its present predicament. In a continuous obsession with external threat and short-run power politics, all underwritten by external support, Pakistan has neglected long-term economic development. Especially in the contemporary global economy, this has proven a fatal error. Military security has always had an economic basis, and states neglect the goal of increasing prosperity at their peril.[19] The imperative to prosper through trade and investment is larger than ever.

Strong and Weak States

The measure of success or failure of the state is based on its ability to provide political goods such as internal security, the opportunity for citizens to resolve their disputes with the state and their fellow citizens without recourse to violence, enforceable rule of law, and popular participation in the political process. A strong state is also able to offer public goods, such as education, healthcare, and physical infrastructure. A state is considered "weak" or "failing" if it is not able to offer most of these public goods.[20] The relative autonomy of the state from dominant social classes that live within it is necessary to determine how strong the state is, for a dominant social class will require the state to make policy for the benefit of a small minority rather than for the general good.[21] A strong state has the capability to effect significant social change through state planning and policies, the regulation of social relationships, the extraction of resources, and sometimes coercion. In essence, weak states lack the ability to do these things.[22]

Weak states also tend to have little or no effective control over some parts of their territory. In such areas, the state may have *de jure* authority, but *de facto* power lies with local groups that may not show allegiance to the state. Colonial history is part of the story here: colonial powers drew lines on maps for their own convenience, rather than for what could easily be controlled by a postcolonial government. However, the state's insufficient capabilities in military and civilian institutions are also a primary source of this absence of governmental control. When confronting such regions, states face a difficult challenge: their efforts to integrate their territories can result in repressive measures that alienate the population even further. This "state strength dilemma" can keep states weak.[23] And war-making efforts can likewise weaken states because they bring along several social, economic, and political pathologies in their train.

Despite the fact that much of the state strength in nineteenth century Europe came from war-making efforts, this strategy probably reached its apogee with World War II. Since the war, legitimacy has become more important to state-building. Legitimacy can come from a combination of democracy and welfare, as in Western Europe, or rapid economic development through trade and investment as in East Asia; but one way or another, the state must now provide its citizens with clear benefits. The Western European states reinvented themselves by adding "welfare" to their core functions. They also adopted a liberal-democratic model of governance, adding additional layers of legitimacy to the state. Most Western European states also embraced the three core principles of Immanuel Kant's model for perpetual peace—democracy, economic interdependence, and international institutions—and managed to create a separate peace for their area where organized violence among states is unthinkable.[24] Many of them have also expanded their trading and commercial links with the rest of the world. Their notion of state strength has therefore changed as a result. This transformed view varies greatly from traditional understandings of the strong state as a coercive institution demanding obedience from its citizenry. While there have been antecedents—states that strengthened through legitimacy derived from popular representation and prosperity[25]—it is since World War II that these concepts have taken center stage. In this new perspective, a state's capacity is also a function of its ability to impose its will legitimately and offer public goods to the extent that almost all of society view the state's role positively. Loyalty comes through the benefits that the citizenry receives from the state.

In the post–World War II era, war-making has become ever more counterproductive for state capacity. Excessive focus on national security can destroy a state, as it happened in the case of the Soviet Union.

A state that overmilitarizes itself can seriously hamper state capacity as well as political and economic development. Faster economic development in the postwar era has required integration into the global economic order and the adoption of a developmental state strategy,[26] as in the cases of many of the newly industrializing states in East and Southeast Asia. Granted, states like South Korea and Taiwan, developmental states par excellence, have focused on active military preparations to face existential threats. Crucially, however, neither allowed security to get in the way of prosperity. While each has faced periodic crises with their respective adversaries, neither has engaged in nearly the same degree of open and covert conflict as Pakistan. Neither has fought a full-scale war since 1953. Pakistan and India have fought four. Neither has become embroiled in other regional conflicts, proxy wars, or the promotion of insurgencies, unlike Pakistan's involvement in Afghanistan and Kashmir.

If economic growth is rapid enough, it can to some extent provide an alternative to democracy as a source of legitimacy. Fast growth has taken place in "developmental states," a category that includes nondemocracies and democracies alike.[27] Thus formerly authoritarian Korea and Taiwan and democratic Israel may have become strong states in the war-making context, but they are also states that offer many public goods to the citizenry such as education, healthcare, near-universal employment, and a high standard of living. Economic growth, in turn, can be endangered by a developing state's excessive preoccupation with military and security issues and entanglement in geopolitical conflicts of the great powers, especially if its elites ignore developmental challenges. A developing state, even when it faces powerful external security threats, can grow fast only if it has an economic strategy that makes use of its potential niche in the global marketplace. Such a strategy is sustainable only if the developing country institutes substantial internal reforms that utilize its workforce for modern industrial purposes and make its domestic market business and welfare friendly. State building thus no longer results from a purely coercive capacity but the integrative power of the state drawn from its willingness and ability to invest in its people. During ordinary times, citizens want to know what the state can do for their economic and social welfare and if state elites continuously falter in this mission, they may simply fail to achieve the national cohesion that is essential for building a strong state. This I believe is the fundamental change from the nineteenth century European state to the late twentieth century state. State capacity in today's world can be judged on the basis of the ability of a state to develop and implement policies in order to provide collective goods such as security, order, and welfare to its citizens in a legitimate and effective manner untrammeled by internal or external actors.[28]

How do these arguments explain the Pakistani predicament?

Pakistan's Development

Since its arrival as a nation-state after a bloody partition from India in 1947, Pakistan has been extraordinarily obsessed with security and particularly the military balance with its neighbor. India was nearly four times larger before the 1971 secession of East Pakistan, and since then has been six to eight times larger in most parameters of national strength, for example, size, population, and economy. Pakistan has fought four wars with India—1947–1948, 1965, 1971, and 1999—of which it initiated three (the exception was 1971). Pakistan has also engaged in protracted asymmetric warfare by training and sending insurgents into Indian-controlled Kashmir since 1989. The military elite has attempted continuously to obtain security by striving for strategic parity with its larger neighbor through arms buildup, alignment with great powers, acquisition of nuclear weapons, offering a home base for transnational terrorist networks, engaging in terrorism on its own, and initiating wars and crises to extract territorial concessions. However, war-making in this case appears to have come with strong negatives. It has generated continuous military rule, stunting the growth of a healthy civil society. More specifically, it has destroyed the chances of democracy and civilian institutions taking root, hampered rapid economic growth, and created a garrison state that is bureaucratic and excessively focused on military control over all domains of society.

The enormous focus on external threats has not, as one might have imagined, helped to develop a cohesive nation-state or national unity, bridging ethnic and political divisions for the sake of defense against India. Within 25 years of its emergence as a nation-state, Pakistan lost its eastern portion of Bengal to secession and war, while the western part has experienced several ongoing subnational autonomy movements.

The loss of East Pakistan was largely the result of the efforts by the West Pakistani military and political elite to deprive the eastern side of political and economic autonomy and democratic rights. Granted, external military intervention by India was essential for the bifurcation of Pakistan in 1971. However, fundamentally secession was the result of an excessive focus on military solutions to a political problem: the participation and representation of the large Bengali population.

In 2012, Pakistan is one of the weakest states globally. Its armed forces do not have full control of several parts of the country, especially the northwest areas, with the Taliban forces having occupied over 30% of Pakistani territory in 2009. Pakistan appears among the top of various indexes on state weakness. For instance, the "Failed State Index," an annual report of most failed states by *Foreign Policy* magazine, places Pakistan at number 12 in 2011. This was actually a slight improvement from previous years: Pakistan ranked tenth in 2009 and 2010 and ninth in 2008. This index lists countries' performances in the area of stability on the basis of vulnerability criteria such as refugee flows, poverty, group grievances, factionalism within its elite, the quality of public services, and the capacity of the security apparatus.[29] It should, however, be noted that Pakistan has conventional and nuclear capability sufficient to wage traditional warfare with India, as well as deter its larger neighbor from launching a major attack. Indeed, Pakistan's capabilities are lopsided: it can hold its own against India but is severely constrained in counterinsurgency warfare at home. Pakistan has also faced major difficulties in overcoming the state-to-nation imbalance— that is, there is a mismatch between the formal territorial state and the national groups living in it.[30] This imbalance has also been exacerbated by the elite's active support for territorial revisionism within the region, especially vis-à-vis India and Afghanistan. The blowback effects from these efforts have only increased ethnic and communal problems within Pakistan.

Today, powerful warlords control many parts of the country. The central leadership has little sway over the northwestern areas, while extremist Islamic groups such as the Taliban have become key players in the political system. Conflicts between the key sectarian groups, Sunnis and Shias, and by ethnic groups such as Mohajirs (7.57% of the population) and Baloch (3.57%) have made many Pakistani cities like Karachi,

Peshawar, and Quetta unsafe for their inhabitants. In addition, key ethnic groups such as the Baloch, Sindhis (14.1%), Pashtuns (15.42%), and Seraikis (8.38%) demand autonomy from the Punjabi-dominated (44.68%) country, some more forcefully than others.[31]

What is most puzzling is the insufficiency of Islam as a factor in gluing together the Pakistani society. Neither the national security state approach nor the use of religion has pacified the class and ethnic divisions of Pakistan. Economic benefits have been unevenly divided, making some ethnic groups less successful than others. Most of the ruling class, including the military elite, has always come from the province of Punjab. Before East Pakistan's secession in 1971, that ruling class showed little interest in improving the conditions of Bengalis. Since then it has similarly neglected a just resolution of simmering conflicts in Balochistan and Sindh, among others. The fiercely independent Pashtun tribes in the northwest were never pacified, and the state has not offered a compelling economic or political model to them. More generally, successive rulers of Pakistan followed policies that negatively impacted political and economic development, integration, and long-term security. As a result, Pakistan has fallen behind many of its peers in Asia and Latin America in the arena of economic development despite showing some signs of progress in the 1960s. In 2012 Pakistan stood at 124 among 144 countries in the global competitiveness index.[32] The 2013 Human Development Report assigns Pakistan the 146th rank out of 186 countries (placing it in the lowest category) on the basis of indicators such as life expectancy at birth, mean and expected years of schooling, and per capita income.[33] It is indeed one of the least globalized countries in terms of the core economic categories of trade and investment.

A deeper understanding of Pakistan's development has immense policy significance in the age of transnational terrorism and nuclear proliferation; in both areas, Pakistan has emerged as the single most important source of challenge.[34] Since the 1990s, Pakistan has become the world's biggest hotbed of transnational terrorism, with the connivance of elements of the state. Since 2001, it has also become the home of al-Qaeda and Taliban forces waging war on the Western coalition protecting the Karzai regime in Afghanistan. It has also posed a major challenge in nuclear proliferation, with the A. Q. Khan network illegally transferring nuclear materials to countries such as North Korea, Iran, and Libya. In 2011 Pakistan possessed some 110 nuclear weapons, making it the fifth largest nuclear weapons state. Yet unlike almost every other nuclear state, there is a potential for state failure and the weapons falling into the hands of Islamic radicals.[35] Understanding why this has happened is important for policymakers everywhere.

The larger implication is that the European example of state building is *sui generis* and historically contingent, and has serious weaknesses when applied to either non-European contexts or different time periods.[36] Barring exceptional cases, war and war preparation do not make a state strong. At the very least, the connection between war and development of a strong state must be approached with care: war-making states in the contemporary era have prospered in the face of serious security threats, but largely through restraint and refraining from a hypersensitive approach to security. Continuous preparation for war is an unattractive model, especially in comparison to the generally developmental (or trading) state approach that other nations have followed in recent decades. As the Pakistani case shows, if a state fails to innovate, it can become a geopolitical and security nightmare for its neighbors, other states, and—not least—itself. At a minimum, states need to keep security competition under control or—failing that—compartmentalize it to achieve rapid economic growth and political development. At the policy level, decision-makers need to understand better the negative impact of foreign aid, excessive defense spending, and the pursuit of hyper-realpolitik national security policies.

In the next seven chapters I elucidate on the themes discussed above. I clarify the causes of the Pakistan syndrome, outline the turbulent history of Pakistan, and develop the reasons for its emergence as a garrison state. In the process, I focus on its occasional hybrid democratic governments, the geostrategic impulse that generates the war-making dynamics in Pakistan, and the role of political Islam in Pakistan's development. In addition, I present a short comparison with three Muslim-majority states, Turkey, Indonesia, and Egypt, and two non-Muslim states, South Korea and Taiwan (both of which experienced intense military conflicts somewhat similar to Pakistan), to see why these nations ended up on paths so divergent from the one Pakistan took. In the concluding chapter, I consider the larger implications of the Pakistan model as well as the effects of war and war-making on nation-states in the twenty-first century. Ultimately, we need to know why Pakistan has not made it in the modern world as a strong state and why its model of statecraft and development strategy has become archaic and why it needs fundamental rethinking on the part of its elite and its people if it ever wants to emerge as a peaceful state.

2

The Causes

IN THE MIDNIGHT HOUR of October 4, 2003, a container ship was diverted to the Italian port of Taranto where agents from the American Central Intelligence Agency (CIA) and Britain's MI6 seized five containers destined for Libya in which they found centrifuges to enrich uranium. The materials originated from the network run by Abdul Qadeer Khan, father of Pakistan's nuclear bomb, the world's deadliest and most successful nuclear proliferation ring.[1] Despite this enormous discovery, the United States did not do much to get to the bottom of the scandal, although Washington imposed sanctions on some 13 members of the ring and three companies associated with it.[2] Barring three in Switzerland, no Khan network member has yet been prosecuted successfully, although the International Atomic Energy Agency (IAEA) has been instrumental in enabling some arrests. The George W. Bush administration has been accused of hampering investigations by the Swiss authorities by refusing to provide information to arrest key members of the ring.[3] A.Q. Khan was first pardoned by President Pervez Musharraf in February 2004, but under pressure from the US and IAEA he was placed under house arrest as a scapegoat for five years. In February 2009, he was released from house arrest by President Musharraf, but Pakistan refused to allow him to be interviewed by US law-enforcement officers or IAEA officials.[4]

In March 2003, the United States went to war with Iraq on its alleged nuclear weapons program and has locked horns with North Korea and Iran over their nuclear plans for over two decades. Washington put comprehensive sanctions on Libya as well, and forced the Moammar Gaddafi regime to abandon its nuclear program in December 2003. Why then has Pakistan been let off scot-free, despite being the biggest source of nuclear proliferation in the contemporary era? Why does it remain one of the largest recipients of American aid? The answer lies in Pakistan's geostrategic salience and its elite's willingness and ability to carry out or thwart US policy objectives in the region. Pakistan receives rents for its geopolitical services to the great powers and this has discouraged its leaders from undertaking a more sustainable developmental path. I term this phenomenon "geostrategic curse" and attribute it as fundamentally one of the major reasons for Pakistan remaining a quintessential warrior state, unable to transform itself into a proper democracy or a developmental state.

The "Geostrategic Curse"

Pakistan has simultaneously been blessed and cursed with geostrategic importance for the great powers due to its location and the willingness of its elite to play geopolitical games. But while this geostrategic centrality may have benefited the military, it has not helped the ordinary people of Pakistan. Despite periodic ups and downs in their relationship, during the Cold War era, Pakistan became a key US ally and, beginning in mid-1950s, provided base facilities for spying operations against the Soviet Union. In the 1980s it served as a conduit for the supply of weapons and funds to the Afghan resistance against Soviet occupation. Participation in the geopolitical competition between the US and USSR brought billions of dollars and modern weapons to Pakistan. The military and political elites who gained materially from this interaction had little reason to innovate in either the economy or the political sphere. Nor did they have to reform the semifeudal landlord system in order to extract resources from it. Foreign support was largely sufficient to pay the costs of waging war externally and buttress the warrior state internally. In essence, Pakistan became a *rentier* state, living off the rents provided by its external benefactors for supporting their particular geostrategic goals.[5] The Pakistanis did not follow European examples of internal extraction or the East Asian model of internal innovation and external trade. As the military elite came to dominate the economic and political systems, they had the most to lose if any major economic reform efforts were undertaken. Thus the military-bureaucratic elites have little incentive to develop a liberal economic or political order; it would only undercut their paramount position in Pakistani society. Similar to the oil-rich sheikdoms' "resource curse," geopolitical prominence inflicts a "curse" on a semifeudal state with an intense national-security approach.

Foreign aid curse and *resource curse* are much-discussed concepts in comparative development and sociology. Despite some immediate benefits, excessive foreign aid can generate a number of long-term problems for a country. It can exert a negative impact on democratic institutions and economic development as governments are not under pressure to reform their economic policies or political institutions. As the ruling elites know foreign powers and agencies will bail them out, they can develop the license to spend and cultivate patron-client relationships with important societal sections such as businesses and landed aristocracy.[6]

The easy money that comes from abundant natural resources such as oil has similarly correlated with several pathologies. It is associated with authoritarianism because control over the funds that come from single-resource economies strengthens incumbents. The additional resources allow them to repress dissidents and provide patronage to potential challengers. It hinders the development of the strong and independent middle classes and organized labor movements that are necessary for democracy. At the same time, it undermines the stability necessary for democracy.[7] Many such countries are prone to civil wars as different interest groups jockey to gain access to the wealth generated through natural resources.[8] It has been shown that in Africa alone resource-poor countries such as Benin, Mali, and Madagascar have undergone democratic reforms while resource-rich countries such as Nigeria and Gabon have experienced a decline of democracy.[9]

Similar to natural resources, a state can get easy money because of its vital geostrategic position. Realizing it is extremely valuable to powerful allies, the state's elite does not need to make long-term investments in institutional reform or development in order to survive in the international arena. Instead, it can take advantage of external assistance. This geostrategic curse helps explain why an obsessive focus with military security has failed to make Pakistan more secure or economically prosperous. A clear manifestation of this phenomenon is evident in the low levels of tax collections by the Pakistani state.

Pakistan is one of the world's least effective tax-collecting states. Many of the rich—including the political elite—pay no taxes. According to a *New York Times* report in July 2010, less than 2% of the 170 million Pakistanis paid income taxes. Only 2.5 million were registered to pay taxes although some 10 million should be. This placed Pakistan among one of the lowest tax-paying countries in the world and in terms of taxes as a ratio of the gross domestic product it scored slightly below Sierra Leone.[10] Pakistan also receives a substantial amount in foreign remittances from Pakistanis working abroad, which only exacerbates the easy money problem. Remittances further decrease the incentive for internal development or the building of capacity of the state to collect taxes.[11] The absence of a proper tax regime makes the governments less accountable to the population. Moreover, it reduces the legitimacy of the government as it does not need to develop larger roots in society.[12]

Between 1960 and 2012 Pakistan received from bilateral and multilateral sources some $73.1 billion (2001 prices). The United States provided over 30% of this aid, with Japan, France, United Kingdom, Germany, the International Development Association (IDA) of the WB, and the IMF serving as other sources. Between 2002 and 2010, Pakistan obtained more than $2 billion per year on average from the United States. Three-quarters of that amount was for military purposes. Only one-tenth was for development (though this proportion has been increasing).[13] According to one study, "the benefits of this aid flows have not stretched to the whole society, which means that foreign aid has failed to improve the economic conditions in Pakistan." The literacy rate still hovers around 50%, while other social indicators, such as employment, health, education, and so forth, show similar stagnation, and even decline, "leaving Pakistan at par with some of the poorest African countries. Pakistan ranks 120th in the human development index constructed by UNDP [United Nations Development Programme]." Foreign aid, in short, has been little used for the development of the economy.[14] Elsewhere, it has been argued that though aid has driven some economic growth in Pakistan, it has also reduced savings rates and led to long-run problems in debt repayment.[15] Some have argued that from early on, Pakistan's development has been shaped by external donors as the elite formulated a policy called "functional inequality" in collaboration with the donors. This policy has been focused on income redistribution in favor of profits in order to raise private savings, and it has been one that benefited the higher income groups of the society. This policy neglected health and education, although this has changed slightly since the late 1980s. Policy conditionality was rarely part of the donors' emphasis given their focus on geopolitical issues.[16]

Pakistan's alliance relationship with the United States has been pivotal in gaining aid from other nations and international institutions. In conjunction with the United States, allies such as the United Kingdom, Germany, and Japan would also offer financial support to Pakistan, especially during periods when Pakistan was crucial to US geopolitical interests. International financial institutions such as the IMF and the WB often took cues from Washington to offer financial aid to Pakistan. The aid has provided legitimacy to the military regimes in particular. In the past, even private investors went by US official declarations of stability offered by military regimes.[17]

If aid has not helped the Pakistani people, whom has it benefited? The answer seems to be the political and economic elite of Pakistan itself. A study on US military aid to Pakistan since September 11, 2001, has concluded that such aid has in fact disincentivized democratization and that the Pakistani military has not used most of the funds for fighting terror, as promised. Rather, it has engaged in corrupt practices, rendering counter-terrorism efforts a failure. As the study concludes, "over half of the money—54.9 percent—was spent on fighter aircraft [such as F-16 and other systems including antiship, antimissile capabilities], over a quarter—26.62 percent—on support and other aircraft, and 10 percent on advanced weapons systems," all meant to fight India rather than terrorist outfits.[18]

A key effect of the "geostrategic curse" is the tendency to continue on the same path of easy money. The Pakistani elite has exhibited a tendency to play "double games" as a way to extract financial resources from its key allies, especially the United States. This is because of a conviction that if the security problem is fully solved then the external ally will shun Pakistan. Viewed in this way, the continuation of the security problem is in the material and corporate interests of the army and the national security establishment. However, the preexisting cleavages in the Pakistani society have been aggravated by the elite's excessive focus on national security threats and the adoption of a hyper-realpolitik strategy to face them. Not all of Pakistan's population has felt the threats the same way. Indeed, as in the case of the Bengali population of East Pakistan, much of the population has itself constituted a threat in the state's eyes. The state's response to its threats has often generated intense internal polarization and violence. The military's desire to maintain a semifeudal system that benefited its own class interests resulted in negligible socioeconomic progress.

As the prime beneficiary of the *rentier* state attributes of the Pakistani economy, the military has displayed little interest in improving the extractive and integrative powers of the state, let alone transforming Pakistani society. Foreign economic and military aid as well as remittances from expatriate Pakistanis have discouraged the military and civilian elites from undertaking the key economic and social reforms necessary for export-driven growth. Unlike European states that became strong through war-making efforts, Pakistan never equated economic sovereignty with national sovereignty. "Export or die" was the mantra that East Asian states adopted, symbolizing the powerful equation of trade with national survival. From the beginning, the Pakistani elite failed to offer effective leadership to change the system because they regarded foreign alliances and aid as sufficient for maintaining their geopolitical status. Elite neglect of social development thus mattered, but social divisions and the relative absence of civil society institutions made the task of development even more difficult.

The frequent military coups and subsequent military rule did not help matters either in terms of getting out of the geostrategic curse. External security threats, both presumed and actual, have been the basis for both Pakistan's frequent episodes of military rule and its inability to develop a viable democratic order. Even when civilian governments were in charge, the military never gave up control, resulting in a hybrid governance structure.[19] The military became the strongest political and economic actor in Pakistan as a result of this preoccupation with security. Active involvement in proxy wars and insurgencies such as in Afghanistan and Kashmir created a massive infrastructure for terrorism and violence while weapons flowed into the Pakistani society, and parallel forms of authority emerged over time. The state has not been able to assert its power over civil society. Multiple forms of violence emanating from different sectarian groups characterize Pakistani society today, which have further eroded the authority of the state.

The military is not only the security provider but has also emerged as a key economic force in Pakistani society. Senior military officers are given land grants by the state, and over the years they have emerged as a major land-owning class. They have a presence in all other key businesses as well.[20] The economic domination of the military class has meant that major economic changes like those undertaken by Korea and Taiwan are not in the interests of the military elite. The semifeudal land-owning system is thus perpetuated in order to protect the interests of that elite. Since the 1980s, the military has also made pacts with radical Islamic and ethnic-based groups with no interest in modernizing society in order to continue their rule, to persist in their struggle against India, and to obtain strategic depth in Afghanistan.[21] These extremist groups do seek social transformation but not on a developmental path. Instead they hope to transform Pakistan into a bastion of fundamentalist Islam or an Islamic emirate while they struggle against one another as well as with India and the West. The notion of a welfare or developmental state does not appear in the lexicon of the Pakistani elite's calculations.

The Role of Ideas

The second key factor in understanding Pakistan's dilemma is in the realm of ideas and strategic assumptions. Ideas, defined as "shared beliefs," provide the basis for the elite's understanding of the cause and effect of national issues and their solutions. The core ideas provide the rationale for pursuing particular national strategies and agendas. They can act as "blinders" on the elite and help reduce the number of alternative courses of action they would consider facing a situation.[22] Exploring ideas thus offers an understanding of the elite's policy preferences and the specific goals they seek. They are also reflected in the institutions elites create and the methods they adopt to achieve their national goals and objectives.[23] In this sense, shared ideas that the elites hold about their particular situation affect their strategies in dealing with it. Over a period of time, ideas also get embedded in institutional structures, assuming rigidity until new ideas emerge that can uproot the existing ones.

The dominant idea of the Pakistani elite is drawn heavily from a Hobbesian worldview with a religious coloration. From this perspective, intense conflict is the nature of inter-state politics and the preservation of the state from predatory adversaries is the primary function of the state. The Hobbesian world is characterized by extreme enmities as the enemies are presumed to deny existential right to oneself and would not limit using unlimited violence.[24] International relations are characterized by a state of war of all against all; a period of peace is an interval to the next war; state interests are zero sum (i.e., interests of one state preclude the interests of the other); and a state is free to pursue its goals vis-à-vis another without moral or legal considerations.[25] This is in contrast to the Lockean worldview, where rivalry can exist but is not based on unlimited violence or the fear of the enemy's willingness to deny one the right to sovereignty. The Kantian worldview is the most advanced in terms of cooperation as states settle disputes without war and would fight as a team against a common enemy.[26]

In subsequent chapters I will discuss the reasons why the Pakistani elite has developed a Hobbesian worldview, and why Lockean or Kantian views have little room in their perspectives. The perceived existential rivalry with a larger India and the desire to achieve strategic parity with this neighbor are the main source of the Pakistani elite's mindset. However, some Islamic notions of warfare are also deeply entrenched in this worldview, given Islam's experience of expansion from a small region of Arabia in the face of enormous challenges and larger and stronger enemies.

Stephen P. Cohen, a leading scholar on Pakistan, has identified the core ideas driving the security oriented approach of the Pakistani "establishment," which really consists of a small group of 500-odd decision makers. These ideas—"operational codes"—have undergone some changes over the years, but most have remained stable. According to this logic, the chief national security problem is the military threat from India. This threat requires the army to hold the dominant position in domestic society, both in terms of political clout and resource allocation. The army also demands that Kashmir be incorporated to fulfill the original vision of Pakistan and sees other Islamic countries as Pakistan's natural allies. The armed forces of Pakistan are the model for Pakistani society as a whole: "selfless, disciplined, obedient, and competent." Deep-rooted social or economic reforms, including land reforms and universal literacy, are too risky to pursue for a country already facing massive external threats. The state must give the Pakistanis correct history lessons through tight control over the media and academia. Many of these ideas on governance are paternalistic and heavily borrowed from the policies of the British Raj.[27]

The key approach to security that prevails among the Pakistani elite, then, has several deeper elements.

First, the Pakistani state is a successor to the millennia-old Muslim rule in South Asia, especially the Mughal Empire.[28] Iqbal Akhund puts it neatly: "The Pakistani Muslim thinks of himself as heir to the Muslim empire, descended from a race of conquerors and rulers."[29] At independence many Pakistanis considered Mohamed Ali Jinnah as a successor to the great Mughal emperors and they wanted him to reestablish the Muslim glory which had disappeared since the eighteenth century and in particular after the 1857 Mutiny, when the British took away many privileges of the ruling Muslims monarchies.[30]

Second, Pakistan is a state built for the protection of Muslim interests (largely Sunni) and not other religious groups. This means minorities within the country (including other Muslim denominations such as Shia and Ahmadi) are expected to accept a subsidiary role. General Muhammad Zia-ul-Haq states this in the context of the military in an extreme version:

> The professional soldier in a Muslim army, pursuing the goals of a Muslim state, CANNOT become 'professional' if in all his activities he does not take on 'the color of Allah.' The non-military citizen of a Muslim state must, likewise, be aware of the kind of soldier that his country must produce and the ONLY pattern of war that his country's armed forces may wage.[31]

Third, as a state built on Islamic principles it should also strive for the protection of Islamic ideas and fellow Muslim countries on a global scale. This was especially evident in the policies of Zulfikar Ali Bhutto following the 1971 war with India.[32] Many Pakistanis believe that similar to Western countries' support for democratic groups across the world, Pakistan, founded on Islamic identity, has a "civilizational responsibility" to support Islamic causes at home and abroad.[33] More extreme positions include that of Zia-ul-Haq, who "dreamed like a Mughal emperor of recreating a 'Sunni Muslim space between infidel Hindustan,' 'heretic' [because Shia] Iran, and 'Christian Russia.'" He also hoped that "the message of the Afghan Mujahedeen would spread into Central Asia, revive Islam, and create a new Pakistan-led Islamic block of nations."[34]

Fourth, the conflict with India is natural, and to avoid defeat strategic parity and a balance of power with its larger neighbor are necessary. Such parity is both achievable and a desirable objective even if it exacts a high cost on the state and society.[35] While the size differential with India is large, it can be overcome through pursuing asymmetric strategies, alliance relationships with major powers, and the acquisition of advanced weapons systems (including nuclear arms). Further, religious and ideological strength adds to Pakistan's balancing efforts.

Fifth, India is unlikely to honor the partition agreement of 1947 permanently and may even attempt to overturn it. Hence, the defense of the country against India should always be the priority of the Pakistani state. Statements by Hindu fundamentalists on "Akhand Bharat" (Greater India) and India's past interventionist policies in East Pakistan, Sri Lanka, and Maldives are evidence of this Indian mindset. There is also a belief that one day Hindu India (due to its inherent contradictions emanating from the caste system and communal and regional differences) will decline and will be forced to concede as previous Indian rulers did in military encounters with Islamic invaders during the previous millennium. Accordingly, Pakistan, especially since the time of Zia-ul-Haq, pursued a two-track policy of engaging in clandestine operations to weaken India while appearing to be willing to negotiate peace. The former Pakistani ambassador to the US Hussain Haqqani revealed a number of Pakistani military writings to this effect. They suggested that India has many weaknesses and cutting India down to its proper size was feasible.[36] Lieutenant Colonel Javed Hassan, who studied more than two thousand years of Indian history for the army's Faculty of Research and Doctrinal Studies, claimed that "India has a poor track record at projection of power beyond its frontier and what is worse a hopeless performance in protecting its own freedom and sovereignty" (although Hindus show "incorrigible militarism"). In addition, India has not been able to "resort to the warfare of the weak" and lacks "revolutionary fervor." India has thus "displayed consistent failure" in the "use of violence as a means to the achievement of the aim."[37] Haqqani's conversations with figures like former Inter-Services Intelligence (ISI) chief Hamid Gul also support Hassan's argument that "India was hostage to a centrifugal rather than a centripetal tradition," and "with some encouragement, the alienated regions of India could become centers of insurgencies that would, at best, dismember India and, at last weaken India's ability to seek regional dominance for years to come."[38] Many who argue for balancing India believe that in the longer run Pakistan is the "sturdier of the two states, even if it is smaller, because of its religious unity and strong international friends." Hence in the "longer term India will be the first to crack."[39] Some hardliners believe that the Indian political system is not viable, its "loose federalism" is a sign of weakness. Also, they think that India can be intimidated by force and Pakistan's possession of a larger nuclear force than India allows it to engage in lower level military probes such as the 1999 Kargil operations.[40]

Sixth, as the weaker aggrieved party, striking first is needed and the use of force for territorial recovery is a justifiable strategy, morally, and ethically. This has a religious sanctity as well. In the book, *The Quranic Concept of War*, Brigadier S. K. Malik states:

> The Holy Quran wishes to see the Muslim armies always in an upper-most, dominating and commanding position over those of their adversaries. . . The Book wants the Muslims to retain the initiative to themselves through bold, aggressive but calculated and deliberate planning and conduct of war. We shall later see that, despite the gross inferiority of his numbers and material, the Holy Prophet (peace be upon him) never let the initiative to pass on to his adversaries.[41]

Seventh, Afghanistan should under all circumstances be brought within the Pakistani orbit, lest India make it its ally and thereby upset Pakistan's security on both borders. Afghanistan provides strategic depth in the contestation with India. Finally, peace with India and Afghanistan is desirable, but only if they concede territory and largely on Pakistani terms. Gaining contested territory from India is also necessary for preventing Indian hegemony in the region. Zulfikar Ali Bhutto's views represent this strand of thinking within the Pakistani elite: "If a Muslim majority area can remain a part of India, then the *raison d'être* of Pakistan collapses . . . Pakistan is incomplete without Jammu and Kashmir both territorially and ideologically . . . [Accepting the Indian control of Jammu and Kashmir] would be the first major step in establishing Indian leadership in our parts, with Pakistan and other neighboring states becoming Indian satellites."[42]

These hyper-realpolitik ideas, which are embraced by a large section of the state elite, encourage them to pursue a military-first approach to problem solving with a pronounced emphasis on visible territorial revisionism, irrespective of the consequences for the regional order. The warrior state flows directly from this logic.[43]

The warrior state ideal and the military security-first approach the elite upholds generate consequences for both the political development of the country and its external behavior. Militaries in such states tend to hold views based on worst-case assumptions about the intentions and capabilities of their enemies,[44] and the Pakistani military is highly prone to this phenomenon. They assume that Indian intentions are generally malign and hence focus sharply on Indian capabilities (even though such capabilities may not be purely Pakistan-centric). For instance, former President Ayub Khan stated: "In matters of defense, countries do not formulate their policies on the basis of intentions of others; it is their capability which must be taken into account. If a big country like India has the capability to attack Pakistan, the intentions can always change, pact or no pact. A 'no-war pact' can make sense only if it is accompanied by an agreement about the maintenance of forces at a specified level."[45] These India-centric ideas based on worst-case assumptions continue to this day.

Little, if any, thought is given to the possibility that Pakistan's obsession with military security, with countering India at every turn, could itself provoke hostile responses from its adversary—the classic "security dilemma."[46] Nor is the triangular nature of the security dilemma problem involving India, Pakistan, and China given any consideration, and that Pakistan's alignment with China may be provoking India to respond negatively toward Pakistan.[47] The lack of understanding of the unintended consequences of one's own actions is a problem in rivalries of this nature. There is also little effort made to understand the opponent's domestic politics or changing strategic calculations in the global environment. All this means that the Pakistani Army must be prepared for the next war, which can happen without warning. War being the *raison d'être* of the army, and the fact that highly professionalized and organized groups tend to value their activity as the most important one in society—none more so than the military, given its pivotal role as the security provider—only exacerbates these problems.

A warrior state creates several social, political, and psychological pathologies. Military elites are highly prone to groupthink given that they are small groups based on consensus, cohesion, and decision-making unity. They tend to exploit windows of opportunity whenever presented. They also do not often learn from past mistakes—chivalry demands that failure be followed only by greater effort in the future. They tend to assign a low weight to diplomacy and to the political settlement of territorial disputes. They are prone to false optimism even when the balance of forces is against them. In addition, they could consider allies as genuinely interested in their cause and falsely expect their military support in times of war. They are also likely to believe that the "balance of will" is in their favor and underestimate the will of the opponent to fight.[48] The army in a semifeudal developing country that operates like a warrior state is especially susceptible to believing myths about national security threats. In time, it becomes the core national actor in both the political and economic realms. Unless there are countervailing power centers that can take on the military by emphasizing the need to abandon a hyper-realpolitik approach, the military will not change its policies.

The absence of strong demand for institutional reforms thus acts as a major impediment to change in a country like Pakistan. These demands usually come from powerful social and political groups and they can succeed during brief windows of opportunity such as a national crisis.[49] Activism by an internationally oriented civil society comprising progressive political parties, with the support of powerful elements of the middle and business classes is essential for change. Indeed, civil society needs to have the ideas, power, and inclination to demand new democratic institutions and continuously defend such institutions from attacks by the military. From time to time, a form of social revolution has to take place for a society to transform. These revolutions are "revolts from below" that can produce rapid social transformation.[50] If a state has a semifeudal system and the military emerges as a powerful economic actor, extracting resources from land and geostrategic ventures, it will have little interest in modernizing or pursuing economic and political reforms. Such states are not good at extracting internal resources either, especially if external aid is sufficient to pay for militarization and security competition. A weak civil society can simply perpetuate this system.

Unlike the war-making European states, which had to draw on resources internally and externally and innovate internally, the Pakistani elite has failed to extract or innovate because outside aid largely compensated for economic shortfalls. A weak state has been the result of these processes. The demand for institutional reform has not been strong enough to force the military to abandon either its commitment to national dominance or its security-first approach. Political parties, whenever they have assumed power, have been almost invariably corrupt. They also failed to cultivate strong party cadres that were effective at democratic outreach. Pakistan's weak civil society groups occasionally managed to make small-scale changes, but often retreated after their initial activism. In short, the military has remained the powerhouse of the country even when civilians hold office. Although there have been several religion or ethnic-based rebellions and conflicts in Pakistan, the middle and working classes are too weak to wage a social revolution that would overthrow the warrior state and generate a true democratic order. They are also vulnerable to nationalist or religious myths and hyperbole propagated by the military and the national security managers.

Pressures for revolutionary change can also come from outside. In this case, the main source of such a demand should have been the United States, the core supporter of Pakistan. Secondary supporters, such as China or Saudi Arabia, are unlikely to pressure for institutional reform given their own aversion to democracy. US policy has been one of "lost opportunities" and misguided priorities. Washington has generally found the Pakistani military a useful ally in geopolitical conflicts or in the pursuit of short-term regional policies. Powerful stakeholders in both countries developed links that allowed the perpetuation of the status quo, as little thought ever went into how to create a proper democracy in Pakistan. American policymakers in fact preferred the Pakistani army to the country's ramshackle group of political parties—after all, the former was the more reliable partner in the United States' various geopolitical conflicts over the years. The complexities in this relationship are many, but the Pakistani Army always had the shrewdness and dexterity to function as a loyal ally of the United States despite occasional ruptures in the relationship. Powerful sympathizers in Washington never saw a democratic Pakistan as feasible or desirable due to the overwhelming need for Pakistan to be on the American side, whether against the Soviet Union or the Taliban. Much of this is the result of US policymakers' preference for quick and dirty solutions instead of a more far-reaching policy based on a deeper analysis of Pakistan's problems. The United States has almost exclusively employed one readymade instrument—military and economic aid. This is in sharp contrast with US policies in Korea and Taiwan in the 1960s and 1970s, where US agencies such as the United States Agency for International Development (USAID) demanded structural change and economic integration with the world market. American and Western-controlled global financial institutions such as the IMF and WB occasionally made demands on Pakistan, and set conditions for loan disbursement, but were not strong enough as they had to bow to the pressures of their lead donor members. Similarly, China and Saudi Arabia have also helped perpetuate the system by supporting Pakistan for balance of power or religious/ideological reasons.

Comparing Pakistan

Is the Pakistani case unique, or are there other similar examples in the developing world? The experiences of other countries, especially in the Middle East and Asia, shed a great deal of light on Pakistan. Despite some differences in strategic circumstances, several military-dominated Muslim countries including Turkey, Egypt, and Indonesia—and non-Muslim states such as South Korea and Taiwan—are useful comparative cases. South Korea and Turkey both experienced wars and crises since their formation as nation-states, faced enduring rivalries with their neighbors, and have been targets of great power politics. But they approached their security and economic policies differently. Both of these states prioritized military security and created elaborate institutions for the provision of it. Both started off as weak states, but over a period of time, they acquired more state capacity than Pakistan did. Like Pakistan, Turkey and South Korea have both been members of US-led alliances and received substantial economic aid from the United States. While South Korea also faced an existential security threat and had a deep alliance with Washington, its elites managed to transform the national economy. Indeed this transformation was partly *driven* by the security imperative—the opposite of Pakistan's experience.

Unlike Pakistan, Korea used its alliance relationship with a great power patron for market access and economic reforms. Japanese colonialism had helped to create the preconditions for what Atul Kohli calls a "cohesive-capitalist, growth promoting state."[51] Turkey, despite the military's powerful control over society, has managed to experience some economic development, but not nearly as much as South Korea. In the political arena, Mustafa Kemal Atatürk's modernization led to a highly transformed state. This overwhelmingly Muslim country did not become an Islamic republic as in the Pakistani case.[52] The Turkish elites successfully avoided many pitfalls associated with a religious state. Instead, they embraced modernity and secularism (even at the price of heavy repression) and advocated economic integration with the West. In the early twenty-first century Turkey has further democratized by allowing a quasi-Islamic party to retain power and engage in democratic elections, although the current government has been accused in recent years of democratic retreat that in spring 2013 has produced mass protests.

Caveats

One major criticism in applying the European model of war and the strong state to the developing world is the contrast between the amount of time the European political entities took to become cohesive units— over 400 years—versus a short postcolonial history in most of the developing world. Pakistan has been independent for only 66 years.[53] This objection may be partially correct but it has many problems. In the pre-World War II era, economic and political development had a much longer gestation period than now. In the postwar period, economic and political development has been rapid, and states have been able to grow out of their centuries-old poverty and political underdevelopment in a shorter time span. Indeed, one of the core reasons for this rapidity—the development of the global economy and global export markets—is central to understanding state formation in the world today. South Korea, Taiwan, and several states in the Southeast Asia region attest to this trend. Even China has made immense progress in a short historical span, beginning in 1979 when it initiated economic reforms. Stages of development are more compressed now and a state does not need several decades or centuries to grow. In addition, we cannot simply expect time alone to produce development. Many African and Latin American states have grown weaker rather than stronger over time.[54] In Latin America, states have been around as independent entities for over 150 years, yet most remain weak. This tells us that time is not a sufficient factor in making a state stronger. In other words, the availability of more time need not strengthen a developing state. Other factors may be at work. A developing country, even when it faces extreme national security challenges, can become cohesive and strong through a developmental path as the East Asian experience powerfully shows.

The Pakistani elite proved to be astute in one thing—milking the geostrategic rent, but not developing or extracting sufficient resources from its society. The major allies would not allow it to go bankrupt and force its leaders to reform. During the past two decades Pakistan came very close to bankruptcy at least twice. In 2008 in view of the impending failure to repay its foreign debt, the IMF under the influence of the United States came up with a rescue plan to provide some $7.5 billion in loans.[55] In 2013, Pakistan once again needed IMF bailout of some $5.3 billion in view of its rapidly deteriorating balance of payment situation. Washington, on several occasions, backed off from its own threats to stop aid fearing collapse of Pakistan's economy and losing its pivotal support for America's so-called vital security interests, be it in Afghanistan, or vis-à-vis the erstwhile Soviet Union. The economic sustenance of Pakistan by the United States, China, and their allies as well as international aid agencies serves their short-term strategic interests, but it has destroyed the transformation of a country that has immense potential. The failure to transform means Pakistan will remain a major challenge to global and regional peace for decades to come. If Pakistan has any chance to prosper, the geostrategic curse must go along with the hyper-realpolitik ideas the elite holds about security and national purpose.

3

A Turbulent History

IN OCTOBER 1958, in what amounted to a bloodless coup, General Mohammad Ayub Khan was appointed chief martial law administrator by President Iskander Mirza through a proclamation. Within a few weeks the military ruler dismissed the president and sent him into exile. Ayub Khan and his supporters believed that a country like Pakistan did not need Western-style democracy, but instead a political system focused on stability and development.[1] The same story was repeated in July 1977 when General Zia-ul-Haq dismissed the elected government of Zulfikar Ali Bhutto and proclaimed military rule. Subsequently, Bhutto was hanged by the military regime for the alleged crime of murdering a political opponent. And then again in November 1999, Pervez Musharraf, chairman of the Joint Chiefs of Staff Committee of the Armed Forces, staged a coup against the civilian government of Nawaz Sharif. Sharif was arrested and sent into exile for his order to prevent General Musharraf's airplane from landing in Karachi on his return from a trip to Sri Lanka in his desperate effort to dismiss the general.

For over half of its existence as an independent country, Pakistan has been ruled by the military which promised much yet delivered little. The military believed that Pakistan could not afford a democratic system and must focus on stability and security through military means as long as it had external and internal enemies. Following the May 2013 national elections, the question still looms large: Will the story of military coups replay or will the men in arms remain in the barracks and concede their de facto power? Will they ever allow themselves to be under the control of elected civilian leaders?

The fundamental issue here is that during the past 66 years of Pakistan's existence, the country's political elite has been unable to create strong and legitimate democratic political institutions. State structures remain at best, poorly developed. The manipulative behavior of the political elite and the behind-the-scenes activities of the military and its spy agency, the ISI, have further weakened democracy. Weak and/or dysfunctional social and political institutions, in turn, have allowed for the emergence of violent extremist groups that have made Pakistan a hotbed of religious, ethnic, and sectarian conflict.

Nation-building and national integration are multifaceted processes. Myron Weiner has identified several crucial steps toward full national integration, defined as: "the process of bringing together culturally and socially discrete groups into a single territorial unit and the establishment of a national identity." These involve: territorial integration, that is, the establishment of national central authority over subordinate political units and regions; value integration of various cultural groups comprising the state; and elite mass integration of goals and values, especially through institution building.[2] In the Pakistani case, all these elements have been difficult to obtain. The Pakistani leaders, according to Khalid Bin Sayeed, a pioneering scholar of Pakistani politics, have not been very interested in building proper democratic institutions but instead focused on creating authoritarian state structures such as the bureaucracy and the army, both inherited from the British Raj.[3] Sayeed does not explicitly state the fundamental issue here: the Pakistani military and political elites have been extraordinarily preoccupied with creating a warrior state and an ideological state in the Hobbesian image, and not a welfare-oriented, developmental state.

In the late twentieth century, employing coercion to strengthen a nation-state became a much less successful method than it had been in previous eras. Thus multinational states that managed to become strong or integrated used methods like a proper federal setup enshrined in constitutional guarantees, or a mechanism known as consociationalism, which allowed them to share power among different sociopolitical groups in proportion to their size. The model that the Pakistani elite adopted privileged the top-down idea of state while it might have been more beneficial to follow a power-sharing approach relying on accommodation and the respect of political and economic diversity of the country.[4]

The story of Pakistan's tumultous evolution as a nation-state is fraught with leadership failures and institutional lapses. It has therefore persisted as a weak yet authoritarian state with multiple developmental and security challenges. An examination of the turning points in Pakistan's history, the political elites that have been the major players on its national stage, and their policies since 1947 is crucial if we are to understand Pakistan's story.

The Emergence of the Pakistani State

The emergence of Pakistan was a cataclysmic event for South Asia. The partition of the Indian subcontinent which gave birth to the country saw an estimated 14.5 million people uprooted, moving between India and Pakistan.[5] Mass displacement was accompanied by unimaginable violence of genocidal proportions, meted out by Muslims, Hindus, and Sikhs toward one another in the absence of effective state control. The estimates of deaths vary between a million to 1.5 million[6] as there has been no accurate count. While the violence was not state-sponsored, the complicity of state authorities and agents of the state cannot be fully ruled out. The leaders of both India and Pakistan were tragically late in condemning the mayhem that sections of their populations carried out with impunity. While three states—the retreating British, and the successor states of India and Pakistan—vied with each other for resources and positions in the fluid situations, their demobilized armies also played a role in the violence.[7]

The independent state of Pakistan was the result of a political and ideological movement that began as an idea in 1929, and became a forceful demand after 1937, with a formal declaration in Lahore in March 1940 at the All-India Muslim League conference. The demand itself was the result of a confluence of conflicting personalities and their competing strategies in the peculiar sociopolitical circumstances prevalent in pre-independent India. Interestingly, the demand for Pakistan came from Muslim leaders of Muslim-*minority* provinces of British India—the United Provinces (today's Indian states of Uttar Pradesh and Uttarakhand) and Bihar. Sentiment for a separate Muslim state had been, in contrast, relatively muted among the Muslim majority provinces of Punjab and to some extent Bengal, areas that would eventually form the core territories of Pakistan.[8] While the League therefore had the task of building support in Muslim majority areas of Pakistan before it, garnering such sympathy proved initially difficult given that the Muslim leaders of the United Provinces had more say and representation in the Muslim League than did those from Punjab or Bengal.[9]

Jinnah's Unfinished Political Project

The founding father of Pakistan, Mohammed Ali Jinnah, began his quest for an independent Pakistan in 1937, when his demand for a coalition partnership based on a separate electorate for Muslims was turned down by the Indian National Congress. Much has been written about Jinnah's personality and the role he played in the partition saga.[10] It is still a matter of debate as to how and why Jinnah, initially a leader of the Congress Party and supporter of Hindu-Muslim unity, turned against both to initiate a struggle for a separate religion-based political project that would divide India. The stated reasons for the rupture included Jinnah's unhappiness with the Congress' support for the Khilafat movement (which sought to restore the Ottoman Caliphate in Turkey, which Kemal Atatürk's secular regime had overthrown after World War I), the rise of Hindu fundamentalism, especially in popular culture and literature, and Congress leaders' alleged "arrogance" toward Muslims.[11] Interestingly, it was Mohandas Gandhi who supported Muslim revivalism as represented by the Khilafat movement, much to the chagrin of many of his supporters in the Congress party. Jinnah was also critical of Congress leaders' use of Hindu symbols.[12] In particular, Gandhi evoked the Hindu god Ram even though the Congress leader's nonviolent strategy was heavily influenced by ideals from other religions and belief systems.

Although Jinnah had left the Congress in 1920, it was not until 1934, when he returned from four years practicing law in England, that he became active in Muslim politics and took over the reins of the Muslim League. By 1937 Jinnah had become influenced by the writings of Muslim poet Muhammad Iqbal, who had been the first major intellectual figure to propose Pakistan, a state meant to protect the rights of Muslims in the subcontinent. Iqbal wrote several letters to Jinnah in 1937, persuading him to take the lead in creating Pakistan along religious/communal lines, and soon Jinnah began to articulate the idea in his use of phrases like "the magic power of the Muslims," and "the moon of Pakistan is rising." These correspondences would change the way Jinnah would look at the issue of a separate state for Muslims.[13]

The Congress leaders on their part were incredulous at Jinnah and his ambition to carve out a separate state based on communal ideology. Their insistence that the Congress was a secular party and that independent India would be a secular state where Muslim rights would be adequately protected did not impress Jinnah or his supporters. Perhaps the most salient example of Congress' lack of inclusiveness from Jinnah's point of view lay in the aftermath of the provincial elections held in 1937. These elections were conducted under the 1935 Government of India Act, which had given partial autonomy to Indians in the British Provinces. Jinnah's Muslim League managed to win in only one out of the 11 provinces where elections were held and only 108 of the 485 seats that had been reserved for Muslims. In the Northwest Frontier Province and Sind it had no success, while in the majority Muslim province of Bengal it won only 39 of the 119 seats reserved for Muslims. The Congress, on the other hand, won a majority in five, and was able to form governments in seven out of 11 provinces.[14] Factionalism and lack of leadership were blamed for the failure of the Muslim League in the elections. The Muslim League hoped for joining coalition ministries along with the Congress where the latter had won. But this hope was in vain, and a source of great disappointment for party adherents.[15]

Indeed, the Congress Party's unwillingness to form coalition governments with the League can be considered a pivotal event in coalescing the Muslim political elite in support of the creation of a separate state. The Congress, by opposing electoral arrangements on communal lines, had unwittingly laid the roots of conflict with Jinnah, laying bare a fundamental disagreement over the meaning of democracy and self-rule. While the Congress sought to create a democratic order in independent India based on majoritarian and secular principles where each vote counted equally, the Muslim League advocated a system of representative government based on communal membership where minority votes would be given greater weight to compensate for their numerical inferiority. It wanted parity or equal weight in electoral rights for the minority Muslim population with the majority Hindu electorate. Without this extra weight, the Muslim League believed, Muslims were vulnerable to being denied their due political rights. Majority rule based on equal voting rights, it was argued, would have been akin to an acceptance of Hindu rule given their majority status.

The Congress leadership also appeared to be unaware of the depth of this concern among the Muslim leadership. Nor did they seem willing to consider electoral models that might have placated the League's demands by guaranteeing different ethnic groups a key role in governance. This was in part due to the strong secular identity that underlay the Congress, which was composed of members from all religious groups, including many prominent Muslims. The Congress leadership had also, however, decided that given their party's majority, the fact that the Muslim League had fared poorly in the recent elections, and that enough Muslim representation could be drawn from within their own ranks, meant that there was little need to accede to the League's demand for coalition governments.[16] However, Congress had underestimated the extent of Muslim desire for equal representation based on the notion of religious parity, and Jinnah's willingness to escalate this demand to the next level—independence for Muslim majority provinces. Finally, Congress leaders also underestimated the possibility of Britain throwing its weight behind the idea of Pakistan, especially given that Jinnah supported Britain's war efforts while the Congress opposed them. This difference made Jinnah a better strategic bet in the British calculus.[17] At the same time, the very idea of Muslim separateness formed a basis to apply the divide-and-rule policy practiced by the British colonial rulers, especially since 1909 when they introduced a policy of separate communal electorates for the religious communities.

Events leading to the demand for an independent Pakistan now occurred in rapid succession. First, in 1938, the Muslim League repudiated the federal scheme envisaged in the 1935 Act which envisaged a weak setup consisting of some Indian princely states and British-controlled provinces. Then, in September 1939, it again "irrevocably opposed" any federal arrangement, and in March 1940, at its Lahore conference, passed the "Pakistan Resolution" demanding in plain terms the partition of India along communal lines.[18] These demands grew more fervent with the Congress Party's rejection of the Cripps Mission offer in March 1942 of an interim government and final constitutional settlement after World War II. The mission, led by cabinet minister Stafford Cripps, was sent by Britain to obtain the support of Indian leaders for Britain's war efforts. The Congress' refusal on the ground that the party leaders were not consulted prior to the entry of British India to the war was followed by its launching of the Quit India Movement in August 1942, which demanded immediate independence with communal problems to be addressed only afterward. The Quit India Movement was launched at the time of Britain's most difficult phase in the war, when it was unclear whether it could win against Hitler. This helped undermine British sympathy for a unified India (a topic that Indian historiography has thus far ignored). In the 1946 elections for the interim assembly, the League, in a major turnaround of fortunes from its 1937 rout, captured 446 out of 495 seats allocated to Muslims, highlighting its meteoric rise in a short period of time through rapid mass mobilization.[19]

Jinnah's desire for Muslim-majority provinces to join Pakistan entirely, with the remaining Indian Muslims migrating to Pakistan, did not materialize in reality. A huge proportion of the Muslim population in India (unlike their Hindu and Sikh counterparts in Pakistani territories) chose to remain. Equally disheartening from a Pakistani perspective was the failure to acquire all of Punjab and Bengal but only areas of those two provinces where Muslims formed a majority. Nevertheless, Jinnah had strategically used one of the most powerful symbols of identity, religion, to engineer the partition of the subcontinent. In that sense, there was an element of political brilliance attached to Jinnah and his brand of nationalism, if one sets aside the enormous human tragedy that befell Hindus, Muslims, and Sikhs alike in the territories that would be divided as a consequence. Perhaps more importantly, the manner in which partition took place also laid the foundation for an intractable and enduring rivalry between the two newborn states, as India-Pakistan relations have remained strained even after 66 years of existence as independent states, interspersed by occasional, and tragically unsuccessful, efforts at reconciliation.[20] Pakistan's search for strategic parity with India continues to this day. The consequences of this rivalry for the internal development and external policies of Pakistan will be discussed in Chapters 4 and 5.

Jinnah's initial desire was to carve out several parts of British and Princely India and unite them in a centralized system. There are unanswered questions, however, regarding the type of political order he intended to eventually create in the new state. Some have argued that he was in essence democratic and secular, while others suggest Jinnah sought to adopt a top-down approach and build a semi-authoritarian state based on the vice-regal system inherited from the British colonial rulers. Still others believe, based on his writings, that Jinnah had not given much thought to these issues at all.[21] His few speeches do, however, leave the clear impression that he wanted to create an Islamic state, but not a theocracy run by Mullahs. Accordingly, although the last Viceroy of India Lord Louis Mountbatten referred to Jinnah as a modern-day Akbar the Great (the seventeenth-century Mughal emperor renowned for his tolerance for different religions), Jinnah rejected the comparison.[22]

Despite the occasional reference to tolerance and the fact that he led a Western lifestyle, Jinnah was clearly not a secularist in the strict sense. For him Islam was "Our bedrock and sheet anchor,"[23] and he would therefore declare in 1944: "We do not want any flag excepting the League flag of the Crescent and Star. Islam is our guide and the complete code of our life. We do not want any red or yellow flag. We do not want any isms, Socialisms, Communisms or National Socialisms."[24] In April 1946 Jinnah embraced "in the name of Allah the Beneficent, the Merciful" as the League pledge for Pakistan.[25] In general, after the creation of Pakistan references to the Quran and the Prophet became increasingly prominent in Jinnah's speeches,[26] and even if Jinnah had held on to a somewhat broad view of minority rights, those simply did not manifest themselves in any constitutional or institutional guarantees during his short reign as governor general of the new state. In any event, Jinnah died in September 1948, barely 12 months after the state was formed. While his contribution to Pakistan' initial state formation was huge, in terms of lasting institution-building in a positive sense, his impact had been virtually nonexistent.

As a new state, Pakistan suffered from many debilitating structural and institutional weaknesses. One of them was the absence of a strong development-oriented bureaucracy. At the time of partition, Pakistan faced an immediate shortage of bureaucratic talent, with the number of officials of the Indian Civil Service (ICS) who decided to migrate to Pakistan proving grossly inadequate to ensure the state's effective functioning.[27] The new state had some 17% of the population of former British India.[28] But only 95 out of the 1,157 Indian civil service officers opted for Pakistan. To this figure, 50 British civil servants were added on a temporary basis.[29] It received 30% of the British Indian Army, 40% of the navy, and 20% of the air force.[30] However, its share of military infrastructure, arms and ammunition, and training establishments was meager, owing to their larger concentrations in geographical locations within independent India. For instance, of the 46 military training establishments only seven were located in Pakistan, while all three command workshops as well as 35 of 40 ordnance depots similarly found themselves in India.[31] All these deficiencies were of course superimposed on more basic weaknesses. At independence, Pakistan had less than 10% of undivided India's industrial base. In an effort to encourage industrialization, an import substitution policy was adopted from the beginning, which focused on developing indigenous industries by importing machinery from abroad, taking away precious state resources. Investments in areas like education and health were given very low priority.[32]

Despite their initial weakness, though, the military and bureaucratic elite that emerged would subsequently end up with much more power than the civilian political elite, with the failure of political parties, especially the Muslim League, to entrench themselves in the political system and acquire legitimacy in the eyes of the people. To Pakistan's misfortune, however, neither the bureaucracy nor the army proved to be development-oriented. Instead, they geared themselves largely toward the furtherance of national security objectives as well as their own corporatist interests—that is, enhancing their wealth and power over other societal groups.

Part of the blame for this has to lie at Jinnah's door, with his poor record of nourishing a future political leadership. As Hamza Alavi has succinctly put it: "Inevitably, the officials on whom he [Jinnah] had to rely had a virtually free hand in dealing with the business of government. He had collected around him in the Muslim League, spineless men on whom he could rely little and who were in no position to assert themselves as the nation's political leadership . . . Jinnah's unintentional contribution to the future of Pakistan was a demotion of the political leadership in favor of the bureaucracy."[33] Additionally, some have argued, by adopting the British governor general-based model of governance, which gave considerable power to the executive branch, Jinnah was acting upon his people's wishes for him to be more a king than a democratic leader, reminiscent of the *Shehenshah* or "absolute King" of the Mughal era, and thereby restore the lost glory of the Muslims in the subcontinent.[34] This vice-regal system in turn ensured a concentration of power in the executive and the bureaucratic actors who were tasked with carrying out the day-to-day governance of the country.

1947–1948: The First Kashmir War

In many ways the warrior state had begun its formation during Jinnah's time itself. The pivotal event early on was the first Kashmir War in 1947–1948. The Pakistani state unofficially organized and aided the incursion of tribal mujahedeen forces from the Northwest Frontier Province into Kashmir in October 1947, a majority Muslim princely state ruled by a Hindu Maharaja, Hari Singh. The Maharaja had been, ever since the partition plan was announced, dithering on the decision of joining his state to either India or Pakistan or declaring independence. In late October 1947, in the face of the impending collapse of his state from the mujahedeen invasion, Hari Singh invited India to intervene militarily and protect his state. Indian intervention, which took place only after the Maharaja had agreed to provisionally accede to India, prevented the state from being completely overrun by the invaders, now joined by regular Pakistani forces. Nearly 60% of the state ended up in Indian hands and the rest of the territory in Pakistan (now called Azad Kashmir and Gilgit-Baltistan) when a ceasefire was eventually agreed to by the two parties on the last day of 1948.[35] Subsequently, China gained control of some 17% of Kashmir's original contested territory after the 1962 war with India and Pakistan ceded some areas in Northern Kashmir to China in 1963 in a border agreement.

To the Pakistani elite, Kashmir should have been part of Pakistan under the partition deal. Its refusal to join Pakistan was seen as a violation of the letter and spirit of the partition agreement. For New Delhi, the accession of a majority Muslim state validated the idea of a secular India, which Pakistan's use of force sought to deny. However, Indian policy generated much ambiguity. New Delhi initially proposed a plebiscite among Kashmiris, but withdrew that offer after realizing that the majority of Kashmiris might opt for independence, and that Pakistan would not abandon control over Azad Kashmir.

This first war in Kashmir was pivotal as it made the Pakistan army's chief *raison d'être* to gain Kashmir from India. It generated a sense among Pakistanis that their state was incomplete, and that India had failed to reconcile itself to the principle behind partition. Subsequent Indian policies in Kashmir and the region further helped to reinforce the military's prime role in Pakistan's political order. The territorial gains in Kashmir gave the military leaders confidence that they could take on a larger India and still prevail. For India, on the other hand, the use of force by Pakistan for territorial conquest served as a potent indication that the state that was emerging on its western and eastern borders was an adversary. The subsequent hardening of India's position might have been due to the initial use of force by Pakistan to obtain Kashmir and then later on bringing external powers—the United States and China—as allies to the subcontinent, upsetting India's aspirations for a regional leadership role.[36]

The conflict with India consumed a large part of Jinnah's reign. The inability of either side to fully win the wars they fought or find a diplomatic solution would most adversely affect Pakistan in the long run. As the weaker party, its focus would become one of attaining military strength vis-à-vis the larger neighbor through arming and alliance building. Pakistan's quest for parity prompted an enormous commitment of resources and the creation of a garrison or warrior state. This war would also create the later Pakistani strategy of asymmetric war, using nonstate actors against India to redress the power imbalance between the two.

The Post-Jinnah Polity

From the very beginning, the Pakistani ruling elite exhibited antidemocratic tendencies. Extraordinary powers were conferred on the governor general until March 1949, which included the power to suspend a provincial government, a power that was invoked several times. Jinnah's successor as governor general was Khawaja Nazimuddin (September 1948–October 1951), a Bengali leader from East Pakistan. Nazimuddin commanded little authority, leaving effective power in the hands of the Prime Minister Liaquat Ali Khan, who was also president of the Muslim League and the bureaucracy.[37] Khan was assassinated in October 1951, upon which Nazimuddin assumed power as prime minister, allowing ex-bureaucrat Malik Ghulam Muhammad to become the governor general. The governor general dismissed the Nazimuddin government in April 1953 and Muhammad Ali Bogra, Pakistan's ambassador to the United States, became the next prime minister. The prime minister, his cabinet, and their portfolios were all determined by the governor general, and the National Assembly rubber-stamped those decisions. During Bogra's term in office, the Mutual Aid Assistance agreement with the United States was signed (May 1954), and Pakistan joined the Southeast Asia Treaty Organization (SEATO) in September 1954 and the Central Treaty Organization (CENTO) or Baghdad Pact in February 1955, both of which are now defunct. Under the 1956 Constitution, the governor general post was replaced by a president. But both these positions were held by bureaucrats, Ghulam Muhammad (October 1951–October 1955) and his successor, General Iskander Mirza (October 1955–March 1956), whose power came from the support of bureaucracy and the army and not from any political party.[38] This early failure to create an elite structure with roots in political parties turned out to be pivotal to damaging the emerging state, as political participation was stifled and the bureaucracy-army combination assumed the mantle of the state from that point onward.

The First Military Takeover: 1958

The major weakness of the Pakistani political order was the dearth of strong political leaders or political parties with a deep democratic sense or commitment. There were four governors general and seven prime ministers between 1947 and 1958, the most crucial period of state formation in terms of institution-building. These weak civilian leaders, most of whom were drawn from the bureaucracy, lacked legitimacy and popular appeal. They also made no serious efforts to nurture democratic political processes, which required active political parties. The prime ministers and governors general jockeyed among themselves as to who should hold more authority. Some prime ministers were dismissed by the governors general at will. The party politicians were viewed rather contemptuously by the military-bureaucratic elite, their bickering among themselves regarded as undermining national unity and national security.

The main purpose of the state was national security (a rare source of consensus among all the political parties and the bureaucratic elite), ensuring that defense spending took the biggest chunk of the national budget. Pakistan's defense expenditure during 1948–1959 was 59% of total governmental expenditure, growing by 116% during this period.[39] Indeed, in his Defense Policy Statement in August 1953, Prime Minister Bogra declared that "he would much rather starve the country than allow any weakening of its defense."[40]

The political and bureaucratic elite's realpolitik worldview led them to assign to the Army a prominent role in political decision making, especially with regard to the emerging strategic relationship with the United States. The US-Soviet Cold War rivalry had deepened in the 1950s, and Washington was seeking allies among the developing countries. Pakistan jumped at the chance. Meanwhile, India, under Jawaharlal Nehru, was busy with the Afro-Asian movement, which later became the nonaligned movement. India resisted pressures to align with either superpower. Army General Mohammed Ayub Khan emerged as a key decision-maker and was given considerable power by the civilian leaders not only in defense, but in foreign policy in general. Ayub Khan, as a British-trained military persona, would also play a crucial role in concluding the 1954 Defense Treaty with the United States.[41] This treaty would result in major arms shipments and economic and military aid to Pakistan. By the second half of 1950s, the three A's—"Allah, Army, and America"—would emerge as the most powerful rallying forces in determining the destiny of Pakistan.

General Ayub Khan was appointed chief martial law administrator by President Iskander Mirza in October 1958, in a proclamation equivalent to a coup d'état. The proclamation of martial law and the military takeover of power were momentous events for the state in Pakistan as they killed the possibility of a nascent democracy emerging, with a military subservient to civilian control. Within a few weeks of the coup Ayub Khan managed to dismiss Mirza as president and then have him exiled. Some have contended that the United States persuaded Ayub to dismiss Mirza, whom Washington regarded as a liability.[42] Interestingly, Governor General Ghulam Muhammad had already approached General Ayub Khan to assume power four years prior, but the latter had turned it down. Ayub Khan and his supporters thought that a country like Pakistan did not need Western-style democracy, but instead a political system focused on stability and development.[43]

By this period, the warrior state began to show its tentacles more powerfully. It had a major influence on Pakistan's internal and external policies in the next decade or so. In 1962, when China and India went to war, Ayub Khan seriously considered an attack on India in order to conquer Indian-controlled Kashmir. This plan was sensed and opposed by US President John F. Kennedy, who pressured him to abandon the military adventure. Later, Khan regretted not making use of the opportunity to settle the Kashmir conflict.[44] In view of US' attempts to befriend India following the 1962 war by way of arms transfers, Ayub made friendly overtures to China. In March 1963, he signed a border agreement with China, ceding 750 square miles of territory in Kashmir and in effect "making China a party" to the Kashmir dispute.[45]

However, war was a constant theme for the military-controlled state. India's charismatic Prime Minister Nehru died in 1964, creating a void in New Delhi's political leadership. His successor Lal Bahadur Shastri was perceived in Pakistan to be a weak leader. Militarily, too, India was considerably weakened after its defeat in the 1962 war with China. Although there was limited military and economic support from the United States and the United Kingdom, the defeat was a highly demoralizing event for India, especially for Nehru. It seriously damaged his credentials as the leader of the developing world. India was also going through enormous economic challenges, including famine. Pakistan, on the other hand, had received a considerable quantity of arms from the United States, weapons which were qualitatively superior to India's arsenal. They included 200 top-of-the-line M-47/48 Patton tanks, 12 high-performance F-104A Starfighters, and 92 F-86 Sabre aircraft (many equipped with state-of-the-art Sidewinder air-to-air missiles) and twelve T-33 jet trainer aircraft.[46] A short window of opportunity had arisen. It is not surprising that, in congruence with the warrior state's approach toward security, jumping through windows of opportunity was an acceptable option.

The 1965 War

The warrior state tested its military mettle in the 1965 war with India. As a prelude to the war, in March 1965, Pakistan launched a limited incursion into the Rann of Kutch region of Gujarat. A military stalemate resulted, but the biggest lesson learnt was that India would concede territory under pressure, as New Delhi agreed to international arbitration of the dispute. Following this "success," Operation Gibraltar was conceived largely by civilians and a small group of decision makers who included Foreign Minister Zulfikar Ali Bhutto, Foreign Secretary Aziz Ahmed, and the commanding officer for the Kashmir area, General Akhtar Malik. Apparently, none of the other ministers of the Ayub Khan's cabinet was aware of it.[47] The plan consisted of sending 7,000 to 8,000 specially trained mujahid soldiers into Indian Kashmir to dislocate and disorganize the Indian army by sabotaging Indian military installations and communication facilities. They would follow this by distributing arms to the Kashmiri liberation volunteers. Once the guerrilla operation gained momentum, it was expected that India would find the control of Kashmir too difficult to sustain and would seek a conciliatory settlement, especially under international pressure.[48] The decision-makers made several assumptions: that there was widespread support among the Kashmiris in favor of Pakistani intervention; that war would be limited to Kashmir; that India would not escalate the conflict to the vulnerable international border; that Pakistan's qualitative superiority in armaments would compensate for India's quantitative superiority; and that friendly countries such as China and the United States would come to Pakistan's support, the latter more in political terms.[49]

These assumptions would prove to be wrong. Indian forces struck back by opening a second front on the international border in the Punjab, and were able to get close to the Pakistani city of Lahore. Pakistan, as a result, had to pull out its troops from the Kashmir theater, thereby nullifying the limited advances it had made. The superpowers would diplomatically convince both states to agree to a ceasefire. A meeting was held at the Soviet Central Asian city of Tashkent in January 1966, attended by Ayub Khan and Shastri, where a ceasefire agreement was signed. Pakistan gained little territorially and the status quo ante was restored. Most importantly, neither of Pakistan's strategic allies, China or the United States, would come to the rescue of its military adventurism. The latter in fact imposed an economic embargo on Pakistan, and military transfers and economic aid to Pakistan were curtailed. This put pressure on Pakistan to agree to a ceasefire after 17 days of fighting.

The failure in the 1965 war exposed the military and the weaknesses of the warrior state. The war, however, had a perverse effect on Pakistan. It laid the beginnings of a deep slide toward greater militarization, hybrid democracy, and a national morass that has bedeviled Pakistan ever since. Expectations of an easy victory against a weak-kneed India were shattered, and the Ayub regime got delegitimized by its failure. The Tashkent Declaration between India and Pakistan of January 1966 was perceived by the Pakistani public as a betrayal and a failure to make gains from war on the part of the Ayub regime. Major unrest followed. The popular disillusionment arose from the earlier government propaganda that Pakistan was on the verge of a historic victory. In response to the unrest, Ayub imposed a state of emergency, including censorship, political detentions and the suspension of basic rights.[50]

The Supreme Court of Pakistan made Ayub's continued rule difficult by declaring many of his acts unconstitutional. The Bengali population in East Pakistan, separated by over a thousand miles of Indian territory, had also become increasingly restive, treated as they were as second-class citizens by the West Pakistani political elite in both the political and economic arenas. There was also a sense in East Pakistan that the 1965 war had nothing to do with them and they were dragged into a conflict to fulfill the desires of the West Pakistani political/military elite. They also realized that they were left undefended during the war. The war revealed to East Pakistan the absurdity of the strategic slogan that "the defense of the East lies in the West."[51]

East Pakistani alienation had deep roots in the way Pakistan was constituted and controlled from the Western side. Although they comprised about 54% of the population of Pakistan, as Rounaq Jahan notes, "at the time of independence the Bengalis had little representation in the civil-military bureaucracy, the professions, or the entrepreneurial class. As a result, the Punjabis and the migrants from northern and Western India—who 'modernized' early—though ethnically and linguistically a minority, became the national elite of Pakistan from the outset."[52] Pakistan's power structure gave limited participation to the Bengalis, with some rare exceptions like Nazimuddin and Mirza, and the policy of "one state, one government, one economy, one language, one culture" helped to precipitate Bengali alienation.[53] Bengali discontent widened as a result of the lack of effective political participation and cultural policies imposed by West Pakistan. In particular, western elites' imposition of Urdu while simultaneously denigrating the Bengali language widened the chasm between both parts of Pakistan. This and the denial of adequate legislative representation were two major issues that caused friction between the eastern and western wings of Pakistan early on.

Despite political unrest and a preoccupation with military security, Pakistan witnessed some economic progress during the Ayub era, largely due to foreign assistance and industrial development. The average annual growth rate from 1959–1960 to 1966–1967 was 5.2%, compared to the 2.2% of 1950–1951 to 1957–1958 period. The manufacturing sector grew by 16.2% and per capita income increased by 3.8% in the 1960s. GDP growth was 6.6% and 7.9% for the years 1959–1960 and 1964–1965 while per capita income grew by 4.8% during 1964–1965. This, however, did not result in much qualitative improvement in the lives of the majority as the wealth was concentrated largely in the upper strata of landowning classes.[54] Despite the praise that Ayub's developmental model received, the seeming success evaporated when one took a closer look at the results. A number of constituencies were excluded from mainstream political and economic life, and the country lacked proper institutions to deal with their increasing demands.[55] Critics also pointed out the aggressive capitalist model generated huge income disparities across regions. Industrial growth was concentrated in central Punjab, while agricultural growth occurred in central Punjab and Karachi. It led to a sense of "utter neglect and betrayal" in other regions, especially in East Pakistan.[56] The rampant inequality, which was accompanied by inflation, led to major political tensions and mass protests by students, workers, and lawyers in 1968. However, the landed elite scuttled Ayub's proposed land reforms, which would have mitigated some of the problems.[57]

The Prelude to the 1971 Bangladesh War

Dramatic changes took place in Pakistan during the period from 1965 to 1971. Having lost his legitimacy in the 1965 war, in March 1969 Ayub Khan resigned, granting his Commander in Chief Yahya Khan the reins of power. Yahya Khan was entrusted with defending the country from external and internal threats alike. The same month, Yahya Khan imposed martial law. This was followed by promulgation of the Legal Framework Order (LFO) of 1970. The LFO provided for elections for a house to frame a new Constitution and act as a legislature.[58] Elections were held for the creation of a Constituent Assembly in the months of December 1970 and January 1971. In the elections, East Pakistan's Sheikh Mujibur Rahman would emerge as the overall winner with 160 seats, although in West Pakistan, the Pakistan People's Party (PPP) led by Zulfikar Ali Bhutto was the frontrunner with 81 seats. The West Pakistani elite—especially Bhutto—refused to accord Rahman the victor's status, let him form a government or lead the Constituent Assembly. Bhutto insisted on a coalition government which did not materialize. This led Mujibur Rahman to launch a movement for the political autonomy and eventual independence of East Pakistan, something that he achieved largely through the military and political support of India.[59]

The response of the warrior state was military repression and the killing of thousands of Bengalis. Mass rapes and other human rights abuses by members of the Pakistani Army were rampant. India gave strong support to the independence movement, including covert military aid. During the bitter civil war, over 10 million refugees fled to India, creating considerable strain on the Indira Gandhi government. War between India and Pakistan appeared imminent. By November 1971, India had intervened with troops, and on December 3, 1971, Pakistan declared war on both Eastern and Western fronts. The Indian army, led by General Sam Manekshaw and locally commandeered by Lieutenant General Jagjit Singh Aurora, led a short blitzkrieg operation lasting 13 days, thoroughly defeating the Pakistani army in East Pakistan and liberating Bangladesh on December 16, 1971. Some 93,000 Pakistani troops surrendered to India, resulting in national humiliation to the Pakistani people, especially the Army, the supposed custodian of Pakistan's security.[60] The country lost its eastern portion and more than half of its population. This pivotal event profoundly harmed Pakistan's future relations with India. Much of the Pakistani historiography blamed India for the partition of their country. A secret report by former Chief Justice Hamoodur Rehman, commissioned by Zulfikar Ali Bhutto, never saw the light of the day. The army's own review report confined to the Western side blamed the late starting of the war on that front as a cause for Pakistan's disastrous performance on the Eastern side.[61] In Pakistani discourse on the subject, even today there is very little attention paid to why the Bengali population got so disenchanted with the West Pakistani elite in the first place and fought a bloody war of independence.

The Bangladesh War and Its Impact

The secession of East Pakistan was a crucial event that only strengthened the warrior nature of the Pakistani state. Although at the postwar Shimla conference in 1972 Prime Minister Zulfikar Ali Bhutto agreed to respect the Line of Control in Kashmir and seek an eventual resolution of conflict with India through bilateral negotiations, his policy became increasingly belligerent after returning home. Strategic parity with India was temporarily lost as a result of the war and the loss of the eastern half of the country. India's intervention was viewed as a great treachery, strengthening the assumption among the elite that India was yet to reconcile itself to the 1947 partition agreement. The fear now was that New Delhi might attempt to engage in bifurcating Pakistan once again if Pakistan did not become militarily stronger. From the Pakistani perspective, its great power allies (the United States and China) did not help sufficiently to stop India from winning in Bangladesh, although the Nixon administration had sent the Seventh Fleet led by USS Enterprise to the Bay of Bengal in an overt act of coercive diplomacy against India.[62]

The lessons learned in this case were somewhat perverse: that conflict with India was inevitable and that Pakistan had to become stronger once again for waging the next war. The response of Bhutto was to launch a nuclear weapons program as a "great equalizer," a capability that would reestablish strategic parity with India. In January 1972, he held a meeting of nuclear scientists and engineers in Multan, where the decision was made to launch a nuclear weapons program. In 1965 he had already declared that if India goes nuclear Pakistan would build one even if it has to go hungry and eat grass.[63] At the Multan meeting, Bhutto asked the scientists how long it would take to build the bomb as Pakistan was waging a 1,000-year war with India.[64] Bhutto had strong faith in balance of power politics. To him, "a small state under pressure from a great or global power should handle its affairs adroitly; propose a limited cooperative relationship to the hostile power and thus dissuade it from being hostile; muster the support of other small states and sympathetic great and global powers to resist the hostile power if it persists in its policy of pressure; see and take such opportunities as the current conflict among the global powers themselves seems to offer; be more cordial with those who support its causes than with those who do not."[65] The elite concluded that defeat was due to the treachery of the opponent, the relative inability of Pakistan's own forces to wage the war properly, and the lack of support from allies. The next time around, these factors could be altered through a different approach to conflict.[66] In addition, Pakistan's leaders considered revenge to be an acceptable motivation for military behavior. Paying back India in kind became the elite's obsession. The opportunity came in the early 1980s when the Sikh nationalists of the Indian state of Punjab started the Khalistan movement to create a separate state and then again in 1989 when the Kashmiri militant groups launched their violent separatist movement; both Pakistan supported covertly.[67]

Bhutto attempted to introduce several internal reforms in line with his populist and socialist ideology. In January 1972 the Bhutto government instituted a social-democracy model by nationalizing industrial units in heavy metals, heavy engineering, heavy electricals, and gas, in addition to nationalizing several private banks. But the most significant effort was in land reform. Initially, the allowed individual holdings were reduced to 150 irrigated and 300 unirrigated acres and in January 1977, the maximum ceiling was further reduced to 100 and 200 acres of irrigated and unirrigated land respectively.[68] Bhutto's policy initiatives did not produce any radical economic changes. The landholding classes offered only token land surrenders. They transferred land to family members or even to fake tenants, and benefited from tax breaks, loans and compensation for doing so.[69] Bhutto's brand of socialism hurt large industrialists, actually benefited landowners, and only provided marginal assistance to the poor.[70] Ultimately, Bhutto alienated his own supporters because his economic and social reforms did not have the backing of the constituency that brought him to power. Many left his PPP for the Pakistan National Alliance, a nine-party opposition coalition.[71]

The Indian military victory in 1971 generated a temporary period of calm on the subcontinent. Pakistan was much weaker than before: the eastern portion of its territory lost, its armed forces demoralized, and its political elite groping for a second chance to build a national security state and reestablish strategic parity with India. The military retreated temporarily from domestic politics. However, the civilians did not make use of this opportunity to transform Pakistan in fundamental ways. Instead of changing national policies in the face of defeat, they proceeded largely in the same fashion. The military defeat was not decisive enough as in the case of Germany and Japan in 1945 at the hands of the Allied forces. Still, it created a limited military and strategic dominance of India and some believe that peace through the preponderance of the larger power emerged temporarily in South Asia.[72] This, however, would not last. In 1979, Pakistan once again was thrust into geopolitical prominence due to a great power conflict in the neighborhood.

The 1977 Zia Coup

The military was waiting in the wings to stage a coup, as was evident when the civilian rulers' rank incompetence mounted. The opportunity came in July 1977 when General Muhammad Zia-ul-Haq, a zealot in uniform with military competence, ousted Bhutto's democratically elected government. The popular agitation by the opposition parties and Bhutto's repressive approach provided an opportunity for such a coup. Zia not only destroyed civilian rule, but sent Bhutto to jail on trumped-up charges of connivance in the murder of a political opponent and then allowed him to be hanged on April 4, 1979.[73] After six years of direct military rule, Zia appointed Mohammed Khan Junejo as prime minister following the elections in February 1985, which were conducted on a nonpolitical party basis, while continuing as president.

The Zia coup was facilitated by a new class of army officers who came from the middle and lower middle classes, largely from the Punjab, who held a different value system than the army officers under Ayub Khan and Yahya Khan. These officers, like many in the middle class, felt that the PPP was pursuing "un-Islamic policies" and that Bhutto was disrespecting the "ideology of Pakistan" through his so-called socialist policies.[74]

Zia-ul-Haq continued the hyper-national security state policies and accelerated the covert nuclear weapons program. But Zia's major policy innovation was the introduction of Sharia laws and the Islamization of Pakistan's educational system. In that pursuit, he was helped by Saudi Arabia and its strict Wahabbi sect of Islamic preachers. More moderate elements of Islam were subjugated to this more orthodox view, and a generation of Pakistanis would grow up in a system of madrassas that his policies helped to set up. Many of them proved to be great seminaries of hatred, focusing almost exclusively on medieval teachings. The contemporary predicament of Pakistan in fact can partially be attributed to this one ruler whose policies have had a profoundly debilitating—and lasting—impact on the Pakistani body politic, its relations with neighbors, and even global security in the early twenty-first century. In many respects, Zia is akin to Aurangzeb, the Mughal ruler who introduced extreme Islamic ideas in South Asia in the seventeenth century and destroyed all the progress his predecessors, such as Akbar, had achieved in establishing intercommunal harmony.

Zia's policy approaches toward Afghanistan and the United States attest to the earlier contention that the Pakistani elite has often made moves that looked brilliant and successful in the short term, but which in the long run have brought major disaster to the country's unity and security and overall political development toward a tolerant, democratically oriented developmental state.

Pakistan and the War in Afghanistan

Geopolitics and national strategy came together in a major turning point in December 1979. The Soviet Union, under Leonid Brezhnev, had by that time become increasingly angered by the failures of the communist regime which had come into power in Afghanistan in the previous year, the inefficiencies and excesses of which had driven the Afghan population toward rebellion. Moreover, the Soviets suspected that the Afghan leadership was increasingly tilting toward the United States. The Soviet response was the launching of an ill-fated and poorly conceived invasion of Afghanistan that involved also the installation of a sympathizer in office, Babrak Karmal.[75]

As the rebellion in Afghanistan against the communist regime had intensified over 1978–1979, the United States had remained skeptical of the prospects of a Soviet entry into the country, and Washington had limited itself to some logistical support for the rebellion through the CIA.[76] The response to the unexpected invasion itself, however, was swift. President Jimmy Carter immediately demanded Soviet withdrawal from Afghanistan, and by January 1980 had proclaimed a doctrine which stated that any attempt by an external power (read the Soviet Union) to gain control of the Persian Gulf would be considered a direct threat to the vital interests of the United States, to which Washington would respond accordingly. The administration, asserting that the Soviet Union had broken the detente commitments and used the Afghan political window of opportunity for its geopolitical expansion to the Gulf region, immediately imposed economic sanctions and other punitive diplomatic measures against Moscow.[77]

Earlier in the year the United States had already lost its staunch ally, the Shah of Iran, to the Islamic Revolution led by Ayatollah Ruhollah Khomeini. The Soviet invasion added to the fears in the United States of losing international credibility. Overnight, Pakistan would emerge as the frontline state in America's fight against the Soviet Union in this resurrected Cold War environment. Pakistan's warrior state, with its links to the radical mujahedeen forces in Afghanistan, became an instantly useful tool for the United States and Western allies in their war against the Soviet Union. Zia was a very successful asymmetric bargainer with the United States. Washington under President Ronald Reagan provided a considerable amount of economic and military aid to Pakistan, which in return would act as a conduit for the supply of arms and ammunition to the Afghan mujahedeen. In all, from 1982 to 1989, conservative estimates suggest that the United States supplied military weapons alone worth US$5 billion to the mujahedeen directly, and around $5.7 billion worth through Pakistan. US direct military and economic assistance to Pakistan over the 1980s amounted to over $7.2 billion, leaving it only behind Israel, Egypt, and Turkey in aid received from Washington.[78]

Further, under a secret agreement with the Saudis, Riyadh had agreed to match US outlays toward the Afghan effort dollar for dollar, virtually doubling the amount of aid that was flowing to the mujahedeen. Interestingly, all of this aid was being funneled not directly from the CIA to the mujahedeen, but rather on Zia's insistence, through the ISI in Pakistan, which gave the latter immense control over the disbursal of weapons and resources to Afghan rebels.[79]

The United States closed its eyes to Zia's accelerated pursuit of nuclear weapons. Washington's policies indirectly helped the Islamization of Pakistan as Zia engaged with different mujahedeen groups in both Afghanistan and in Pakistan. Zia used the war in Afghanistan to gain the support of Pakistan's Islamist parties, thereby weakening opposition to his tenuous rule. Radical Muslim groups became more powerful within Pakistan's increasingly permissive environment. Thousands of Muslim young men who came from all over the Arab and Muslim world for training in Pakistan would later become the backbone of al-Qaeda. Indeed, the mujahedeen, some of whom would subsequently form the core of the Taliban, received considerable support from Washington, especially the CIA, in its covert war in Afghanistan.

The American military drive against the Soviet Union was a major success, forcing Moscow to withdraw from Afghanistan, and eventually helping to bring about the collapse of the Warsaw Pact and the Soviet Union as a state. The end of the Cold War owes much to the Soviet Union's failure in Afghanistan. To the Pakistani elite, this showed the power of asymmetric war as well as the utility of pursuing grand geopolitical projects. In that process, however, Pakistan was transformed in a perverse way into a well-entrenched warrior state. It became a source of transnational Islamist terrorism and nuclear proliferation. Pakistan also stood as a testament to the debilitating effects that poor developing countries with major internal structural problems experienced when entangling in superpower rivalries. In the short run, Pakistan had won a tactical victory and economic and military aid, but in the long run, the Afghan war would destroy any chance of Pakistan emerging as a normal state with a development-oriented elite in charge. The "geostrategic curse" imprinted its stamp on Pakistan's trajectory.

The Post-Afghan War Pakistan

The Soviet retreat from Afghanistan in 1989 heralded momentous changes to the international system. It helped to end the Cold War and led to the eventual collapse of the Soviet Union. For Pakistan, it was disastrous as it released thousands of mujahedeen warriors into its society, with over a million refugees serving as an easy recruiting ground for Jihadist groups. Pakistan's support of the mujahedeen has essentially created a war economy where narcotics and weapons became the most valuable currency, thereby further entrenching the warrior state. Washington made no real effort to settle the politically and strategically empty space created by the Soviet retreat. Its failure to do so would later haunt America, helping to facilitate the September 11, 2001, attacks by al-Qaeda warriors supported by the Taliban, an entity which Islamabad had helped create.

Afghanistan's ongoing civil conflict only helped to accelerate the weakening of Pakistan. It offered a major opportunity to the Pakistani military leaders, working within a hyper-realpolitik framework, to exploit their influence in Afghanistan. They were not interested in developing a secular or democratic Afghanistan, but a theocratic country under their hegemony. The bogeyman was India as the prevailing assumption has been that if Pakistan did not control events in Afghanistan, India would make use of them and extend its influence to Pakistan's western border. This notion of border security was derived from the British-era idea that the creation of weak vassals and buffers in the periphery was essential for the colonial state's defense in South Asia. What was missing was an understanding that a weak Afghanistan would also produce blowback effects on Pakistan. The ruling Taliban's radical program drew in concerned outside forces intent on containing it. In turn, the involvement of outside actors would only reinforce the Pakistani elite's sense of encirclement and its commitment to hyper-realpolitik foreign policy. Ultimately, the Pakistani elite's fears over its northwestern border became a self-fulfilling prophecy.

The sudden death of General Zia on August 17, 1988, in a plane crash under mysterious circumstances opened up a limited window of opportunity for democratic progress in Pakistan. The two major parties reemerged, the PPP and the Pakistan Muslim League (PML). Benazir

Bhutto, the daughter of Zulfikar Ali Bhutto, assumed the prime ministership in a PPP-led government following the elections in November 1988 and was reelected in the 1993 parliamentary elections. She had an unmatched opportunity to transform the warrior state, but failed miserably. The warrior state readily reasserted itself in this hybrid arrangement. Bhutto accommodated herself to the model with surprising ease, as was evident in her Afghanistan, Kashmir, and nuclear weapons policies. The key to this reassertion by the military and the ISI was Pakistan's policy of supporting the Taliban against the Northern Alliance straight through to their eventual Afghanistan victory in September 1996. Though considered the most secular leader of Pakistan since her father, Benazir Bhutto supported the Taliban in what Ahmed Rashid calls "a rash and presumptuous policy to create a new western-orientated trade and pipeline route from Turkmenistan through southern Afghanistan to Pakistan, for which the Taliban would provide security."[80]

Benazir Bhutto also increased support for insurgents in Indian-controlled Kashmir and helped create several terrorist organizations like the *Lashkar e-taiba* (LeT) and *Jaish-e-Mohammed* (JeM). These terrorist groups would later haunt Pakistan itself. Their initial aim was to fight India in Kashmir, using the opportunity provided by the unrest there, but eventually their goals came to include global jihad in conjunction with al-Qaeda and other terrorist groups.[81] Bhutto was possibly placating to the military hardliners in the hope of avoiding a coup.

Under Bhutto, the nuclear program was also augmented with the help of China and North Korea, although the program was not under her control. She appeared to have helped the Pakistani nuclear scientist Abdul Qadeer Khan in transferring nuclear materials to North Korea, Libya and Iran in return for missiles and economic benefits. The Khan network consisted of 50-odd associates working from different parts of the world. Its clients included North Korea, Iran, Iraq, and Libya. It had nodal points in the United Arab Emirates, Malaysia, Turkey, and South Africa and the network held more than 50 workshops around the world, with Dubai serving as the main reexporting platform. The Khan Research Laboratories and their affiliated firms provided several components to North Korea, Iran, Iraq, and Libya for building nuclear weapons.[82] New revelations implicated Benazir Bhutto in working in collaboration with A. Q. Khan to make possible a nuclear-missile swap with North Korea. In an interview with journalist Shyam Bhatia, Bhutto mentioned that she carried scientific data about uranium enrichment on CDs in her overcoat to Pyongyang in 1993 and brought back critical missile information from North Korea, although she recanted this story in subsequent interviews with him.[83] The nuclear materials in question were related to North Korea's gas centrifuge uranium enrichment program. She twice visited North Korea to obtain Nodong missiles in a barter deal. The unwillingness on the part of the Pakistani government, especially under General Pervez Musharraf (who had been a major player in the Pakistani military during this period), to allow the interrogation of Khan by credible prosecutors strengthens the argument that Khan was not working alone as a rogue scientist interested in enriching himself.[84]

Bhutto's government did not last long. She was dismissed by civilian president Farooq Leghari in November 1996 at the behest of the army and the ISI. Nawaz Sharif of the PML emerged as the winner in the subsequent elections. Sharif attempted to reassert civilian control over the military, only to fail miserably in the end. He ordered nuclear tests in May 1998 in response to India's own nuclear tests two weeks earlier. Following a short period of rhetoric and bravado, Sharif met with India's Prime Minister Atal Bihari Vajpayee in February 1999 and together they launched the so-called Lahore peace process.

The military leadership under General Musharraf was unhappy with the civilian effort to change the direction of foreign policy and in the spring of 1999 launched a military offensive at a vulnerable point for India in Kashmir—Kargil. With the help of Pakistani soldiers pretending to be Kashmiri freedom fighters, Pakistan occupied the Kargil Heights, which were not protected by India in the winter and spring seasons. With that occupation, they were able to cut off the Leh-Srinagar road, a major artery connecting the Vale of Kashmir and Ladakh. India, under Prime Minister Vajpayee, responded strongly and after a bitter skirmish ejected the Pakistani intruders from most of their positions. However, this was not an easy victory. US President Bill Clinton had to persuade Sharif to ask his army to withdraw, as India was about to escalate the conflict. Not surprisingly, some worried about the possibility of a nuclear war. Clinton met with Sharif on July 4, 1999, the US Independence Day, and convinced him to go back and seek unconditional withdrawal. His agreement to do so immediately made Sharif unpopular with the army. Although it was a brilliant tactical move and caught India by surprise, the attack on Kargil exposed the failure of the Pakistani military to think strategically.[85] The failure of Pakistan at Kargil created a major political backlash. Sharif's relationship with General Musharraf deteriorated dramatically. In October 1999 Musharraf staged a successful coup and deposed the Sharif regime. The coup occurred while Sharif made an unsuccessful attempt to stop Musharraf from returning to Pakistan from an official visit to Sri Lanka by not letting his aircraft land in the country. Musharraf's loyal soldiers mounted the coup and arrested Sharif who would then be deported to Saudi Arabia after a brief jail term. Now in power, Musharraf promised the eventual restoration of democracy and political order, claiming he was taking cues from the founder of modern Turkey, Kamal Atatürk.

September 11, 2001, Attacks and Their Aftermath

Pakistan once again became prominent geopolitically after the September 11, 2001, terrorist attacks in New York and Washington, America's citadels of economic and military power. Musharraf's initial response was to rebuff American overtures to abandon the Taliban and al-Qaeda. But the United States changed the mix of threats and carrots, and by November 2001, Pakistan had agreed to help the United States topple the Taliban and al-Qaeda in Afghanistan. US Deputy Secretary of State Richard Armitage was said to have carried the tough message to Pakistan that it would be bombed to the stone age if it refused to support the war on al-Qaeda and the Taliban in Afghanistan.[86] In that month, the United States launched a major offensive on Afghanistan, unseating the Taliban and pushing their forces as well as al-Qaeda leader Osama bin Laden into Pakistan's poorly controlled northwest territories including Khyber Pakhtunkhwa and Waziristan. The United States installed a government in Afghanistan under Hamid Karzai, whose control over the fractious country was and remains very weak. This support brought immediate financial rewards to Pakistan; by January 2002 it obtained some $3 billion as debt relief and rescheduling of interest payments.[87] However, the United States-led coalition's war efforts were made much more difficult due to the unwillingness of the Pakistani military and the ISI to fully abandon the Taliban and instead keep them in reserve as a strategic asset.

In July 2010, Wikileaks released some 100,000 intelligence documents relating to Afghanistan and scores dealing with Pakistan's involvement with the Taliban. Several documents implicated the ISI in maintaining contacts with the Taliban, encouraging them to engage in some attacks, and providing suicide bombers with accessories like motorbikes—despite receiving billions of dollars from Washington to combat terrorism. The ISI was also incriminated for meeting "directly with the Taliban in secret strategy sessions to organize networks of militant groups that fight against American soldiers in Afghanistan, and even hatch plots to assassinate Afghan leaders." The reports revealed that "the Pakistani military has acted as both ally and enemy, as its spy agency runs what American officials have long suspected is a double game—appeasing certain American demands for cooperation while angling to exert influence in Afghanistan through many of the same insurgent networks that the Americans are fighting to eliminate."[88]

Despite this half-hearted fight against the Taliban, the Pakistani army still appeared to keep some elements of the Jihadist forces alive for its war in Kashmir and potentially in Afghanistan, making a distinction between "good Taliban" and "bad Taliban." The Taliban's biggest mistake was crossing the line and attempting to spread its power in the traditional areas of the army's control. The tendency to play "double games" has been abundantly clear in the Pakistani military and ISI's war on terrorism. A February 2012 secret report by the North Atlantic Treaty Organization (NATO), entitled *State of the Taliban*, suggested that the ISI has been directly helping the Taliban. Based on interrogation of 4,000 captured Taliban, al-Qaeda members, foreign fighters, and civilians, the report revealed that "Pakistan's manipulation of Taliban senior leadership continues unabatedly," and that the "ISI is thoroughly aware of Taliban activities and the whereabouts of all senior Taliban personnel. The Haqqani family, for example, resides immediately west of the ISI office at the airfield in Miram Sha, Pakistan."[89]

Meanwhile, major political changes occurred in Pakistan in 2007. Civil society emerged as a key player for a brief period, catalyzing this change. In November 2007 Musharraf declared an emergency, suspended the constitution, and dismissed the popular Chief Justice

Iftikhar Muhammad Chaudhry. This resulted in a campaign by lawyers for Chaudhry's reinstatement. Major political unrest and street demonstrations spearheaded by lawyers led to the resignation of Musharraf and the reemergence of both Bhutto and Sharif in the political sphere. Fears of a rigged election, like the one in 2002 that allowed him to remain president, were not realized even though Musharraf received the support of the pro-Taliban Jamiat Ulema-e-Islam (JUI). Bhutto was assassinated in a subsequent election rally in Rawalpindi on December 27, 2007, two weeks before the elections, and in her place her husband Asif Ali Zardari assumed the leadership of the party and subsequently the presidency of the country—thanks in part to sympathy votes in the delayed 2008 elections. Zardari's coalition with Nawaz Sharif did not last long. In late 2008, the rupture between the two leaders caused Sharif to abandon the coalition and join the opposition. Zardari's appointment of Yousaf Raza Gilani as prime minister augured a period of relative calm in the Pakistani political landscape.

Ironically, Pakistan's democratic elections and political transitions have made things worse domestically. Its democratically oriented civil society has emerged much weaker, and the middle class has become increasingly sympathetic to extremism. An example was the January 2011 assassination of the governor of Punjab, Salmaan Taseer, who opposed the blasphemy laws from the Zia era, which promised jail terms and execution of Christians and other minorities for alleged acts or statements against the Quran and the Prophet Muhammad. The governor daringly opposed the execution sentence of a Christian woman for alleged desecration of the Quran. His assassin was cheered by large segments of Pakistani society, including several lawyers who had fought against the Musharraf regime. In March 2011, the minister for minority affairs, Shahbaz Bhatti, a token Christian, was gunned down by Islamist extremists, an act that also received very limited national condemnation.[90]

During this period, the Pakistani Taliban effectively took over significant portions of the country. Nearly 30% of the country was under their control, including Swat, a popular tourist destination 107 miles from Islamabad. This sudden change of control forced an about-face in the Pakistani military, as they realized that an Islamist takeover would end their own power as well. Under considerable US pressure and aided by economic support, the military launched an offensive to remove the

Taliban, and was fairly successful in pushing them back by 2011. A major turning point came in May 2011, when US Navy SEALs entered the garrison city of Abbottabad by helicopter and killed Osama bin Laden, who was living just 500 yards from the Pakistan Military Academy. The Pakistani military's response was intense denial of any culpability. The military leadership put pressure on the civilian leadership to take a more defensive posture while blaming it for not defending Pakistan's sovereignty. The opportunity to rein in the military, however, was lost as the warrior state reinvigorated itself. The government responded by arresting informants and cutting off NATO supply routes. A deep freeze in relations with Washington ensued. Yet despite repeated coup scares, the civil-military ruling arrangement continued in spring 2012.[91]

Still, Taliban forces have managed to maintain their control over many interior regions of Afghanistan and continue to successfully orchestrate military strikes on NATO forces. Within Pakistan, the Taliban still poses many challenges, one being the opposition to girls' education—which is absolutely essential to economic development. (In October 2012 they shot and wounded Malala Yousafzai, a 15-year-old girl from Swat who had been campaigning for girls' education, bringing the matter to international attention.) The attacks on minority Shia community by the Taliban increased manifold during this period. During the past five years more than 1,000 Shiites from the Hazara community were killed in the city of Quetta alone. The year 2012 witnessed a high number of killings of Shia across Pakistan, in which some 396 were killed in 113 targeted attacks, and the Pakistani state has not been forthcoming to protect the community.[92] In February 2013, in an act of defiance, relatives refused to bury 84 Shiites killed in Quetta for several days but this did not have any lasting impact.[93]

US President Barack Obama has set 2014 as the deadline to withdraw from Afghanistan, opening the possibility of a Taliban victory (assuming a civil war ensues). Even if the Afghan government and the Taliban come to some sort of power-sharing agreement, it is unlikely to be long-lasting given the Taliban's ambitious goals. Although Pakistan has supported the US-led war and the peace process, it has focused mostly on creating a weak Afghanistan that would remain under its thumb.[94] In keeping with this strategic goal, some Islamist elements in the Pakistani army and the ISI would also like to see the Taliban win in Afghanistan. They ignore the reality that such an outcome in Afghanistan will inflict much damage on Pakistan itself. If the Taliban gain control over Afghanistan, Pakistan will get a tactical ally, but one that has the potential to further "Talibanize" Pakistan itself. A resurgent coalition of former Northern Alliance forces—with the support of India, Russia, several Central Asian states, the United States, and probably Iran—would oppose such a state. If the Taliban does not win outright and continues to fight, Pakistan will likely carry on its double game of tepidly supporting United States–backed forces while simultaneously undermining them by backing the Taliban. In either instance, the warrior state mentality will retain its hold over Pakistan, with Islamist forces enjoying sway over Pakistani politics. Limited tactical victories or a substantial strategic victory in Afghanistan will, however, not enable Pakistan to transform itself into a unified and tolerant state.

Meanwhile in early 2012, some movement has occurred in the peace process with India. Pakistan agreed to open trade with India by offering the most-favored nation (MFN) status, and during official visits of the leaders of the two countries, a settlement of some of the long-standing conflicts such as Siachen and Sir Creek border areas looked possible. In January 2013, the army in its Green Book, considered as the doctrinal manual and most authoritative publication where officers write about strategic issues, acknowledged internal threats as the greatest risk to the country's security[95] although this may well be in rhetoric only. The Pakistani army chief, General Ashfaq Parvez Kayani, even spoke of the "peaceful co-existence" of India and Pakistan following an avalanche disaster in the Siachen that killed some 135 Pakistani soldiers.[96] Skeptics can point to several such past efforts. Many of them were on the cusp of success, only to be thwarted by elements within the ISI or the army in collusion with the many terrorist organizations that Pakistan has allowed to mushroom in the country over the years. The skeptics may well be right; border tensions once again flared up in 2013, with mutual killings of Pakistani and Indian soldiers (reportedly, some were beheadings).[97]

The domestic political sphere got even murkier with the dismissal of Prime Minister Yousaf Raza Gilani in June 2012 by the Supreme Court. The court argued that the government failed to prosecute the president for his alleged corrupt activities involving Swiss banks. His successor,

Raja Pervez Ashraf, also faced major challenges from the Supreme Court, which ordered his arrest for allegedly committing bribery in his role as minister for water and power (the order was never carried out).[98] During this time a Pakistani expatriate cleric from Canada, Tahirul Qadri, appeared with a massive street rally demanding the immediate ouster of the government. He was pacified only after the government agreed to dissolve the National Assembly and hand over power to a caretaker government in March in preparation for the May 2013 elections.[99]

Through all of this, the Pakistani media has been remarkably resilient, with the English media especially and social media producing highly critical news reports and analysis. Some believe that as a result, the military may have far more difficulty engineering another coup anytime soon. The array of television channels, radio stations, and social media available through Internet and mobile phone networks has brought a measurable degree of dynamism to the Pakistani media space.[100] That said, the jihadists have also been able to effectively disseminate their message through the same social media.[101]

The May elections were marred by major violence against somewhat secular political parties, especially the Awami National Party (ANP), Muttahida Qaumi Movement (MQM), and the PPP. Nearly 300 people were killed and 885 injured between January 1 and May 15 in some 148 reported terrorist attacks by Taliban and Baloch insurgents. During the election campaign the Pakistani Taliban (Tehreek-i-Taliban), which then had established itself in the Waziristan region, declared a war on all political parties except Nawaz Sharif's Pakistan Muslim League-Nawaz (PML-N) and cricket-star turned politician Imran Khan's Tehreek-i-Insaf (PTI) party. Fearing Taliban violence, many politicians, including the President, Asif Ali Zardari, canceled electioneering, while his son, Bilwal Bhutto Zardari, the chairman of the PPP, left the country altogether.[102] One silver lining in all these events was the army not manipulating the electoral process, unlike in many previous elections. Former military ruler Pervez Musharraf returned, hoping to lead his political party, All Pakistan Muslim League, in the elections. He was disqualified from standing for elections in several constituencies by the election commission and eventually was placed under house arrest for charges such as his alleged complicity in the murder of political opponents, including Benazir Bhutto.[103] What is noteworthy is the absence of active army support for General Musharraf—one of its own illustrious former members—in his struggle against the judiciary and civilian authorities.

Despite the violence, the elections saw a voter turnout of 60% (rather high in the Pakistani context), with a large number of young people voting for the first time. Sharif's PML-N emerged as the largest party in the National Assembly and with the support of smaller parties and independents was able to form a government. Memories of his previous government during 1997–1999 suggest that Sharif may have to tread a very careful line with the military and the ISI, the two institutions that want to retain their control over foreign and security policies. The Pakistani Taliban and other extremist groups are also of much concern as they could intensify their attacks on minorities as well as semisecular politicians. Sharif's initiatives for peace with India could produce a backlash with the military and his efforts to control the military top brass could also result in attempts to undermine his regime. How Sharif handles the Afghan situation is another big issue. Pakistan's economy is in deep crisis and the daily lives of people are affected by long electric shutdowns ranging from 12 to 18 hours a day. Pakistan's power generating capacity is only 9,000 MW out of a total demand of 16,000 MW. The chances of increasing power supply look dim for months or even years. This has further hurt Pakistan's economy, especially its exports, and deterred investments.[104] However, it is remarkable that a successor government was formed through the electoral process and all political parties seem to be willing to abide by the electoral verdict. Pakistan has miles to cross before calling itself a true democracy and it may never become one. The troubled structural foundations of Pakistan, which I discuss in subsequent chapters, as well as the hyper-realpolitik and illiberal views the elite holds are part of the reasons for this skeptical prognosis.

Although the army has retreated somewhat and is reluctant to take power away from civilians, it is difficult to determine if it has really given up control, whether direct or indirect. Nor can we predict whether or not it will attempt a coup if its real interests are threatened by the civilian elite, especially vis-à-vis India, or if Pakistan's economic conditions deteriorate to the point where a massive popular uprising against the civilian government becomes likely. Asif Ali Zardari's civilian government was the first one in Pakistani history to finish a full term, yet

Pakistan remains a state in perpetual crisis. Its trajectory is highly uncertain given the ongoing war in Afghanistan and its own political instability. The absence of economic opportunity for Pakistan's burgeoning youth population, who are mostly uneducated in technical subjects, makes it even harder for them to carve out a niche in the global marketplace. Export-led growth is unlikely to happen either. For our analysis, it is imperative to explain why Pakistan emerged the way it did and why it failed to develop a cohesive, prosperous, and tolerant nation-state. The next chapter explores the reasons why Pakistan remains a garrison state despite occasional hybrid democratic rule.

4

The Garrison State

IN JULY 1996, Prime Minister Benazir Bhutto attended a war game in Pakistan's army headquarters in Rawalpindi during which Pervez Musharraf, a lieutenant-general at that time, attempted to impress upon Bhutto the need to take military action in Kashmir. He reportedly told her that the "time window for the resolution of the Kashmir dispute is short," because "with passage of time, the India-Pakistan equation" in both military and economic dimensions is going against Pakistan. He warned: "the differential is increasing and the window will close."[1] Although Bhutto refused to act, Musharraf never gave up his plan to launch a military operation in Kashmir. The opportunity came in the spring of 1999 when Musharraf was the chairman of the Joint Chiefs, he was able to send in specially trained forces and occupy the Kargil heights on the Indian side of Kashmir under nuclear cover and in complete surprise. The then Prime Minister Nawaz Sharif claimed he came to know about this operation only after it had begun in May 1999, although the preparations had started in January 1999.[2] Even if Sharif's account is accurate, it is still a puzzle as to why the prime minister would approve of such an operation almost at the same time he was in peace talks with the Indian leader Atal Bihari Vajpayee in Lahore. More importantly, how was the army able to engage in such a pivotal offensive on its own without the full connivance of the civilian leaders?

A somewhat similar episode occurred in 1965 when a small group, led by Foreign Minister Zulfikar Ali Bhutto and a few military commanders, convinced the military ruler Ayub Khan to launch an offensive in Kashmir. It was called "Operation Gibraltar" and meant to take advantage of the unrest in the Indian-controlled province and the small window of opportunity arising from Pakistan's acquisition of high-quality weaponry from the United States. According to Bhutto, Pakistan had to act because "militarily" to achieve a "big push" Pakistan was superior in the area of armor to India because of the military assistance it was getting. As the Kashmir issue was not being resolved peacefully and "we had this military advantage, we were getting blamed for it." India's new ordnance factories were not in "full production and once they did India would have been too strong to be beaten."[3] Making use of military windows of opportunities against an adversary is the quintessential character of a garrison state that is often driven by the offensive military doctrine of "strike first, ask questions later." Pakistan's warrior state has been deeply entrenched in the political, social, and economic order of the country since the 1950s. Although several national elections have been held, and some civilian governments have been allowed to function periodically, a proper democratic system is yet to be established with the military under full civilian control. The puzzle is why?

Despite some limited attempts at democracy, from its early days Pakistan repeatedly found it immensely difficult to create or sustain viable democratic institutions. Indeed, it quickly became a garrison state where the ultimate authority rested with the military as the most powerful political and social institution, with the many privileges and risks that come with such a status. Since 1958, Pakistan has alternated between elected governments and military rule, but democratic governance has been neither complete nor sustainable. The army has always been lurking behind the elected governments, holding real political power and the capacity to control the fate of the civilian elite. If the civilians failed to comply, the army would unleash its ultimate sword—coup d'état. Even under civilian rule, the army and its spy wing, the ISI, never gave up their power over crucial national security and foreign policy matters, including the control of the atomic weapons that the country obtained in the 1980s.

Today, a leading scholar of Pakistan calls the military-intelligence establishment of the country the "deep state" which can "pick and choose policy toward extremists, refusing to fight those who will confront India on its behalf as well as those Taliban who kill Western and Afghan soldiers in the war next-door" in Afghanistan.[4] Those civilian rulers who dared to seriously challenge the military establishment risk assassination, as happened to Zulfikar Ali Bhutto and Benazir Bhutto, or exile, as in the cases of Benazir Bhutto and Nawaz Sharif. Fear of army retribution has acted as a major deterrent to civilian leaders from undertaking meaningful reforms to make Pakistan a true democracy where the military would be under the control of elected civilian leaders.

The key players in the Pakistani political spectrum as well as its powerful external supporters such as the United States showed little interest in making it a true democracy. As Stephen Cohen puts it: "Most of the key power players in Pakistan respected democracy and wished Pakistan to be democratic, but they were not willing to make it so." To Cohen, these included the powerful army, civilian bureaucrats, and the civilian governments that came to power periodically. For the United States in particular, a "pro-Western Pakistan, a stable Pakistan, a prosperous Pakistan, and a democratic Pakistan were all desirable, but in that order."[5] None of the other powerful backers of Pakistan, China and Saudi Arabia in particular, had any interest in encouraging democracy in Pakistan because they themselves abhorred democratic values. The donors, especially the United States and the international financial institutions such as the IMF and WB, rarely if ever made democracy a condition for economic aid. With only a weak civil society in favor of liberal democracy, Pakistan has had little chance to develop a coherent democratic system.

Pakistan ended up as a garrison or praetorian state and whenever the military ceded power to elected civilian governments, it did so only partially. This left Pakistan a hybrid democratic model where the ultimate power rested not with the people but with the military as a veto player in any decisions the civilian government would take. Even in the second decade of the twenty-first century, Pakistan retains many of the features of a garrison state, while many previously military-controlled states in Latin America and Asia have transformed to democracies during the 1980s and 1990s. This puzzle cannot be explained without exploring the particular societal context and geostrategic circumstances under which Pakistan exists as a nation-state.

What Is a Garrison State?

A garrison state is characterized as a state which is preoccupied with danger, one in which the "specialists on violence" are the most powerful societal group; the main function of the ruling elite is to "skillfully guid[e] the minds of men . . . [through] symbolic manipulation" and prevent the full utilization of state resources for non-military purposes.[6] *Praetorian state* is another term commonly used for a state dominated by the military. According to Amos Perlmutter, a praetorian state is one in which the military frequently intervenes in national politics and dominates the political system while professional officers emerge as a ruling class and play a leading role in the country's institutions. He classifies praetorian states into two, the "arbitrator type" and the "ruler type." The "arbitrator type" tends to be more professionally oriented, without a stated ideology, and intervenes occasionally with a time limit on army rule and then returns to the barracks. The "ruler type" maintains continuous rule. The arbitrator type does not necessarily leave ultimate control even when it entrusts power with a civilian government.[7] Using this framework, the Pakistani military at the present time can be characterized as an arbitrator type, as it controls the levers of power even when it is not in charge of the formal government. But for half of Pakistan's history it has been of the ruler type.

In my view, although the concepts of "praetorian state" and "garrison state" are somewhat similar, the garrison state is a more appropriate term for Pakistan as it describes a state with a deeper penetration by the military as the most dominant actor in society, where military values and culture dominate the societal ethos profoundly. A praetorian state may exist without military values penetrating deeply into the society. In that sense, Pakistan is a great example of a garrison state with military ethos deeply ingrained in its society and its culture.

A garrison state may periodically give civilians some amount of power, especially during periods when the military is unable to provide sufficient economic and social benefits or public goods to the population. It is then that various vocal segments of society issue demands for political rights or concessions. In order to mollify these demands, as in the Pakistani case, civilian rule can be established with the military still in command behind the scenes, especially on issues of national security and foreign policy. Thus the military wields a veto, and can overrule or suppress the civilian government's own veto. This has substantial ramifications for the conduct of international conflict, as it offers the military an extra-institutionality, disregarding rules, laws and constitution.[8]

Indeed, international conflict is an important spur to the formation and persistence of garrison states. Countries that face incessant threats and conflicts, or have ambitious geopolitical agendas, are especially vulnerable to the formation of garrison states. In this milieu, the military elite develops managerial qualities and strengthens its position in society, resulting in the increased centrality in society of the specialists on violence. The constant readiness for war would generate militarization of the civil order and a higher community deference for military men.[9] Militarism is invariably developed by a garrison state, defined as "an attitude and a set of institutions which regard war and the preparation for war as a normal and desirable social activity."[10] Succeeding generations "accept the military model of society," while the civilian institutions show an inability to "civilianize" the military.[11] Public opinion is not developed or respected, political parties have limited or no control, the legislature and judiciary have less power than the executive and elections are no more than plebiscites.[12] Further, civilian life is deeply penetrated by the military, be it in politics or business, closing the gap between the two realms, and the military ally with key industrial and economic corporations.[13]

A garrison state is the quintessential national security state, concerned primarily about the protection of national borders, physical assets, and core values, largely through traditional military means.[14] The state elite in a national security state works chiefly based on the premise that in a Hobbesian anarchical international system, the self-help principle, rules, i.e. each state takes care of its own security as no higher authority can protect them, nor can they rely on the goodwill of others. Use of force may be essential to protect oneself.[15] States are constantly concerned about their position relative to other states. While states have other purposes, such as providing domestic order and welfare, national security, especially from external threats, takes priority over all others in the hierarchy of state interests, as without territorial security, all national values would suffer.[16] Threats and counterthreats are the main topics of discourse, while offensive doctrines, based on the logic of first strike and jumping through windows of opportunity, are sought in order to maximize one's strategic goals.

Granted, democracies can be staunch national security states. The United States and Israel certainly place considerable weight on these concerns, although civilians have dominance over the military in decision-making in these countries in national security matters.[17] But a garrison state, with its constant preoccupation with danger, takes concern about national security to a fever pitch. It is authoritarian in character, with the military never completely subservient to civilian authority.

In the twentieth century, some paradigmatic national security states have pursued a trading state strategy as well, showing that garrison states can be intensely capitalist and not necessarily always feudal.[18] Such states include Korea and Taiwan (especially prior to their democratization in the 1980s) and China since 1979. While these states privilege national security, they also have reformed internally and engaged in extensive trading activity internationally in order to bolster their countries' economic and developmental goals. In Chapter 7, I will make comparisons between Pakistan and a few such states. Those states where proper full-scale democratic transitions have taken place and where the military is under civilian control can no longer be called garrison states, even when a focus on national security remains a key characteristic.

A garrison state may also be a partial democracy, combining military control with elements of electoral democracy. Pakistan is primarily a garrison state, alternating periodically between straight military rule and hybrid democracy. However, its democratic institutions are weak, owing largely to the garrison nature of the polity.

The Democratic Deficit

Pakistan's garrison state has intermittently allowed for democratic elections and civilian rule. However, even when civilian governments were in charge, they were not fully in control of the key levers of state power. The military always lurked in the background, controlling many domains, especially national security. Civilian rulers have typically placated a military that presumably would challenge any of the civilians' attempts to reduce its power. Under such a system, the country can never become truly democratic—civil-military relations can deteriorate at any time and the military can easily reassert its control.

The Pakistani case shows that even a full-fledged military regime can toy with some form of democracy in order to gain legitimacy. The first major experiment with limited democracy in Pakistan was during the Ayub Khan period (1958–1969). Ayub's military regime promulgated a system called "Basic Democracy." Elections were held in January 1960 for "Basic Democracies Councils," with 80,000 members. The different layers of this system consisted of divisional, district, municipal, towns and war councils, representing the different sections and administrative structures of the country. These councils would then elect the president. In such an election in February 1960, Ayub won by a vote of 95.6%. From February 1960 to March 1962, representatives of the council organized, interacted with officials, and advanced plans for development schemes.[19]

Ayub Khan's Basic Democracy system was a cunning model designed to legitimize military control while at the same time providing the illusion of public participation. It was neither basic nor democratic, because it simply did not follow the key principles of democratic rule—the freedom to contest elections by independent political parties. It was a top-down model designed by the military and its chief so that real democratic forces would not emerge as a challenge to the garrison state. Thus it was during Ayub's tenure that the formalization of the garrison state occurred. Significantly, "he made manifest what had already been implicit during the 1950s—the dominant role of the military and the civilian bureaucracy in Pakistan."[20] Other military rulers, including Zia-ul-Haq and Pervez Musharraf, similarly utilized elections, often through manipulated and handpicked candidates, and the excessive involvement of military officers in civilian activities. Zia's party-less elections in 1985 and similar exercise under Musharraf further weakened political parties like the PPP that could appeal to broader constituencies. In this process, the military rulers strengthened groups and organizations that are based on narrow sectarian and ethnic identities. The military in Pakistan has become a well-entrenched institution by keeping control over many civilian departments. Under Musharraf, this process continued at a fast pace. In 2003, a large number of civilian positions in the ministries of defense, communications, foreign affairs, education, information, interior, food and agriculture, information technology, petroleum, science and technology, and revenue were held by military officials.[21]

Studies based on the curriculum at the National Defense College and their key internal publication, the Green Book, show the deep-rooted military involvement in Pakistan's civilian world. Serving and retired military officials, as contributors to various chapters in the internally circulated Green Books, discuss the inability of civilian politicians to prevent regionalism and instability. This distrust of the civilian political elite is a persistent theme in Pakistani military officers' discourse and writings. Some writers in the Green Book draw on the examples of China, Indonesia, Egypt, Israel, and Turkey as examples of militaries that contribute to all the key aspects of national development.[22]

In fact, much of Pakistan's strategic behavior can be traced to the system of ideas contained in various Green Books, which show a deep attachment to radical Islamic thinking among many military officers. For example, an article in the 1991 Green Book by Commodore Tariq Majid proposed the creation of a volunteer people's force of all able-bodied men to strengthen military operations and the ISI-backed jihadist networks. In the 1994 Green Book, Brigadier Saifi Ahmad Naqvi argued: "the existence and survival of Pakistan depend upon complete implementation of Islamic ideology in true sense. If the ideology is not preserved then the very existence of Pakistan becomes doubtful," and it is the duty of the army not only to protect the territorial boundaries but also the "ideological frontiers to which the country owes its existence."[23]

Pakistan's education system generally extols and valorizes the military's vision. Schools tend to ignore South Asia's rich history prior to the major Muslim invasions (which started around 1000 A.D.) and portray India and Hinduism in a negative light. This portrayal has helped to perpetuate the garrison state in Pakistan. Some of these history textbooks even contend that Pakistan was first established when the Arab armies led by Mohammad bin Qasim occupied Sind and Multan in the eighth century.[24] A study in 2003 of Pakistani school textbooks in social studies and civics found a multitude of historical distortions, especially regarding Hindus and India. The books also encourage as well as glorify war and the use of force. The study's authors found that the glorification of war and military were pervasive, evidenced by such courses as "Fundamentals of War" and "Defense of Pakistan," both of which featured in textbooks issued during Zulfikar Ali Bhutto's presidency in the 1970s. Such textbooks demonstrate the pervasiveness of Pakistan's warrior state ideology even under civilian governments.[25]

Pakistan's hybrid democracy is a system in which, procedurally, the civilians may have the upper hand, but the military can never be under their full control. Although civilian rule was established based on elections, the governments of Zulfikar Ali Bhutto, Benazir Bhutto, and Nawaz Sharif were hybrid in many respects. The role of the army has been paramount in the Pakistani system, and fear of an army coup restrained these governments from undertaking any major initiatives against the wishes of the armed forces. The governments led by President Asif Ali Zardari (2008–2013) and his prime ministers, Yousaf Raza Gilani (2008–2012) and Raja Pervez Ashraf (2012–2013), have also been hybrid in many respects. The army has retained key national functions and called the shots in many areas of national policy and, when threatened, has invoked its right to stage a coup. For instance, the "memogate" scandal involving the former ambassador of Pakistan to the United States, Hussain Haqqani, almost resulted in the overthrow of the elected government in early 2012. The security forces alleged that the ambassador had asked a Pakistani expatriate businessman to contact US military officials in order to prevent a coup following the assassination of Osama bin Laden. The businessman dutifully informed the ISI and the military leadership, which led to a severe reaction against the civilian government. The military forced the civilian government to let Haqqani resign, and a bruising investigation of the affair ensued.[26] The ambassador first took refuge in the prime minister's residence but later fled the country, fearing his incarceration. This event showed the fragility of civilian rule in Pakistan and the coup threat that the military always wields. Another instance of military's ultimate control was revealed in November 2008, following the Mumbai terrorist attacks, when Zardari made a statement in favor of Pakistan declaring a no-first-use nuclear policy, which the military vehemently opposed. Unsurprisingly, Zardari abandoned the idea for good.[27]

A democracy is incomplete if the elected government does not have full control over the apparatus of the state. Leading scholars of democratic transition Juan Linz and Alfred Stepan contend that transition to full democracy is complete only when general agreement is reached on procedures for elections, when a government comes to power through popular elections that are free and fair, the government has de facto authority to make policies and the three branches of government—legislature, executive, and judiciary—do not have to share power with other state institutions, such as the military.[28] They warn against the "electoralist fallacy," where free elections, a necessary condition for democratic transitions, are considered as a sufficient condition for democracy. A good example is Guatemala where, at the time they were writing, even though the military had relinquished formal control of power, it "retains such extensive prerogatives that the democratically elected government is not even *de jure* sovereign."[29] In a garrison state like Pakistan, the military thus holds onto many levers of power, and serves as the ultimate arbiter, with the coup d'état as veto. Due to internal or external pressures, the military may allow the civilian government to run major functions of the government. But when it comes to defense and foreign affairs, the military has the ultimate say. When a country's main preoccupation is national security, this power amounts to de facto control over governance.

Explanations

There are several explanations for Pakistan's status as a rare garrison-*cum*-hybrid democratic state today, even when such states have been in retreat in many parts of the world. In the Post-War era, the largest number of garrison states existed in Latin America, but a wave of democratization had ended most of them by the 1990s, including in Argentina, Brazil and Chile. These garrison states had few external enemies; their core mission was protection against internal opponents seeking to generate social disorder, especially against the well-entrenched military oligarchy.[30]

A National Security Explanation

A national security explanation posits that garrison states emerge and persist in response to external or internal threats. The Pakistani elite faced or perceived enormous security challenges from powerful neighboring India and, to a limited extent, Afghanistan. Due to the size differential with India and the ongoing conflict over Kashmir, it needed to devote considerably more energy to the military sector than other areas. Due to its strategic location, Pakistan also got entangled in the Cold War alliance with the United States and then with China. Both phenomena reinforced the concept that a strong army was absolutely necessary given the hostile external environment. There is some merit to this argument. In the first decade of Pakistan's existence, feuding political parties and bureaucratic elites agreed on one thing—Pakistan must privilege national security over everything else lest India may try to impose its hegemony. There was also a strong sense that Pakistan was created to protect Islam and Islamic civilization and that "if she perished or India succeeded in extending her hegemony over Pakistan, repercussions would also be felt in other Islamic countries. Therefore, the political and religious leaders claimed, the defence of Pakistan was the defence of Islam."[31] The Pakistani military relies on the national security imperative to rationalize its dominance over the Pakistani politics and social life. The Chief of Army Staff Ashfaq Parvez Kayani stated in October 2011: "we cannot base our strategies on any good intentions, no matter how noble they may be, as intentions can change overnight. Our strategy has to be based on India's capability."[32] This existential logic of the military—it must be prepared for any eventuality given India's capabilities—allows it to stay on as the key power-wielding force in the Pakistani society.

While there is much merit in this national security argument, it only offers a broad macro-level explanation for the rise and persistence of a garrison state, for many countries facing perceived existential threats or external hegemony have chosen to become democratic and developmental states even when retaining their focus on security.

An Institutionalist Explanation

An institutionalist explanation contends that the fundamental basis of the garrison state is the military institution itself. If a country gives highest salience to national security and it does not possess well-established civil-military rules, the chances of a garrison state emerging are high. Civilian control thus becomes crucial in preventing the state from emerging as a garrison state. The specialization that the military enjoys as custodian of national security offers it advantages with which other specialized social groups cannot compete. If the military is politicized, it will institutionalize its power and continue to do so as long as it can.[33] In a society as divisive as Pakistan, where political forces are extremely polarized, it is not surprising that the army, with superior organization, centralized command, discipline, and esprit de corps, has been able to maintain its dominant position for such a long time. Many of the sham elections the military regimes conducted were to formalize and legitimize their rule. After all, military regimes tend to both lack political legitimacy and lose effectiveness over time due to the lack of sustained popular support.

The institutionalist explanation is very much based on a bureaucratic conception of state authority. The garrison state emerges as the military becomes well-entrenched as a major stakeholder of power due to bureaucratic and organizational reasons. Militaries in many situations tend to espouse offensive doctrines since winning wars often requires striking first. Elevating national security to the highest salience is in the interests of the military, in order to maximize resources from the national economy. It also offers "increased prestige," and "heightened self-image" to the army.[34] As beneficiaries of the system, military officers are thus unlikely to abandon power, and instead simply engage in solidifying their position and demanding ever-increasing allocations of the national budget.

In Pakistan, a powerful secondary military bureaucratic organization emerged in the form of the ISI. It was established in 1948, but it acquired legitimacy and strength in the 1980s as part of the United States-led mujahedeen struggle against the Soviet occupation of Afghanistan. The ISI is often referred to as the country's "big brother," frequently functioning with a level of authority that makes it "a state within a state." Beyond intelligence gathering, it has been playing a critical role in the country's foreign policy from Afghanistan to Kashmir. Both under civilian and military rule, it has played by its own rules. Indeed, it has helped to overthrow civilian governments.[35] The ISI has been accused of subverting the political system and suppressing political groups that the military doesn't approve of, setting up alliances with extreme right-wing and religious groups, and influencing the media and journalistic community through manipulation and coercion. All efforts by civilian governments to tame the ISI have thus far failed.[36] The ISI is believed to have played a big role in the training and dispatching of terrorists to India's financial capital Mumbai in 2008 which killed some 166 people, including 28 foreigners. The ISI's role in the attacks were revealed during the trial and sentencing of David Headley, a Pakistani-American who helped in the scouting of targets in Mumbai for the Lashkar e-taiba (LeT) terrorists from Pakistan who conducted the attack.[37] Prior to that incident, ISI was involved in an audacious attack on the Indian Parliament in December 2001 by the LeT and another terrorist group, Jaish-e-Muhammad, which almost led to a war between the two nuclear-armed countries.[38]

While there is much merit in the institutionalist explanation, it is still unclear why and how these institutions gained such an upper hand in Pakistan. Further, why has the Pakistani military not lost its legitimacy—political and moral—completely to govern despite its many failures? After all, other military regimes across the developing world have collapsed because of their inability to bring either sustained peace or development.

A Historical-Cultural Explanation

Another sort of explanation for the emergence of a garrison state in Pakistan emphasizes deep structural and cultural factors. In societies with long histories of conflict and political domination by the military, the veneration of militarism and the military virtues can easily become pervasive. The largest segment of the Pakistani army elite comes from the Punjab, the province which dominated the armed forces of British India. The Pakistani elite—a combination of officers, bureaucrats and landlords, also drawn largely from the Punjab—inherited a culture that extolled military virtues and touted the efficacy of military solutions to conflict. Thus they tend to regard the martial traditions of the Punjab as a fundamental cultural feature of Pakistani life. It is therefore not surprising that Pakistan evolved into a garrison state.[39]

According to this perspective, following the 1857 Indian Revolt, Punjab became the "sword arm of the Raj" by providing the largest number of troops for British colonial rule. In fact, from early nineteenth century till the end of World War II, between 50 and 60% of the soldiers of the British Indian army was drawn from the province.[40] The extent of the Punjab's militarization became evident in the high levels of violence that occurred there during the 1947 partition. The initial civil-military regime that was formed in Pakistan was heavily drawn from this left-over army and the bureaucrats. This colonial legacy also allowed the Punjabi-controlled oligarchy comprising the army and the bureaucracy to dominate post-independent Pakistan. The landed aristocracy of the province remained extremely powerful in the post-independent era, and they, collaborated with the army and bureaucracy.[41]

Yet there may be something to the configuration of the Pakistani military as a Punjabi-dominant one. Even today the majority of officers come from the Punjab followed by the Northwest Frontier Province (currently known as Khyber Pakhtunkhwa).[42] Even though Punjab's share had declined marginally by 2005, the province still accounted for 60% of all new officers. The Northwest Frontier Province with 22%, Sindh with 10%, Baluchistan with 5%, and the Federally Administered Tribal Areas, the Federal Capital, and Azad Kashmir constituted the rest.[43] A question arises: why did India, which also inherited the British army, not become a garrison state? It is true that the Indian armed forces drew heavily from different parts of the country, and the conscious effort by first Prime Minister Jawaharlal Nehru and his successors to place the army under strict civilian control, made the big difference. The rise of a warrior state in Pakistan may have been contributed to by the cultural-historical factor discussed above, but it is not necessarily the sole critical variable for the persistence of such a state as countries with deep military history and culture have changed in modern times. However, this factor in conjunction with other external and internal conditions may be necessary for a comprehensive understanding of the warrior state of Pakistan.

Civilian Weakness

Outwardly, Pakistan typifies all these causes in one form or another. However, an important reason for the persistence of the garrison state in Pakistan is institutional in the form of weak political parties and civilian leaders. Pakistan always had a weak civilian political elite, not really able to tame the military. The civilian leadership has been inept from the beginning of the state. It was difficult to establish proper civilian institutions, as the military would not allow their growth and would blame them for the country's failures even though the military itself often wielded actual power. The nationalist elite that fought for independence in 1947 declined their position quickly and the oligarchic power elite that emerged had a narrow societal base and the high concentration of land ownership by them made it relatively easy for this power elite to capture the state and its wealth.[44]

The military in a country like Pakistan presents itself as the alternative to dysfunctional civilian rule. Political parties were seen by the military as agents of disunity. Samuel Huntington has argued that militaries tend to rely on "consensus by command" and "community without politics." Often by criticizing and downgrading politics, the military prevents society from developing strong democratic political order.[45] This applies well to the Pakistani case. It was initially the elected president who invited the military to stage a coup. It was President Iskander Mirza (with a background in the military and the bureaucracy) who invited Army General Ayub Khan into key decision-making bodies and then asked him to take over the levers of power in October 1958 when he was installed as chief martial law administrator. Mirza abrogated the constitution in October 1958, arguing that the constitution was unworkable and that it contained many dangerous compromises that would lead to the disintegration of Pakistan "if the inherent malaise is not removed." Ayub called upon the "valiant Armed Forces of Pakistan" to rescue the country. He stated: "I have learned to admire their patriotism and loyalty. I am putting a great strain on them. I fully realize this, but I ask you, Officers and men of the Armed Forces, on your service depends the future existence of Pakistan as an independent nation and a bastion in these parts of the Free World."[46]

Democratic institutions and norms face a wide array of opponents in Pakistan. These include the deeply entrenched feudal system, the military, the black market economy, corrupt bureaucracy, dysfunctional and personality-based party politics, and in recent years the Islamic fundamentalist groups that have gained in support among various sections of the society.[47] Pakistan's democratic institutions have not been strong enough to counter this set of adversaries. Generals, having once gained power, are reluctant to part with it. When they do resign their posts and try to civilianize, they ensure transfer of power to those who agree with them, meaning that they can continue to pressure the civilian governments into making pro-military policies even after they withdraw to the barracks. Indeed, they have sought to formalize this power through legal arrangements.[48]

The Pakistani political system has so far not produced a strong civilian leader who could take on the military and who had the integrity and vision to unite the society behind him or her. The early civilian leaders, mostly bureaucratic functionaries, bought into the myth of the military as the only force capable of bringing Pakistan together as a strong Islamic state. The civilians themselves, in turn, showed reluctance to play by democratic rules. The Muslim League could not emerge as a unifying party given the geographical divide of Pakistan. Popular elections would have meant the loss of control to the numerical superiority of East Pakistan, an eventuality which was anathema to the civil-military bureaucracy and landed aristocracy in West Pakistan. More importantly, the Muslim League discouraged the formation of an opposition party by characterizing such formations as "tantamount to opposition to Pakistan."[49] This is neatly covered in Prime Minister Liaquat Ali Khan's statement: "The formation of new political parties in opposition to the Muslim League is against the best interests of Pakistan. If the Muslim League is not made strong and powerful and the mushroom growth of parties is not checked immediately, I assure you that Pakistan, which was achieved after great sacrifices, will not survive."[50]

Based on narrow sectional interests of protecting their turf, the military and West Pakistani politicians failed to honor the results of a rare example of a proper election in 1970. The numerical majority of East Pakistan produced a result against the perceived interests of Pakistan's dominant elite. The Awami League won a majority in parliament, with 160 of East Pakistan's 162 seats in the National Assembly, while Bhutto's PPP won 81 of the 132 seats assigned to the West. Bhutto's opposition to forming a coalition government and his unwillingness to cede power to the Awami League killed that experiment, leading to Yahya Khan suspending the National Assembly. This led to the intensified campaign for liberation by the Awami League, military suppression of the Bangladeshi movement, Indian intervention, and the eventual secession of Bangladesh.[51]

Zulfikar Ali Bhutto's assumption of power in the rump Pakistan in 1971, first as president and then as prime minister, produced a democratic phase for six years. But his policies did not create a permanent democratic structure or civilian control over the military. In a sense, this democratic period actually strengthened the military's role, as Bhutto could not contain mass agitations without the army's support. His dismissal of the Baluchistan provincial government resulted in a major uprising which he contained by using the military. His regime also saw the rise of fundamentalist Islamic groups opposed to his populist and socialist reforms. His winning the 1977 elections was widely branded as rigged and corrupted, causing massive demonstrations and an eventual military take-over by Zia-ul-Haq in July 1977.[52] Thus Bhutto, a leader who probably could have strengthened democracy, helped to only invigorate the authoritarianism and Islamic radicalism which would bedevil Pakistan in subsequent years.[53] His populist interpretation of Islam—for example, couching nationalization schemes as "Islamic socialism"; declaring Ahmadis a non-Muslim minority; presenting himself as a leader of other Islamic states; and privileging Pakistan's Islamic identity over all others—all contributed to this process. In addition, Bhutto consistently linked Pakistan's fate and identity with the Middle East in order to advance his foreign policy goals and reorient Pakistan's national identity after the breakup of the country.[54]

Rarely, if ever, have any Pakistani civilian leaders shown courage to stand up to the military. In fact, many danced to the tune of the military's favorite causes more intensely than the military regimes themselves. Benazir Bhutto is a prime example: supporting the Taliban in Afghanistan, helping to create Jihadi outfits to fight India in Kashmir, and allowing nuclear transfers to North Korea, Iran, and Libya. On relations with India, even though some civilian leaders wanted to pursue peace, they still had to take a hardline position to placate the army.[55]

An Economic Interpretation

While the emergence of the garrison state can be explained on the basis of the political weakness of the civilian elite, an explanation is still needed for the continued dominance of the military, which sets Pakistan apart from many other authoritarian countries that have abandoned military rule. The Pakistani military's overwhelming political dominance also has its roots in the way military officers are compensated in the country. Army officers and top bureaucrats are granted land; generals and bureaucrats emerge as key businessmen in the country, cultivating links with foreign and domestic corporations and placing themselves on their governing boards.[56] Moreover, military rule in Pakistan in many instances has witnessed high Gross Domestic Product (GDP) growth rates. This should not surprise us. During military rule, the US-Pakistani alliance has usually grown stronger, allowing the Pakistanis to extract "geostrategic rents" as payment for their support against America's adversaries.[57]

The Pakistani army has deeply entrenched itself as the lead societal and economic actor in the areas of education, health care, disaster relief, and infrastructure. It runs a vast array of institutions: military schools and colleges, teacher training institutes, the Army Education Press, the National Institute of Modern Languages, the National University of Science and Technology, cadet colleges, and the Fauji Foundation-run educational and health care institutions. The Army Medical Corps runs a broad network of hospitals and specialized institutions. The military also manages major relief operations after natural disasters such as floods and earthquakes. It also plays the largest role in Pakistan's logistics, transportation, and communication infrastructure. Finally, it is tightly bound with the local finance and banking sectors, which manage the military's extensive commercial interests.[58]

Ayesha Siddiqa details three levels at which the military's economic activities run: direct involvement, engagement through subsidiaries, and through activities of individual officers or ex-officers. In the first category, the army directly controls the National Logistics Cell (NLC), which Siddiqa describes as "the largest goods transportation company in the country," with a large public-sector fleet of transportation vehicles. In addition, it builds roads, bridges, and wheat storage facilities.[59] The other organizations the military directly manages include the Frontier Works organization, which is entrusted with the building of the Karakorum highway which connects China's Xinjiang with Pakistan's Gilgi-Baltistan and Khyber Pakhtunkhwa regions; the Special Communications Organization for expanding telecommunication networks in Azad Kashmir; and a number of small- and medium-sized cooperatives that cover everything from gas stations to highway tolls. Officers often angle to join corporate boards as well.

The best known of the military's corporate subsidiaries include the Fauji Foundation, the Army Welfare Trust, the Shaheen Foundation, and the Baharia Foundation. Each has several companies attached to it, and they cover nearly every dimension of industrial activity in Pakistan.[60] These business activities have entrenched the army's dominant role. They produce what Siddiqa calls "Milibus": "activities that transfer resources and opportunities from the public and private sectors to an individual or a group within the military, without following the norms of public accountability and for the purposes of personal gratification."[61] The military thus enriches itself at the expense of the rest of society, crowding out legitimate public- and private-sector enterprise that could serve as alternative constituencies and power bases. These entities have not only ensured that the army has a vested interest in maintaining the system, they have also enhanced the army's ability to dominate it. True reform would threaten too many officers' profits to be very likely. True, the military being a more disciplined institution can offer services more efficiently, especially in situations of national calamities. According to a former director of the Fauji Foundation, Tariq Waseem Ghazi, the Foundation is the biggest corporate entity in Pakistan, and it remits the largest amount of tax to the government and takes care of some three million retired military personnel by setting up schools and hospitals in a country where delivery of services is very poor. He also defended the Foundation by arguing that if the interests of the retired military personnel are not taken care of, it would be extremely difficult to obtain new recruits.[62]

The economic explanation for the persistence of the military's dominant role in society and the weakness of the democratic order is quite convincing. The consequences that strong civilian rule would bring are what most concerns the military. Also, redistributive taxation—a likely consequence of proper democratization—would imperil the military's wealth and reduce its oversized share of economic power.[63]

The semi-feudal structure of Pakistan's economy has also meant that pro-democracy forces remain relatively weak. Many argue that a strong middle class—a bourgeoisie—is necessary for democracy to sustain and consolidate. In Barrington Moore's classical formulation, "a vigorous and independent class of town dwellers has been an indispensable element in the growth of parliamentary democracy. No bourgeois, no democracy."[64] It is true that this argument is not universally shared. Some contend instead that it is the working class, or more precisely the organized labor, that is key to democratic development and consolidation. For instance, a study on class and democracy by sociologists Dietrich Rueschemeyer, Evelyne Huber Stephens, and John D. Stephens concludes that the middle class plays an ambiguous role in the creation and consolidation of democracy. Middle classes generally want proper representation for themselves, but their attitude toward lower classes tends to be utilitarian and transactional. The study finds the landed upper class as the most opposed to democracy because of fear of losing their cheap labor supply.[65] Both theories agree that democracy depends on progressive social forces who become aroused when their material interests are at stake.[66]

The middle class is usually the driver of democratic movements, but sometimes it can be co-opted by the ruling elite and become a reactionary force.[67] At independence, Pakistan simply lacked a middle class capable of challenging the dominance of the military and the bureaucracy. Hamza Alavi, a pioneering Pakistani sociologist, argues that unlike India's Congress Party, which had the bourgeoisie as its core membership, the Pakistani bourgeoisie could not succeed in establishing their representation through political parties as the parties were dominated by the landowning class. For instance, in 1968 some 22 families controlled 66% of the country's industrial resources and 80% of its banking assets.[68] The landowning class has been a major interest group in Pakistan, although they lost some power following the 1958 coup. They not only owned huge tracts of land, but controlled the vote banks within them. Although this has changed somewhat since the land reforms of 1958, the landed gentry still command most of the electoral power in Pakistan.[69] The fear of redistribution is particularly strong among the landed elite. Since it is not as difficult to tax land as it is to tax capital, landowners are generally more averse than capital owners to democracy.[70]

The Pakistani Middle Class and Civil Society

Why has the Pakistani civil society and the small but growing middle class not risen up in sufficient force to compel the military to abandon

its chokehold on political power once and for all? Pakistan's democratically oriented civil society, which draws largely from the middle and
upper classes, has at times showed mettle, but typically abandoned its
efforts once the conditions under civilian rule deteriorated or the military
showed enough determination to recapture power. This lack of sustained
middle class activism is a puzzle. Is it that the middle class remains small
and as weak as it was at independence? Is it that the military-led elite
has managed to co-opt the middle class into its fold? Or is it that the
middle class has bought into the ideology of the warrior state typified by
the hyper-realpolitik view of the army with its powerful religious ethos?

A small middle class does exist in Pakistan. According to one estimate, some 30 million people out of a population of 170 million have
an average per capita income between $8,000 and $10,000 (measured
in purchasing power parity),[71] although it is difficult to corroborate this
number. There are also expatriate Pakistanis who live in many Western
countries and in the Gulf. They are, however, divided along sectarian
lines. Although the variegated middle class is ideologically diverse, there
is a strong Islamist current in much of it. Also, the struggle with India
over Kashmir resonates very strongly among both the middle class and
the diaspora. In fact, the middle class has shown an increasing tendency
toward radicalism, evidenced by the growing belief that Pakistan is
engaged in a just war with India to liberate Kashmir. They see the use of
asymmetric means like terrorism as justifiable even if innocent civilians
die.[72] A 2008 survey of 141 families of killed militants revealed that they
generally came from well-educated families and not from madrassas.[73]
Many in the middle class seem to concur with the military's view that
India, given an opportunity, wants to undermine Pakistan. Through
their zeal, they appear willing to allow the military to establish either a
full-fledged garrison state or a hybrid (read military-controlled) civilian
democracy. From the early years of Pakistan's existence, a general
antipathy toward political parties developed among the general public,
including the middle class. Public opinion was in favor of Ayub's takeover in 1958, with a majority thinking that "the army might succeed in
providing clean and stable government to the people." That is why an
overwhelming majority supported the referendum in 1960 establishing
a form of controlled democracy called "Basic Democracy system," by
General Ayub Khan.[74]

It must be acknowledged that occasionally the urban middle class showed an interest in democracy and civil rights. Even when sympathizing with Islamic ideas, many in the middle class oppose implementation of Sharia laws. Corruption is rampant among the civilian leadership and this affects the way the public looks upon the political system. President Zardari has been called "Mr. Ten Percent," implying he got a cut for government contracts that he facilitated during his wife Benazir Bhutto's term as prime minister. The public is cognizant of this extensive corruption and mismanagement by civilian leaders. They also find the military a better guarantor of internal order in Pakistan. This perception, however, has changed somewhat during certain periods such as Musharraf's term in office. However, many among the generation of Pakistanis educated (especially in madrassas) since the Zia era believe in extremism and religious intolerance, as is evident in the widespread support for the blasphemy law which targets non-Muslims for any acts or allegations defiling the Quran or the Prophet Muhammad and the praise for the assassination of Salmaan Taseer, a prominent opponent of such laws. To be sure, fear of retribution prevents some moderate, middle-class voices from criticizing the extremists. Even a majority of the youth prefers Islamic law and military rule as a British Council survey found out in April 2013.[75] Surprisingly, the youth supported the campaign by cricket-star-turned-politician Imran Khan in the May 2013 elections,[76] showing that their disenchantment may be partially caused by the inability of established political parties to bring prosperity, employment, or corruption-free governments. They also are agitated by the US policies in the region, especially the increased use of unmanned drone aircraft by the Barack Obama administration, which have killed scores of civilians since 2004, and the complicity of the Pakistani government in those attacks.

Consequences

Pakistan's persistence as a garrison state/hybrid democracy has major consequences for its own developmental path and its relations with its neighbors as well as the rest of the world. A garrison state can suffer from sociopolitical pathologies that are difficult to erase even when a desire for democratic reforms exists. Notable among these pathologies is the excessive militarization of society. This militarization can be manifested in the day-to-day affairs of the state and magnification of a narrowly defined military security over all other national goals.

The dominance of the military has significant consequences for foreign policy in a country like Pakistan. Militaries tend to focus on other states' capabilities, not their intentions, to assess threats. They generally emphasize taking advantage of windows of opportunity.[77] And they often seek to marginalize non-military agencies in foreign policy.[78] When governments are dominated by the military, they can adopt a hyper-realpolitik worldview. As Julian Schofield, drawing from the work of Robert Jervis, argues, military governments could use threats to promote further threats: "if the adversary retreated, the success is attributed to the use of force rather than some other factor; if the adversary did not, it will often be argued that the threat was insufficient."[79] As such, they generally do not consider the possibility that threats themselves might be provocative. Militaries tend to generate a number of myths, believing in their own propaganda, underestimate their role in provoking hostility, and their spin doctors spread "self-serving falsehoods," often trusted by an ill-informed public who cannot reject the bogus arguments.[80]

With regard to conflict and coercive behavior, garrison states tend to be poor learners from past experience. They believe that defeats in war are caused by the treachery of the opponent, the relative inability of one's own forces to wage the war properly, or a lack of support from allies. There is a belief that the next time around these factors can be changed through a harder coercive approach. Russell Leng argues that the Pakistani military demonstrates dysfunctional learning with respect to the utility of coercive bargaining. The Pakistani military and political elites seem to follow a pattern whereby, after each conflict with India, they convince themselves that the next time they just have to try harder in order to win. The lessons they learned lead to more crisis behavior. For instance, the lesson learned from the 1965 Rann of Kutch conflict was that India conceding to international arbitration of the disputed land in Gujrat was due to Hindu passivity and was vulnerable to additional military pressures. The launching of the 1965 Kashmir offensive was the result of that calculation.[81] A similar logic in recent years was applied to India's caution when reacting to the Kargil offensive and Pakistan's increasing nuclear capability.[82] In addition, for the Pakistani military elite, revenge is an acceptable form of military behavior.[83] There is also a lack of accepting their errors in military conflicts. For instance, the army's internal reviews after the 1971 war were never published; nor was any military officer punished for the defeat or the egregious violation of human rights of millions of Bengalis, including mass murder and rape.[84]

Another form of dysfunctional learning came from the distorted British-era notions about the martial races of Pakistan and their superiority over the Indian forces. Some during the Ayub era even believed that one Pakistani soldier equaled ten or more Indian soldiers, "distorting the professionalism" of the armed forces. Pakistan was able to convince the US that small amounts of aid could allow them to offset Indian power.[85] During the early years, there was a general public consensus that in the event of a war with India, Pakistan's military would win. According to Rizvi, "this unrealistic view of the military capacity was due to the initial successes of the Army in Kashmir."[86] The perception of the superiority of Pakistani soldiers might have also derived from the historical experience of the poorly equipped early warriors of Islam, who were able to engage in highly successful offensive operations against the formidable empires of Byzantium and Persia. The victories of many Islamic conquerors from Central Asia over Hindu rulers through the millennium might have reinforced this view. Thus the narrative in the 1965 war was that "Muslim forces were innately superior to their Indian counterparts."[87]

Has the garrison state strategy made Pakistan stronger or weaker? Has the military's involvement in politics made national unity possible? The military and its sympathizers tend to argue that had there been no military intervention, Pakistan would have fallen apart. But there is dispute on this point. It is possible that the military might have directly or indirectly undermined the stability and cohesion of Pakistan by helping to strengthen the forces that tear it apart. The Islamist forces that challenge Pakistan today have been supported by the armed forces for their many wars at home and abroad at some point or other.[88]

Conclusions

The continuation of the garrison state punctuated by hybrid democratic governments has been the bane of Pakistan emerging as a coherent state with a strong civil society and democratic credentials. The chief *raison d'être* of the Pakistani state is territorial protection, unlike many modern states that believe in welfare provision or democratic representation as a key function of the state (along with security). The garrison state also ensures that national security is constantly elevated to the topmost priority of the country. Such a state embraces adventurist and ambitious foreign policies that often cause considerable damage to its own people and the social fabric. An intense rivalry with a bigger neighbor is part of the explanation for this behavioral pattern. But rivalry with India alone does not account for why the elite developed hyper-realpolitik ideas and continues to hold on to them, even after multiple reversals over a six-decade-long period of independent existence. The next chapter discusses the military's peculiar strategic approach and some of the deep-rooted causes of its dominance.

5

The Geostrategic Urge

IN JANUARY 1972, just over a month after the surrender of some 93,000 Pakistani troops to India in Dhaka in the concluding days of the Bangladesh liberation war, which saw Pakistan lose its eastern half, Prime Minister Zulfikar Ali Bhutto called a meeting of Pakistan's top atomic scientists in Multan. He reportedly told them that "We are fighting a thousand year war with India, and we will make an atomic bomb even if we have to eat grass. So in how many years can you do it?"[1] In 1979 Bhutto wrote from his jail cell awaiting his execution: "We know that Israel and South Africa have full nuclear capability. The Christian, Jewish, and Hindu civilizations have this capability. The communist powers also possess it. Only the Islamic civilization was without it, but that position was about to change."[2] Bhutto's statements were not hollow proclamations. In May 1998, Pakistan openly tested its nuclear weapons in response to earlier tests by India, following which the then Prime Minister Nawaz Sharif proclaimed: "Today, we have settled a score and have carried out five successful nuclear tests."[3] The acquisition of nuclear arms is only one manifestation of the intensely acrimonious relationship Pakistan has with its larger neighbor, India. To Pakistan, nuclear weapons serve as a great equalizer in this asymmetric rivalry. Catching up with India militarily and diplomatically has been the central piece of Pakistan's security policy since the dawn of independence in 1947.

The causes of the persisting garrison state in Pakistan have to be understood in the context of its enduring rivalry with India, and its simultaneous geostrategic salience for the major powers. Pakistan's most significant geopolitical conflict is with India, which is at least six to seven times larger in most measures of capabilities. Pakistan also has an enduring conflict with Afghanistan and as well a grand strategy of keeping that poor country under its control, a strategy it has partially borrowed from the former British colonial rulers. The conflict with India is about territory, power, status, and national identity. It also is zero-sum. The enduring conflict with India is the central context for Pakistan's pursuit of a highly ambitious realpolitik strategy. It has a perceived need to maintain a constantly vigilant and proactive military policy vis-à-vis India in order to balance its larger adversary at every possible level, including the latter's influence in Afghanistan.

The Pakistani effort, from the beginning of the state's founding in 1947, has been to achieve strategic parity with its larger neighbor. The notion of parity in this context is a broad one. It encompasses both military and political power, as well as regional influence and civilizational status. The desire for parity has deep roots in South Asia's history: it can be traced to nearly a millennium of Islamic conquests and rule of the Indian subcontinent, the demand for a separate Muslim homeland to regain the lost power of the Muslim minority, and the conceptual inheritance of the Mughal rule. The great powers, especially the United States and China, have helped in this quest for parity, and Pakistan's elite has deftly used its relationships with these powers in maintaining a form of truncated power symmetry with India. The quest for strategic parity with its larger neighbor, I argue, has been one of the fundamental reasons why Pakistan remains a quintessential warrior state, unable to transform itself into a moderate, development-oriented, democratic polity. A relatively weaker Pakistan has to expend considerable energy in maintaining strategic parity. Further, its inability to achieve long-term strategic goals vis-à-vis India produces intense nationalism. Over the years, successive governments—including those under civilian rule— have maintained and even intensified military-first policies due to this central focus on parity with India.

Pakistan's competition with India is also one over status. The urge to acquire higher status is part of the challenge here. In international relations, status can be defined as the beliefs, especially held by others, about the valued attributes a state possesses such as military capacity, economic prowess, cultural strength, or diplomatic clout.[4] Even though the status of a given country is very much based on other states' collective perceptions, the people and elite of a state can still believe they have higher or equal status with their peer competitor and can become dissatisfied if they do not obtain the status that they believe they deserve. In an intensely competitive environment, a state can devote considerable energy to obtain the military capabilities that it considers essential for status competition with a rival. It may also engage in aggressive foreign policy behavior to compensate for any status loss that it perceives from other actors as a result of changes in the strategic environment or material capabilities of the adversary.

The historical bases of this competition between Pakistan and India need further clarification. Pakistan is located in the northwest quadrant of the Indian subcontinent, a great theater of imperial conflict and power rivalry through the millennia. The contemporary territory of Pakistan stands as the entryway into India, and several invasions of the subcontinent have passed through it. The Khyber Pass, which is a navigable path through the Hindu Kush Mountains on the Afghan border, is the main entry point to the subcontinent from Central Asia.[5] No wonder this has been one of the main routes of invaders, traders, and migrating populations. Over the years, India has been invaded through today's Pakistani territory by Aryans, Persians, Greeks, Scythians, Parthians, Arabs, Afghans, Turks, Mongols, and the Mughals. The Russian empire also attempted to acquire a warm-water port through British Indian territory in what is now Pakistan, a cause for the "Great Game" policies of constant vigilance and military intrigue pursued by British colonial rulers throughout the nineteenth century.[6] As one historian puts it: "Despite St. Petersburg's repeated assurances that it had no hostile intent towards India, and that each advance was its last, it looked to many as though it was all part of a grand design to bring the whole of Central Asia under Tsarist sway. And once that was accomplished, it was feared, the final advance would begin on India—the greatest of all imperial prizes. For it was no secret that several of the Tsar's ablest generals had drawn up plans for such an invasion, and that to a man the Russian army was raring to go."[7]

The Muslim invasions from the Arab world and Central Asia are critical to understanding the trajectory of the Indian subcontinent and Pakistan's subsequent strategic orientations. As a result of the invasions and Muslim rule, large-scale conversions to Islam took place in northern India, although some of this may have occurred anyway through the preaching of the Muslim Imams who followed the Arab and Central Asian traders. The Sufi preachers from Iran and Central Asia were very influential in bringing the humanistic and pluralistic side of Islam to India.[8]

The invasions began in 712 A.D., when Mohammad bin Qasim, a general from the Umayyad dynasty of Arabia, defeated Raja Dahir of the Sindh region. Nearly three centuries later, starting in 1001, there were a series of invasions into South Asia led by Mahmud of Ghazni. By 1027 he occupied much of northern India, including the Punjab. During each invasion, Ghazni plundered Indian villages and towns, especially Hindu temples where considerable wealth was stored in the form of gold and precious jewels. He destroyed many of the Hindu temples, the most prominent being the Somnath temple of Gujarat in 1024. Less than two centuries later, in 1191, Mohammad Ghauri was defeated by Prithvi Raj Chauhan, but Ghauri exacted revenge the very next year in a victory over Chauhan. From the early 1200s, a succession of Muslim rulers controlled Northern India from Delhi, in what is known as the Delhi Sultanate. The Sultanate remained until 1526 under several Turk-Afghan dynasties such as the Mamluk (1206–1290), the Khalji (1290–1320), the Tughlaq (1320–1414), the Sayyid (1414–51), and the Lodhi (1451–1526). In the interim, in 1398, Timur, the infamous Turko-Mongol ruler from Central Asia, invaded and sacked Delhi.[9]

In 1526, Zahir ud-din Babar from Central Asia established the Mughal Empire in India following his victory in the battle of Panipat against the Lodhis. The Mughal rule would last until 1858, when the British abolished the empire in the aftermath of the 1857 rebellion. The Mughal era is perhaps the most important for our analysis. Some Mughal rulers, such as Jalal ud-din Akbar (1556–1605), were renowned for their tolerance of different faiths. Akbar's rule indeed witnessed major reforms and the spread of religious tolerance toward Hindus and minority Muslim sects such as the Shias. Taxes on non-Muslims, termed *Jizya*, were abolished. The Mughals also lifted an earlier ban on temple building by Hindus. They created a ranked imperial service based on merit rather than birth. Furthermore, the power of imams was undercut, with Akbar declaring himself the final arbiter of Islamic law. The era also witnessed the creation of a syncretic religion, Din-Ilahi, that offended orthodox Sunni Muslims and their Imams. Finally, Akbar initiated the creation of the cash-based *mansabdari* revenue collection system by loyal nonhereditary ranked officers, thus taking away the power of the landed gentry who until then were the chief revenue collectors.

Akbar's successor and son Nurud-din Jahangir (1605–1627) was tolerant as well, despite his deep Sunni faith, as was his son and successor, Shah Jahan (1628–1658). Importantly, these two rulers oversaw the continued expansion of the Mughal empire, and were even more so notable, especially the latter, for their patronage of the arts and architecture. Indeed, Shah Jahan's rule was noteworthy for being the heyday of Mughal architecture, with the building of the Taj Mahal in Agra and the Red Fort (Lal Qila) and the Jama Masjid in Delhi, to name a few of the architectural triumphs of this period. Shah Jahan's son, and successor, Aurangzeb (1658–1707) on the other hand, was a religious zealot. He reintroduced Jizya on Hindus, engaged in many military conquests of Jat, Sikh, and Rajput kingdoms in the periphery of the Mughal empire, and imposed forced conversions to Islam of Hindus and other religious groups. He thus sowed the seeds of eventual decline of the empire. The Mughals impacted the Indian subcontinent in every dimension with their major advances in arts, architecture, and principles of governance. They drew ideas from the Arab world as well as Iran. They were a land power, though, and as a result European naval powers slowly established themselves in the peripheral coastal towns. Ultimately, they would conquer large parts of India once the Mughals went into decline.[10]

With the establishment of British rule in the nineteenth century, Muslims in India saw their political, economic, and social privileges fade. The key event was the 1857 War of Independence (also known as "the Mutiny") involving Muslims along with Hindus. Members of the British East India Company–controlled Bengal Army and the kingdoms such as Oudh (present-day Lucknow and Faizabad regions) actively participated in it. One of the key demands of the mutineers was the restoration of the Mughal emperor Bahadur Shah II's powers (1837–1857) and the return of the Nawab of Oudh his monarchy, which the British had abolished.[11] After the bloody suppression of the revolt, the British sidelined the Muslim community, which then suffered through a precipitous political and economic decline. In the post-revolt era, the British government took over the rule of the East India Company's territories directly, and replaced Persian with English as the language of the administration. Muslim elites were ignored in favor of upper-caste Hindus for the day-to-day running of the empire.[12]

During the last quarter of the nineteenth century, some Muslim elites did emerge as community leaders. Their awakening was evident in the establishment of the Aligarh Muslim University in 1875. Its founder, Sir Syed Ahmed Khan, began it with the intention of educating the Muslim community in modern science and philosophy.[13] This helped foster the creation of a small but powerful Muslim elite which would later spearhead the Pakistan movement. The support Muslims occasionally gave the British made them an ally in the colonial "divide and rule" policy against the Congress Party, whose leaders were spearheading the national independence struggle. The Second World War was an important turning point. The Congress Party, adamantly opposed to British rule, was unwilling to support Britain at war, while the Muslim League was more cooperative. This difference was one of the major factors in Britain's agreeing to divide India and then leave it via a poorly crafted exit strategy. It is noteworthy that the Quit India Movement was launched by the Congress in 1942 at the peak of the war. Gandhi's disenchantment with Britain went back to the Boer War (1899–1902) and World War I (1914–1919); in both of these cases he supported Britain's war efforts, but the Indian nationalist movement did not receive much in return. In my view, Indian historiography has not given enough importance to the differences between the attitudes of the Muslim League and the Congress on the war in explaining Britain's willingness to partition the subcontinent.

British-inherited Strategic Ideas

Great Britain held together the Indian subcontinent for over one and a half century as a patchwork of directly and indirectly controlled territories, the latter consisting of 500-plus princely states, some large, some small. The British strategy in India was based on a number of principles. Chief among them was that Britain would control only certain areas directly but leave the rest to Indian princes who would act as vassals for the empire. A British resident indirectly controlled those princely states even though they were nominally independent. Those residents also played a role in the policy of divide and rule by actively participating in the affairs of the princely states. In the territory of today's Pakistan, some 17 such states existed, while Britain directly controlled much of Punjab, sections of Baluchistan, and the Northwest Frontier Province.

The Northwest Frontier Province assumed major significance for British colonial rulers in the defense of the British Indian territories. The biggest concern for them was the expansion by Tsarist Russia toward India.[14] In their attempts to keep the region free of Russian influence, the British colonial rulers signed several pacts with tribal leaders in the region and maintained Afghanistan as a buffer state. Much of Pakistan's contemporary difficulty in maintaining control over Afghanistan and its own peripheral areas dates back to the British era, when the highly independent-minded tribal populations resisted Britain's effort to establish direct rule over them.

Three wars were fought between Afghanistan's tribal groups and the British. The first (1839–1842) occurred when Britain attempted to install Shah Shuja as the monarch over the more popular Dost Mohammed Khan. Afghan tribes rebelled and forced the British protectors of the Shuja regime and their troops to leave. While the British troops were retreating to Jalalabad, they were attacked by the Afghans. Many were killed while others perished in the extreme cold.[15] The second war occurred between 1878 and 1881. One result of the war was the signing of the Treaty of Gandamak in 1879 which produced partial Afghan sovereignty, although Britain retained hegemony over the kingdom, especially its foreign policy. The British also maintained a presence in Afghanistan and in the northwest frontier region.[16] The Third Afghan War lasted from May till August of 1919, producing an agreement in which Afghanistan accepted the 1893 Durand Line dividing it from British India. It agreed to protect British interests while obtaining its sovereignty.[17] The Anglo-Afghan wars did not result in Britain gaining direct rule of Afghanistan. Eventual agreements were signed to keep local rulers in control in return for preventing the external enemies of the empire from invading India. The inability of outsiders to fully defeat Afghanistan, and the costs suffered in trying to do so, has given it the somewhat exaggerated description "the graveyard of empires." This focus on how Afghanistan affects empires, of course, ignores the severe cost of constant war on this poor, land-locked country.

The Afghanistan-Pakistan borderlands are populated by multiple tribes, mostly belonging to the Pashtun ethnic group. The Pashtuns are intensely tribal and religious, while at the same time very proud of their traditions and practices. They have rarely allowed outsiders to win outright control of their territories. The Pakistani state was never able to assert full control over the Pashtun territories, although juridically many areas where Pashtuns live (Northwest Frontier Province [now known as Khyber Pakhtunkhwa] and parts of Baluchistan) have been in its control since they were added to the Pakistani state by the withdrawing British in 1947. The addition of Pashtun territory to Pakistan occurred over the opposition of Pashtun leaders, especially Khan Abdul Ghaffar Khan, who desired an independent state of Pakhtunistan carved out of portions of Afghanistan and Pakistan where the Pashtuns held a majority. Pakistan rejected Afghanistan's plea for renegotiating the border, arguing that the transfer of power from Britain had made the successor territorial arrangements legitimate.[18]

Today, the Pashtuns are divided between Afghanistan and Pakistan, with a majority living on the Pakistani side. They still exhibit a desire to create an independent Pakhtunistan state, a project that never succeeded due to the steadfast opposition of Pakistan. This project, led by the late Khan Abdul Wali Khan, the son of Ghaffar Khan, has received strong support from Afghanistan and sympathy from India. It has been a major reason for the continuing conflict between Afghanistan and Pakistan. Ghaffar Khan, known as the Frontier Gandhi in India, was against the partition of the subcontinent on the basis of religion and was a supporter of the Indian National Congress. Pakistan's relations with Afghanistan were unfriendly from the beginning as the Afghan rulers supported the creation of Pakhtunistan. Indeed, Afghanistan was the only country that opposed the admission of Pakistan to the UN (although it withdrew that opposition subsequently). Throughout the 1950s, Afghan-Pakistan relations deteriorated. In 1955, diplomatic relations were ruptured after Pakistan decided to merge the Northwest Frontier Province where the Pashtuns lived into a single administrative unit of West Pakistan. There was military mobilization, although war was averted. In 1957, diplomatic relations between Pakistan and Afghanistan were partially ruptured, and in 1961 they were broken off completely, following tribal raids from Pakistan into the Afghan side.[19]

From Afghanistan's perspective, the 1,640-mile-long Durand Line that separates it from Pakistan, created by the British official Mortimer Durand in 1893, did not reflect the demographic structure of the Pashtuns. By allowing Pakistan to take control of the Pashtun-dominated Northwest areas, the British rulers denied the Pashtuns' national aspirations.[20] While Pakistan vehemently argued to reunite the divided Kashmiri population under its control, it refused to give the same right to the divided Pashtun population. The contradiction in its policy was glaring.

In the 1980s, the Pashtuns became the main source of recruitment for the mujahedeen (holy warriors) who fought the Soviet occupation of Afghanistan (later on, the Taliban emerged from the same source). The CIA and ISI aided them throughout the war. Pakistan's alliance with the mujahedeen in the war helped to soften Pashtun nationalism and Pashtun opposition to Pakistan itself. Despite that posture against a common enemy, the Pashtuns themselves have been divided. In their victory over the Northern Alliance—a group dominated by Hazaris, Tajiks and other minority ethnic groups in Afghanistan—the Pashtun/Taliban forces were supported by Pakistan.[21] Pakistan found in the Taliban a powerful ally in its larger regional battle against Indian forces in Kashmir. Islamabad also recognized the Taliban to be a useful asset for controlling Afghanistan, claiming that it provided much-needed "strategic depth" for Pakistan. Their support also quelled demands for the creation of an independent Pakhtunistan.[22]

The notion of "strategic depth" in the Pakistani military's approach toward security is driven partly by its hyper-realpolitik strategic culture. Essentially, Afghanistan cannot be allowed to become a fully independent actor. Instead, it needs to be a vassal of Pakistan, lest it fall into India's orbit. If that were to occur, Pakistan would find itself encircled by unfriendly states. The colonial British rulers wanted to control Afghanistan so as to prevent alleged Russian hegemony or outright takeover. Many of the colonial strategists and young officers of the British Indian Army argued and successfully convinced London that "the only way to halt the Russian advance was by 'forward' policies. This meant getting there first, either by invasion, or by creating compliant 'buffer' states, or satellites, astride the likely invasion routes."[23] The notion is also based on the questionable military idea that if India pushes Pakistan militarily and overruns its territory, it will have a strategic space to fall back upon and wage a defensive war. In this hyper-realpolitik perspective, a weak and subordinate Afghanistan is essential for Pakistan's security.

The theory of "strategic depth" ignores its destabilizing effects on Pakistan, especially in the form of extremism and sectarianism within Pakistan. By supporting the Taliban, Pakistan helped strengthen al-Qaeda in Afghanistan. Pakistani militants provided manpower to both the Taliban and al-Qaeda, while the Pakistani state offered logistical and communications support for training some 30,000 Taliban militants in camps across Afghanistan.[24] On the Pakistani side also the Taliban created its own cadres and engaged in attacks on their opponents and minority Shia groups. Some of Pakistan's internal difficulty since the 1980s stems from the weakness of the Afghan state, especially its inability to control its restive tribal population.

In geopolitical terms, a weak Afghanistan may be attractive to Pakistan's military elite, but it creates intense insecurity and long-term problems for Pakistan itself in terms of refugee flows, fundamentalist Islamic terrorism, and disorder in its border regions. Moreover, it is unlikely that a Taliban-controlled Afghanistan will completely follow the commands of the Pakistani military. Its radicalism is also likely to draw in outside powers into the region. The Pakistani elite has no serious plans for the long-term stabilization of the region. Essentially, their strategy also ignores the fact that Afghanistan is no longer needed as strategic space to fight India along classical lines of warfare. Pakistan has sufficient capacity to deter an Indian offensive. Especially in the context of nuclear weapons, a massive conventional attack on Pakistan would be suicidal for India.

Although Afghanistan appears to be the active contemporary conflict arena for Pakistan, its most significant rivalry is with India. In the next section I analyze this relationship in detail.

Strategic Parity with India

One of the ruling themes in Pakistan's competitive relationship with India is the desire to achieve strategic parity and equal power status with its larger neighbor. According to a Pakistani scholar, the Pakistani strategic community "does not distinguish between equality and strategic parity. Equality, which is more of a political-psychological concept, cannot be achieved without a better military-strategic balance. A powerful India is considered as harmful for Islamabad."[25]

Indeed, the broader reason for Pakistan emerging as a warrior state may owe itself to this underlying cause more than analysts typically acknowledge. When a smaller power attempts to maintain strategic parity and equal power status with its much larger adversary, it invariably has to spend more resources and exert greater efforts at keeping the military balance. Hence, its elite tends to be very insecure, especially when they realize that parity can be achieved only through an intense focus on enhancing the military. Pakistan has used the acquisition of new weaponry (including nuclear weapons since the 1980s), alliances with major powers, and a strategy of asymmetric warfare to maintain strategic parity with India. Imagine a situation in which Mexico wanted to achieve strategic parity with the United States. It would require enormous efforts; with the help of outsiders it may be able to attain some of its goals, but it is likely to hurt Mexicans in the long run. Although Pakistan is not in the exact position as Mexico is in this hypothetical analogy, it faces a major structural inequality in its efforts to create a consistent power balance with India.

The power asymmetry between the two countries is not just material in origin. It also has roots in the perceptions that each side holds of the other. Much of the Pakistani elite believes that India and Pakistan ought to be co-equals geopolitically. It sees relative parity-in military and diplomatic status terms-as a goal worth striving for, even at a high cost to its society. Pakistani leaders are ardent believers in the Westphalian notion of *de jure* equality of states and balance-of-power politics. Accordingly, they view India's aim of achieving major power status, comparable to China, with great alarm, and they marshal all available means to avert this prospect.[26] In recent years, this has manifested in the strident opposition to India becoming a permanent member of the UN Security Council. Pakistan fears that Indian hegemony in the subcontinent will adversely affect its security and power position.[27] India sees Pakistan not as a strategic and geopolitical equal, but as a country destined to remain a regional power.[28] Pakistan's military-intelligence establishment, or the "deep state" as Ahmed Rashid calls it, indeed has ambitions beyond what it can achieve. As Rashid states: "there is perhaps no other political-military elite in the world whose aspirations for great-power regional status, whose desire to overextend and outmatch itself with meager resources, so outstrips reality as that of Pakistan. If it did not have such dire consequences for 170 million Pakistanis and nearly 2 billion people living in South Asia, this magical thinking would be amusing."[29] But for the propping up by major powers, Pakistan would not have been able to match India in any key dimension of national power.

The idea of strategic parity was very much in the plans of Mohammad Ali Jinnah prior to independence in 1947. During the decade before independence, he consistently tried to obtain for Pakistan all of the Muslim-majority provinces within pre-partition India, and the creation of two equal nations, one for Hindus and the other for Muslims. It was the rejection of such calls for parity by the Congress that alienated Jinnah from the party led by Mohandas Gandhi and Jawaharlal Nehru. Jinnah was concerned about a "mutilated and moth-eaten" Pakistan, referring to Congress leaders' proposals for a "Pakistan" sans the Muslim majority provinces of Punjab and Bengal. (Congress argued that the two provinces had too many Hindus to hand over to Pakistan.)[30] In 1946, Jinnah claimed "parity" between the Muslim League and the Congress, and exclusive rights to nominate Muslims to the interim government.[31] The Congress rejected both demands, arguing that it included a good number of Muslim members itself. From the Congress leaders' point of view, the League's claim was also difficult to sustain, given that sizable Muslim minorities would remain in many other parts of India scattered around the vast country and that conceding the claim would undermine Congress' version of secularism. Indeed, almost the same number of Muslims as West Pakistan's population chose to stay back in India at the time of partition. Many Muslims believed in the secular promise of the Congress Party while others who sympathized with Pakistan were deterred by the sheer impracticality of uprooting themselves.

The notion of parity and even superiority may have some deeper historical roots. The legacy of the Mughal rule in India (1526–1858) might have given Jinnah and others a desire to resurrect the past glory of the empire through the newly founded state. According to M. J. Akbar, a noted Indian journalist and Pakistan scholar, the notion of becoming the successor state to the Mughal Empire was reinforced during the pre-partition days with the fear among Muslims that a demographic minority like them would not be able to protect their faith unless they distanced culturally and politically from the overwhelming Hindu majority. To Akbar, the Muslim community as rulers of India for over five centuries had developed a superiority complex. However, the challenges during the British colonial era led to a reversal as they developed more of an inferiority complex.[32] In some respects, then, it is a superiority-inferiority complex that drives Pakistan to its status competition with India.

The sense of entitlement to power seems dominant in the Pakistani elite's conception of its state. For Farzana Shaikh, a prominent Pakistani scholar, the historical roots of the assumption that power was a divinely ordained Muslim prerogative came directly from the Muslim rule in India and it got projected firmly in the collective memory of the Muslim community sustaining the "myth of power as a Muslim birth right."[33] The Muslim leaders like Jinnah refused to accept a subordinate position because of their belief in "the glorious history of Muslim rule and cultural achievement in South Asia." Iqbal Akhund, a former Pakistani diplomat and writer, puts it that since independence, the feeling persisted among Pakistanis that they must compete with India "on an equal footing, and that to accept anything less would be a humiliating betrayal." To Akhund, many Pakistanis think of themselves as heirs to the "Muslim Empire, descended from a race of conquerors and rulers. There is therefore a streak of militarism in Pakistan's ethos, even at the popular level."[34]

The desire for maintaining parity or balancing India also comes out of a strategic assumption that India has not reconciled itself to the partition of the subcontinent in 1947. On December 30, 1947, Pakistan Prime Minister Liaquat Ali Khan wrote to Nehru: "India has never wholeheartedly accepted the partition scheme but her leader paid lip service to it merely in order to get the British troops out of the country . . . India is out to destroy the state of Pakistan which her leaders persistently continue to regard as part of India itself."[35]

This original fear continued in the Pakistani elite's minds. It was only to be reinforced by the experience of 1971, when India helped the bifurcation of the country in a military conflict. Since then, Pakistan's justification for military buildup and acquisition of nuclear weapons was with this end in mind: deterring an Indian military offensive or political pressure aimed at dividing the country once again and thereby achieving overwhelming strategic superiority. However, this conception ignores the dramatic changes that have taken place in the Indian elite's view of Pakistan. Barring the extreme Hindu rightwing group Rashytriya Swayamsevak Sangh (RSS), none talk anymore about a reunited India (*Akhand Bharat*) nor do they consider it a feasible, or even a desirable, option. This does not deny the possibility that some Indian elite still harbor the hope that Pakistan will disintegrate. Regardless, since the economic reforms in the 1990s, India has become a rising economic powerhouse and has sought to transcend its troubled neighborhood. As India obtains more economic and military power as well as diplomatic clout, it appears to have abandoned any real designs on Pakistani territory—but the same rise has only heightened the sense of insecurity among the Pakistani elite.

The search for parity has engendered an ambitious policy to undermine India's unity through asymmetric means, first in the Punjab and then in Indian-controlled Kashmir. The Pakistani military and the ISI have also devised a strategy of inflicting a "thousand cuts" on India, a euphemism for terrorist strikes, as and when necessary to weaken its larger neighbor.[36] The terrorist strike against the Indian Parliament in December 2001 and the Mumbai attacks in November 2008 both had Pakistani stamps on them; the culprits came from Pakistan with proven connections to the ISI.

The Unending Rivalry

The search for parity by Pakistan is also a fundamental reason for the persistence of the India-Pakistan rivalry. There are a number of factors that make Pakistan's quest for parity feasible, factors that have masked the huge asymmetry between the two states in aggregate capabilities. I have argued elsewhere that the India-Pakistan power relationship is characterized by a truncated power asymmetry-that is, based on indicators of power resources such as aggregate military strength, economic capacity, population, and territorial size, the gap is big, but in the military and diplomatic areas it is narrower than generally believed.[37] As a result, there has been relatively little incentive for compromise on the part of both states, especially Pakistan, the main challenger of the regional territorial order.

In terms of aggregate indicators (see Table 5.1), the differential between India and Pakistan is as follows: in population, 6:1; in territorial size, 4:1; in GDP, 9:1; in defense expenditures, 6:1; and in total number of active forces, 2:1. Only in per capita income has the ratio been close at times, but even this ratio is shifting to India's favor.

Despite these glaring disparities in aggregate size and capability, three crucial factors make the power distribution between the two states as one of truncated asymmetry. They are: military balance in the theater of contest (buttressed by geography and terrain); the strategy and tactics of the rivals; and finally, the role of great powers as balancers between the two states.

The two states fought three major wars (1947–1948; 1965; and 1971) and a minor one (1999), and have experienced a number of crises, but none of these events has altered the power equation in any significant way on the western side. The 1971 war had the most pronounced impact, ending in a military debacle for Pakistan and the separation of the eastern wing of its territory. However, the secession of East Pakistan consolidated Pakistan's military assets in the western front, helping it narrow the capability asymmetry with India along the international border and in the Kashmir theater. India was unable to translate its victory in 1971 into a lasting political settlement that could have altered the dynamics of the conflict. At the Shimla conference in 1972, Pakistan's Prime Minister Zulfikar Ali Bhutto managed to extract concessions from India by promising not to raise Kashmir in international forums, a promise on which Pakistan would later renege.[38]

The three most significant variables that make the power equation between India and Pakistan a case of "truncated asymmetry" are: capability in theatre, strategy, and alliance politics. These factors also allow the weaker protagonist to engage in frequent military efforts to upset the territorial status quo. More importantly, these factors allow the Pakistani elite to sustain the idea of strategic parity with India and constantly strive for symmetry, a strategy that only a warrior state can pursue in such a relentless fashion.

Table 5.1 Material Power Capabilities: India and Pakistan (2011)

	Population	Area (sq km)	GDP	GDP (PPP)	GDP per capita (PPP)	Economic Growth	Defense spending	Armed forces (active)
India	1.205 bn.	3,287,263	$1.843 tn.	$4.463 tn.	$3700	7.8%	$31.88 bn.	1.325 mn.
Pakistan	190 mn.	796,095	$204.1 bn.	$488 bn.	$2800	2.4%	$5.16 bn	642,000

(Sources: International Institute for Strategic Studies, *The Military Balance* 2012; CIA, *World Factbook*, 2011. Economic figures in US dollars.) bn: billion; mn: million; tn: trillion

Capabilities

In the South Asian context, although India is larger in physical size, GDP and overall military capability, it is not overwhelmingly preponderant in the conflict's key theater or on the international border. India's overall defense posture against Pakistan until 1965 was based on "matching capabilities." After the 1965 war, India shifted the posture to maintaining "sufficient deterrence" or a "slight edge" in its force deployments. During this period, India had seven divisions deployed, while Pakistan had six; Islamabad enjoyed qualitative superiority in tanks and aircraft. However, this condition had altered by the early 1970s, and the change was a decisive factor in India's military victory in the 1971 war. Since 1971, India has maintained a "slight edge" in both qualitative and quantitative capabilities on its border with Pakistan, although in overall capabilities, India maintained a superior status throughout the 1970s and 1980s.[39] This slight edge, however, has not been sufficient for an adequate defense of Kashmir or to deter limited probes by Pakistan, especially of the asymmetric variety. These limited probes, whether short wars or based on attrition-style guerilla operations, are meant to challenge India's general deterrent capabilities, since its overall superiority does not deter such incursions in the local arena.[40]

The military capabilities the two states deployed against each other have been on an almost equal footing for over four decades. In terms of divisions deployed against each other, there is near parity, as about half of India's land forces are stationed on the border with China or other parts of the large country.[41] The two-front problem is especially acute for India in times of crisis, when India has to keep an eye on Chinese troop movements as well. In contrast, Pakistan can concentrate its military assets along the Indian border, although in 2001, responding to the US war on the Taliban and al-Qaeda in Afghanistan, Islamabad moved a substantial number of troops to the federally administered Waziristan.

The near-parity in troop disposition, especially in the Kashmir theater, gives Pakistan several advantages in limited, asymmetric wars. The Kashmiri terrain permits limited incursions and guerrilla operations to go undetected by the Indian forces. The deployment of certain weapons, especially artillery, allows Pakistan to checkmate India during the initial stages of an armed conflict, and this option has been an asset in short wars. Only in a long war can India muster its aggregate superiority, but this option has been constrained by the diplomatic intervention of great powers and, since the late 1980s, by Pakistan's possession of nuclear weapons. Further, Pakistan enjoys the edge in deployment logistics. The country has an elongated geography, its forces can operate completely within interior lines, and it can mobilize forces into battlefield operations within 96 hours. For the Indian Army it would take between 7 to 10 days to concentrate for war as its "strike formations are based deep inside the country."[42] A former Pakistani Army chief, General Mirza Aslam Beg, confirms this assessment when he states: "out of 370 battalions maintained by India, 210 were committed in Kashmir, and as such India did not have the capability of pre-empting Pakistan . . . While it would take India nine to 10 days to mobilize its army in the event of war with Pakistan, it would take Pakistan no more than four days to do so."[43]

Since the late 1980s, nuclear weapons have emerged as a key factor in the capability equation that reduces the power asymmetry between the two states. In the Pakistani calculus, nuclear weapons and delivery systems, based on short- and medium-range missiles such as Nasr, Ghauri, Hatf, and Shaheen, and on aircraft such as the F-16, allow Islamabad to deter any large offensive that India might launch in response to Pakistan's limited probes. Pakistan also has a nuclear first-use policy, which implies that Islamabad will strike with nuclear weapons in response to a conventional attack by India. New Delhi, on the other hand, follows a no-first-use policy, implying that it would retaliate with nuclear weapons only after absorbing a first strike by its opponent.[44] In 2010, Pakistan tested short-range missiles which can carry tactical nuclear weapons to be deployed on the border to deter an Indian attack. This has once again reinforced the nuclear first-use policy of Pakistan, although officially Islamabad has not declared as much. This discrepancy in nuclear strategies is also a reflection of the two contestants' relative advantages in terms of overall conventional capabilities, as well as the status quo and revisionist orientations of the defender and the challenger respectively.

The conventional capability equation has been changing slowly since 2002, when India embarked on a major defense modernization program that involved purchasing weapons systems aimed at neutralizing

Pakistan's (and China's) military capabilities. Its 15-year-long, $95 billion program envisages the purchase or manufacture of weapons systems that will give it a limited edge in the subcontinent vis-à-vis Pakistan and, to some extent, China. The emphasis is on acquiring airborne warning and control systems, fighter-bomber aircraft, surface-to-air missiles, cruise missiles, and advanced battle tanks. Building up naval capabilities, such as aircraft carriers, is also part of this program.[45] By 2010, India's annual military expenditure amounted to $41.3 billion, 54% higher in real terms than in 2001. Indeed, over the 2006–2010 period India was the world's largest importer of conventional weapons.[46] Such expenditure has prompted questions and scholarly enquiry on whether India is likely to move away from its traditional policy of strategic restraint toward a more assertive military posture.[47]

However, it remains to be seen whether India will achieve military preponderance with respect to theater capability in the near future. Pakistan, with the help of China and the United States, is also building up its conventional military capabilities, although not at the same pace as India given its economic problems. Even if India achieves conventional dominance, however, the nuclear deterrent will still act as a major constraint on any conventional offensive that it might mount in response to Pakistan's asymmetric challenges in Kashmir.[48]

Strategy

Partly due to its status-quo orientation, and partly due to constraints in terms of troop disposition and terrain, the Indian strategy in Kashmir and toward Pakistan has been in general defensive and reactive, while the Pakistani strategy has been one of offensive-defensive. The basic tenet of Islamabad's strategy has been to take the military initiative at crucial junctures, especially by relying on surprise attack. Thus, in 1947–1948 and 1965, short-war calculations were paramount to Pakistan's strategy. In the immediate aftermath of the debacle of the 1971 war, that strategy became untenable for a time. However, in the wake of the 1989 Afghan War, a large number of mujahedeen became available, making an asymmetric strategy based on terrorism and guerilla tactics attractive. Meanwhile, the porous Kashmir border and, following fraudulent elections in 1987, the rise of militant opposition in Indian Kashmir made this strategy feasible.[49] A salient aspect of this Pakistani strategy is covered in the post-1971 "War Directive No.5," which called for a limited land battle using offensive capability in the east or the south and "to muster the capacity to strike a decisive or a forceful tactical blow that could force the adversary to concede strategically."[50] The foundation of Pakistan's Kashmir strategy since the 1980s has been one of asymmetric warfare.

The new strategy was feasible because it offered several advantages to Pakistan. It could support insurgents at a low cost simply by training and encouraging them to enter Indian-controlled areas. For India, the mountainous terrain of Kashmir makes it difficult to seal off the border or conduct counterinsurgency operations effectively. Moreover, India has to rely largely on the Srinagar-Leh road to the area near the Line of Control, and its direct frontal counteroffensives may not succeed in advancing beyond the territory under its control. According to some Indian military commanders, securing some areas of the Kashmir frontline requires a minimum of a 30:1 superiority.[51] Further, the Pakistan military generally perceives India as a "soft state" (despite being "hegemonic"), with several internal problems and insurgent movements that offer opportunities for a determined opponent to engage in asymmetric warfare.[52]

In case of war, the Indian strategy has been to defend Kashmir through conventional means but progressively escalate the conflict toward Pakistan's border along the Punjab and Rajasthan, forcing Islamabad to withdraw its troops from Kashmir. The assumption has been that in any conflict that lasts longer than a few weeks, Pakistan will not be able to sustain the two fronts—one in Kashmir and the other on the international border—and thus India's overall superiority will come to bear on the outcome. The Indians have calculated that the threat of escalation could act as a deterrent, dissuading Pakistan from initiating military hostilities in Kashmir. However, the Indian strategy is constrained given that New Delhi's forces in Kashmir are vulnerable to short, limited offensives. Surprise incursions by Pakistan have been difficult to detect and repel. In 1965, it took India's military escalation toward Lahore to force Pakistan to give up the conflict, and in 1999 India had to deploy considerable manpower and resources to eject the Pakistani intruders from the Kargil Hills. Although the Indian forces succeeded in turning back the Pakistanis from the key mountain tops, Pakistani soldiers were able to hold on to nearly 25% of the area taken.[53] The possibility that India would escalate the conflict in order to cut off Pakistani supply lines to the intruders and mobilize its navy for a blockade prompted Pakistan to threaten nuclear retaliation. As the Pakistani army's position became untenable, Prime Minister Nawaz Sharif approached US President Bill Clinton to intervene. Clinton in turn convinced the Pakistani leader to announce the withdrawal of remaining troops from Indian areas before a complete loss of face.[54] It is fairly certain that even without the US intervention, India would have eventually been able to remove the remaining Pakistani intruders. Indeed, its retaking of the most critical Tiger Hills took place while the Clinton-Sharif talks were going on in Washington.[55]

Since the early 1990s, nuclear weapons have helped strengthen the Pakistani elite's notion of strategic parity. Pakistani leaders have come to believe that they have obtained a "great equalizer" at the strategic level, since their missiles can hit most parts of India. Islamabad's nuclear weapons, according to Pakistani strategists, have "restored a balance of terror in the stand-off with its neighbor, for nuclear deterrence alone' working from the weak to the strong, offers decisive power" without symmetry.[56] Indeed, in the nuclear context, India's earlier conventional posture of deterrence by denial and deterrence by punishment (i.e., its strategy to respond to an attack on Kashmir by escalating the conflict across Pakistan's vulnerable strategic underbelly in the Punjab) may have become less plausible. Pakistan possesses both medium- and short-range nuclear-capable missiles that can hit most of India's cities. The Indians realize this, as evidenced by their having adopted strategies such as full military mobilization and limited war with the hope that Pakistan would suffer economically and militarily in a contest based on long-term, active mobilization.

In fact, in 2011, reports suggested that Pakistan has been able to develop a larger number of nuclear weapons than India by using both plutonium and uranium. Also, it now has missiles capable of reaching almost all parts of India. According to one estimate, in 2011, Pakistan possessed 90–110 nuclear warheads. In a decade or so, the number is expected to grow to 150–200 warheads as the country is in the process of building two new plutonium production reactors and a new reprocessing facility. The delivery systems—both extant or in development—include F-16 and Mirage V aircraft, and ballistic missiles such as Hatf-2 through Hatf-9, which have a range of 180 to 2000 kilometers.[57] Pakistan is also developing and deploying 30-kilometer-range tactical missiles named "Nasr," in an effort to nullify India's strategy of escalation on its international border. These tactical nuclear weapons are considered highly destabilizing, because they come with a much more realistic possibility of use than longer-range weapons—and, if used, would break the tradition of nonuse of nuclear weapons that has been observed by all nuclear powers since 1945.[58]

Following the less-than-satisfactory results from its 2001–2002 full mobilization, code-named *Operation Parakram*, in April 2004 India unofficially unveiled a new military doctrine entitled *Cold Start*. In a future conflict with Pakistan, the doctrine envisages a "blitzkrieg" strategy that would involve joint operations by the Indian Army, Air Force and Navy. It visualizes harnessing the full strike potential of India's defensive and offensive forces, permanent forward deployment of the divisions from their present interior locations to shorten the time required for offensive operations, and concentrated attacks on approximately eight locations.[59] Although the doctrine moves India from a defensive/deterrent to a deterrent/offensive posture, Pakistan's possession of nuclear weapons still acts as a constraint on the effective execution of the doctrine.

The doctrine, although not officially declared, however has increased Pakistan's fears of India's ambitions to cut Pakistan to size. In a way, it has helped to reinforce the Pakistani military's habitual impulse to establish strong control over the government. It reinforces Pakistan's claimed need for strategic depth in Afghanistan. It also has prompted Pakistan to build a larger number of nuclear weapons than needed for a minimum deterrent, and to deploy highly destabilizing tactical nuclear weapons in the border region. The great irony is that the Indian doctrine is simply not practical and is largely made for domestic consumption by making a virtue of a very difficult strategic environment generated by Pakistan's reliance on asymmetric warfare. Finally, the action-reaction effect of the military policies of Pakistan and India is not confined to their relations alone, but also influences the internal dynamics of Pakistan and perpetuate it as a warrior state.

Alliance Politics

A significant factor underlying the truncated asymmetry in the military and strategic position between Pakistan and India is great power alliance politics. More than anything else, support from the United States (and to a lesser extent from China) has allowed the persistence of the notion of strategic parity between the two countries. During the Cold War era, especially in the eyes of Western officialdom and the Western media, India and Pakistan were bracketed as geopolitical equals. The US alignment with Islamabad reinforced this perception of equal status. Since the mid-1950s, Pakistan has enjoyed recurrent alliance support from the United States, and since the 1960s, there has been a de facto alliance between Pakistan and China. These alliance relationships have offered "borrowed power" to Islamabad and have enabled it to reduce the power asymmetry with India. During the 1960s and 1980s, the US alliance helped Pakistan acquire conventional weapons of superior quality to India's. Because of the importance of alliance politics, in the next section I discuss in detail the alliance's implications for the "geostrategic curse" from which Pakistan suffers.

According to Hussain Haqqani, who served as Pakistan's ambassador to Washington, US economic and military support has "encouraged Pakistan's military leaders to overestimate their power potential," and led to their reluctance to accept normal relations with India "even after learning through repeated misadventures that Pakistan can, at best, hold India to a draw in military conflict and cannot defeat it." The aid also has "made Pakistan a rentier state, albeit one that lives off the rents for its strategic location."[60] The next section expands on these points in detail.

The United States and Pakistan

The Cold War provided a major strategic opening to Pakistan's elite to pursue its realpolitik objectives, especially in its efforts to obtain strategic parity with India. The opportunity came in the form of an alliance with the United States, which was desperately looking for strategic partners in Asia-Pacific. The US leaders first assumed that democratic India would join hands with Washington in its fight against communism and the Soviet Union. This proved to be a nonstarter as

India's Prime Minister Jawaharlal Nehru viewed alliances and balance of power competition as antithetical to his country's freshly won independence from colonial rule. Nehru pursued an independent foreign policy and began to bring together the newly emerging countries in Asia and Africa under the nonaligned movement. Nehru took the lead by organizing a major meeting in April 1955 in Bandung, Indonesia, along with Indonesia's Sukarno and Egypt's Gamal Abdel Nasser. US leaders, especially Dwight Eisenhower and Secretary of State John Foster Dulles, were unhappy about it, with Dulles even characterizing it as "immoral."[61]

Sensing a major opportunity, the Pakistani elite began discussions with Washington and in 1954 they struck an alliance.[62] Already, Washington had been providing assistance to Pakistan under the Truman administration's "Point Four" technical assistance program in 1950, and in February 1952 Washington offered Pakistan economic assistance as defense support. The United States found Pakistan's geostrategic location attractive in the context of the conflict with the Soviet Union. During the early stages of the Cold War, Pakistan offered bases and staging posts for US spy planes to watch Soviet nuclear and missile activities. Under Eisenhower and Dulles, Washington initiated the "Northern Tier of Defense" project to upgrade the capacity of the frontline states like Pakistan, Iran, Turkey, and Iraq against the Soviet Union. The Eisenhower Administration treated Pakistan as the "the most allied ally." In 1954, Washington and Karachi concluded a mutual defense agreement, and Pakistan was given membership in the Southeast Asian Treaty Organization (SEATO) and the Central Treaty Organization (CENTO).[63] Ayub Khan stated Pakistan's reasons for joining these alliances bluntly: "The crux of the problem from the very beginning was the Indian attitude of hostility toward us: we had to look for allies to secure our position."[64] The United States promised considerable economic aid and military assistance, all in the name of strengthening Pakistan to fight the Soviets.[65]

This was indeed the beginning of the geostrategic curse discussed in Chapters 1 and 2. The elite, receiving aid money from the US and its allies as well as US-dominated international financial institutions, had little inclination to improve conditions within. It could get sufficient support from Washington and its allies for their maintenance of the garrison state. Taking their cue from official discourse, Western academics and media also treated Pakistan and India as geostrategic equals, reinforcing the idea among the Pakistani elite that the two countries had strategic parity. India's launching of the nonaligned movement and its opposition to many Western positions, especially in Vietnam, had reinforced a negative image of India.

Relations between Pakistan and the United States remained strong until the coming to power of the John F. Kennedy Administration in 1961. CENTO and SEATO did not last long, and Kennedy, in an effort to boost relations with India, downgraded relations with Pakistan.[66] In September 1965 Washington imposed a complete suspension of all economic and military aid on both India and Pakistan because of the Kashmir war.[67] Furthermore, as part of a general reassessment of aid policies toward India and Pakistan, the Lyndon B. Johnson administration in that year postponed the annual pledging session of the Pakistan aid consortium. Its purpose was to provide support for the country's third Five-Year Plan, primarily in response to the India-Pakistan war of that year.[68]

United States–Pakistan relations remained poor during this period until the arrival of the Richard M. Nixon administration in 1969. Nixon and his National Security Advisor Henry Kissinger used Pakistan's links with China to initiate diplomatic engagement with Peking. The duo had also become very hostile to India, which was supporting the East Pakistan liberation movement at the time. In 1971, the United States under Nixon adopted a policy of "tilting" toward Pakistan, and sent the Seventh Fleet to the Bay of Bengal as an act of coercive diplomacy directed at India. This bolstered Pakistan's self-image, but militarily it was of limited use. Nixon and Kissinger viewed every conflict in the developing world, including the one in South Asia, through the Cold War prism and as Soviet inspired. India's friendship with the Soviets made them believe that New Delhi's behavior was Soviet encouraged as well. The Nixon-Kissinger team took no action on the constant telegrams coming from the US consulate in Dhaka revealing the extent of the genocide taking place against the Bengalis at the hands of the Pakistani forces, because of their Cold War calculations, US opening to China, and hatred toward the Indian leaders, especially Indira Gandhi.[69]

The Pakistani debacle in the 1971 Bangladesh war caused some setbacks to US–Pakistani relations, however. The Zulfikar Ali Bhutto regime's socialist and populist rhetoric did not go down too well in post-Watergate, post-Vietnam Washington. The military coup by Zia-ul-Haq in July 1977 was condemned by the Jimmy Carter Administration, which was then spearheading support for human rights movements throughout the world. The administration was also frustrated by India and Pakistan's nuclear weapons programs, and made some unsuccessful attempts to forestall them.

The Soviet invasion of Afghanistan in December 1979 once again put Pakistan in a prominent place in superpower politics. Despite its pivotal geographical location, it was Pakistan's willingness to act as a conduit for support to the anti-Soviet forces, and the availability of asymmetric forces led by the mujahedeen, that gave Pakistan the opportunity to gain geostrategic prominence. The Carter Administration initially offered Pakistan $440 million over a two-year period, which was ridiculed by General Zia-ul-Haq as "peanuts." The Ronald Reagan Administration sweetened the offer eightfold in 1981. Its offer of $3.2 billion was renewed in 1987, with a mix of $1.74 billion in military credits and $2.28 billion in economic grants. Pakistan became the third largest recipient of US aid after Israel and Egypt. During this period, it also received $1.2 billion from Saudi Arabia for offering a 10,000-man contingent for the protection of the Saudi royal family.[70]

The United States played the most significant role in turning Pakistan into a pivotal frontline state in the war against the Soviet Union. The war was waged through an active alliance with fundamentalist Islamists including the Taliban and Osama bin Laden. The unintended consequence of US policy was the emboldening of the warrior state in Pakistan. The success in Afghanistan helped its military elite realize the utility of waging asymmetric war against India and playing "double games" in the Afghan conflict. The Soviet defeat in 1989 to Pakistani-supported asymmetric warfare taught the Pakistani military elite that they could do the same to India in Kashmir. The large number of Arab and other mujahedeen fighters left behind after the Afghan war helped in this process. The Kashmiri insurgency, caused largely by India's failures to conduct free and fair elections in the state, opened up a key opportunity.

The Reagan Administration bent over backwards, sacrificing many of America's liberal principles, to support Pakistan and the mujahedeen in their successful fight against the Soviets. Most importantly, the administration turned a blind eye to Pakistan's nuclear weapons development. Recent works suggest that US intelligence analysts were fully aware of Pakistan's quest for nuclear arms for years, and "successive US administrations closeted this sensitive knowledge to prevent outsiders from deterring the United States from trying to enlist Islamabad to fight successive wars against the Soviet Union and the Taliban."[71] The US treated the nuclear activities of friends and foes differently. A CIA analyst and later Pentagon official, Richard Barlow, who had protested the manipulation of US intelligence on Pakistan's nuclear program and the George H. W. Bush administration's blind eye on them, was dismissed from his job and denied even his state pensions, finally ending up living with his two dogs in a motorhome and working occasionally as a fishing and hunting guide in Nevada and New Mexico. He even claimed that the US government went after him smearing his name, and in that process destroyed his marriage.[72] Some suggest that the United States kept a close watch on the A. Q. Khan network, which spread nuclear materials to Iran, North Korea, and Libya but did very little to stop it.[73] Washington also implicitly encouraged the deeper Islamization of Pakistan as the resistance needed a religiously committed force in Afghanistan to wage the bloody war. This US policy would haunt American and international security later on when the mujahedeen helped deliver Afghanistan into the hands of the Taliban (and by proxy al-Qaeda). Pakistan played a critical role in the organization, training and funding of the mujahedeen, many of whom reconfigured as the Taliban when the war ended. Pakistan offered food, medicine, and fuel; helped to recruit fighters; raised funds from private donors; and provided diplomatic support.[74] The important question is why the supposedly liberal-minded Benazir Bhutto spearheaded this policy toward the Taliban. According to Rasul Rais, the policy showed Bhutto's pragmatism rather than any specific affiliation with Taliban ideology. However, others have argued that she had little control over the Taliban policy, and that the ISI was the key player. Bhutto also appointed an ethnic Pashtun, Nasirullah Babar, as the interior minister. A retired general in the Pakistani army, he was pivotal in developing Pakistan's pro-Taliban policy.[75]

The September 11 Attacks

After a period of benign neglect by the United States a major opportunity for realignment with Washington came to Pakistan in the fall of 2001 following the dastardly attacks on America's economic and military might, the twin towers of the World Trade Center and the Pentagon on September 11. The attackers, although mostly of Saudi descent, were all trained in Afghanistan and Pakistan and were young men determined to wage a new war of jihad at the behest of Osama bin Laden, the leader of al-Qaeda.

Immediately following the attack, the George W. Bush Administration approached Pakistan and asked it to play a leading role in containing the Taliban. General Musharraf, the Pakistani military ruler, initially dilly-dallied, hoping to obtain major economic and military assistance as his predecessor General Zia-ul-Haq had done in 1979. This new conflict in Afghanistan occurred in the background of an improving United States–India relationship. Starting in July 1999, Washington had begun to change its policy toward Pakistan and India, elevating the latter as a more pivotal partner. The Kargil war was a watershed which prompted the Bill Clinton Administration to view the South Asian rivals no longer on equal footing. Pakistan's risk-taking behavior in initiating the war with a nuclear-armed rival was viewed with much alarm in Washington. The Clinton visit to India in March 2000 followed, with the US leader courting both politicians and firms from India's burgeoning high-tech sector. The dialogue between US Deputy Secretary of State under Clinton, Strobe Talbott, and former External Affairs Minister of India Jaswant Singh (June 1998–September 2000) cleared up many mutual misconceptions that had earlier limited the relationship.[76] Both Democrats and Republicans began to view India as a rising power and a potential partner that could serve as a balancer against a rising China. The Bush Administration, especially National Security Advisor Condoleezza Rice, was in favor of upgrading the relationship even further, though this shift was limited by the 9/11 attacks and the subsequent need to placate some of Pakistan's interests.[77] Despite this, United States–India relations have improved substantially under the Bush and Obama presidencies. The 2005 United States–India nuclear accord along with subsequent agreements have removed many of the sanctions imposed on

India since the 1970s. The United States did not bestow these privileges on Pakistan, which unsurprisingly has generated a great deal of concern among the Pakistani elite. US policy toward South Asia was no longer based on parity between India and Pakistan. To address this, Pakistan has redoubled its efforts to establish ties with China as well as to balance against India's growing military and political strength.[78]

The United States–Pakistan relationship underwent major ups and downs during the Obama administration, which intensified its attacks on Taliban and al-Qaeda in both Afghanistan and Pakistan. The United States relied heavily on pilotless drone aircraft, which have killed many innocent Pakistanis and Afghans along with several al-Qaeda and Taliban militants. Yet the drone campaign has largely failed to contain the Taliban. Obama has been more successful against al-Qaeda, killing and capturing a number of al-Qaeda leaders. The United States's biggest victory was the daring killing of Osama bin Laden in Abbottabad, the Pakistani garrison city, in May 2011. This caused much rancor in Pakistan, with civil-military relations plummeting and Pakistan cutting off the NATO supply route to Afghanistan. The United States–India relationship also continued to improve for a while, only to remain low-key as of 2012 due to domestic political and economic considerations in both countries. The future of the US role in the South Asian balance is yet to be determined, as it will depend heavily on the trajectory of China's rise and the outcome of the Afghan War.

China and Pakistan

Pakistan's military and strategic relationship with China has played a crucial role in its balancing of India and has allowed Pakistan to approach a degree of strategic parity. China has maintained its all-weather relationship with Pakistan in order to contain India, even when pursuing a policy of engagement with New Delhi.[79] Chinese support for Pakistan began to increase in the wake of the Sino-Indian war of 1962, the short border conflict which saw China defeating India, although it subsequently withdrew to its former positions unilaterally. The conflict erupted over the undemarcated 2,100-mile long border between the two states, the control of large swaths of territory in the Ladakh and Arunachal Pradesh (formerly known as the Northeast Frontier Agency) and the conflicting interpretations of the British-designed McMahon Line that separated Tibet from India. India's giving asylum to Tibetan refugees, especially their spiritual leader the Dalai Lama, also aggravated the Chinese hostility toward India. This coincided with increased arms transfers from the USSR to India. In the 1965 War, Pakistan expected China to open a second front, although in the end this did not materialize. In 1971, China, along with the United States, supported Pakistan and offered significant material assistance.[80] In the 1980s, China provided significant support to Pakistan's program to develop nuclear weapons and acquire missile technology. In addition, China has been Pakistan's main source of conventional capabilities, including Type-59 tanks, Type-531 armored personnel carriers, missile boats, and F-7P jet fighters. Beijing has provided Pakistan manufacturing facilities for jet trainers, Type-69 tanks, HJ-8 anti-tank missiles, and HN-5A portable surface-to-air missiles. More significantly, China is reported to have given Pakistan a proven nuclear weapon design, enriched uranium, ring magnets for enriching uranium, dual-use diagnostic equipment, and an industrial furnace for nuclear weapons production, even though some of these transfers violated its commitments as a signatory of the Nuclear Non-Proliferation Treaty. Finally, China has provided Pakistan M-11 short-range ballistic missiles and components and is reported to have helped in the production of Ghauri, a ballistic missile with a 1,500-km range.[81] This material and diplomatic support has been crucial in reducing the asymmetry between India's and Pakistan's military capabilities.

Since the 1960s, China has also provided diplomatic cover to its ally, much as the United States does for Israel. By nurturing the India-Pakistan rivalry, China has sought to keep India tied down as a regional power and prevent its elevation to major power status. Balance-of-power and containment considerations are behind these Chinese calculations.[82] The rise of a new great power with nuclear weapons would adversely affect China's preeminent status on the Asian continent. India is the only Asian state which has the potential, and the inclination, to balance China. In Beijing, policymakers believe that they can prevent India's rise as a challenger by deliberately propping up the regimes surrounding India—especially Pakistan—and through the pursuit of policies that would reinforce the perception that India is "weak, indecisive and on the verge of collapse." The main plank of this strategy has been the provision of economic and military support to these states.[83] In recent years, China has been building up Pakistan's conventional weapons capabilities through joint projects for the development of fighter aircraft, battle tanks, and cruise missiles. China's development of the Gwadar Deep Sea Port in the mouth of the Strait of Hormuz has military implications as well.[84] In January 2013 Pakistan handed over management of the port to China, which considers such bases as part of its "string of pearls strategy" in the Indian Ocean region against India and the United States, although the current purpose is ostensibly commercial.[85]

China has argued that its alliance with Pakistan has been in response to what it views as India's imperial designs on territory that is too close to China for comfort.[86] Therefore, China has been the most strident critic among all major powers on the question of recognizing India as a nuclear weapon state, even on a de facto basis. According to Robert Ross, China continues its support for Pakistan by supplying nuclear and missile technology because "China views a credible Pakistani deterrent as the most effective way to guarantee the security of its sole ally in Southern Asia against Indian power."[87] To John Garver, China wants to keep Pakistan independent, powerful, and confident in order to present India with a standing two-front threat.[88] The Chinese calculation appears to be that while India is preoccupied with Pakistan, New Delhi may not be able to develop long-range military capabilities, especially missiles and naval systems, to match those of China. This strategy only works in the short run, however. China's assistance to Pakistan seems to be having a reverse effect, increasing India's determination to develop capabilities that can match China's in the future. Thus China's policies in South Asia may well be working against China's own interests by making India militarily stronger and also encouraging New Delhi to forge a balance-of-power coalition with the United States and other like-minded states in Asia.

The consequences of relative equality, in terms of perception and of actual capability in the theater, have been profound for the persistence of the rivalry and for Pakistan's continuation as a warrior state. For Pakistan, the Kashmir conflict has inflicted severe costs, but these costs have not yet proven unbearable. According to official estimates,

Pakistan spends about 2.5% of its GDP on defense, but this represents 13% of the federal government's expenditures. This amount does not include various hidden costs, such as the nuclear program, or the opportunity costs of military rule and political uncertainty.[89] On the other hand, in the past Islamabad has been able to underwrite some of this defense expenditure with the generous financial and military aid from the United States, China, and Saudi Arabia due to its geostrategic centrality.

The intense desire for strategic parity with India also generates a zero sum perspective among the Pakistani elite (i.e., any gain by India is viewed as a loss to Pakistan). Failure also breeds intense frustration and animosity, calling for additional efforts for war. Pakistan's offensive military doctrine is a reflection of its efforts to achieve parity with India asymmetrically. Nuclear weapons have added the determination to challenge the status quo as and when windows of opportunity arise. An example here illustrates the point. In 1999 while the Lahore peace agreement was signed between Prime Ministers Atal Bihari Vajpayee and Nawaz Sharif, the Pakistani military under the leadership of Pervez Musharraf was plotting an incursion into Kargil to thwart the peace process. Similarly, in 2008 when the civilian president Asif Ali Zardari and Indian leader Manmohan Singh had initiated a peace process, it was thwarted by ISI with the launching of the terrorist strikes on Mumbai.

Conclusions

The geostrategic prominence of Pakistan for the conflicts of the great powers and its alliance relationship with China and the United States has given the Pakistani elite an exaggerated view of its role and status in the world and what it can achieve geopolitically if it pursues crafty policies. The elite has also imbibed the notion of seeking geostrategic parity with India as the cornerstone of its national security strategy. Nuclear possession has enhanced strength to this conception. Added to this is the perception that Pakistan should be the bulwark for the protection of Islam in the world, as it was founded on the principle of the protection of Muslims. When such a world view persists, security is viewed as narrow military security and territorial security, and undermining the security of its neighbors, especially of India and Afghanistan, is viewed as justifiable. India's often poorly crafted reactive policies, such as the *Cold Start* doctrine and its earlier pro-active military intervention in East Pakistan, have also contributed to this way of thinking in Islamabad. When its military or diplomatic efforts do not succeed, the Pakistani elite periodically attempted to engage in further coercive bargaining, encountering obstinacy and resistance on the part of India.

The basic problem is that the structural asymmetry with India cannot be easily bridged despite some factors in Pakistan's favor. The competitive relationship with its neighbor creates intense warrior tendencies among the Pakistani elite. This has led the elite to adopt asymmetric war as a strategy to upset India and its national unity. The unwillingness to accept the territorial status quo also means that conflict becomes an inevitable dynamic in the South Asian milieu. Taking on a bigger power militarily also ensures the predominant role of the military in Pakistani society, while the structural dynamics of truncated asymmetry generate temptations to pursue an offensive military strategy. The prominence that China and the United States give to Islamabad also exaggerates Pakistan's value for the global security order, creating a never-ending obsession with national security and hyper-realpolitik–oriented policies in that country. The financial and military support that the allies have provided allowed the Pakistani elite not to engage in any major structural change in the country's economic or social system. This perceived geostrategic importance in reality has been a "curse" for Pakistan, preventing it from seeking more benign alternative security strategies or developmental paths to greater economic prosperity.

6

Religion and Politics

THE WARRIOR STATE of Pakistan is, in part, built on a religious foundation. The dominant view in Pakistan is that as a Muslim state, Pakistan should exclusively protect Muslim interests. Successive Pakistani rulers, even when they were not devout Muslims, upheld this vision. It has often provided a key source of legitimacy that serves as a substitute for economic prosperity and democratic representation. However, this Islamic identity is contested by the diverse ethnic affiliations of the Pakistanis even though almost all of them are Muslims. The late Pashtun leader Khan Abdul Wali Khan summarized this sentiment nicely when he stated in the early 1990s that he had been a Pashtun for 4,000 years, a Muslim for 1,400 years, and a Pakistani for 40 years.[1] Against this centrifugal tendency is the quest of the Pakistani elite, especially the military, to place religion as the number one source of identity and unity. In the words of Army Chief General Ashfaq Pervez Kayani, "Pakistan was created in the name of Islam and Islam can never be taken out of Pakistan. However, Islam should always remain a unifying force. I assure you that regardless of odds, the Pakistan Army will keep on doing its best towards our common dream for a truly Islamic Republic of Pakistan, as envisioned by the Quaid-i-Azam [Mohammed Ali Jinnah] and Allama Iqbal [poet Muhammad Iqbal]."[2]

The quest for Islamic legitimacy tends to backfire on Pakistan's ruling elite, because a powerful strand within Islamism recognizes no earthly sovereignty. And in a country as divided as Pakistan, with early leaders upholding a quasisecular vision and with deep sectarian and ethnic differences, political Islam has hardly provided national unity. Far from it: to a large degree, Pakistan's many internal conflicts stem from intense competition over how to define the state in Islamic terms. As such, the problems of Pakistan as a warrior state are interwoven with the politics of religion. Pakistan's origins as an Islamic alternative to India's secular model provides a key reason for its intense national security focus, while, at the same time, regrettably failing to serve as an adequate basis for a unified and stable state.

The Pakistani elite could have adopted either a fully Islamic identity or a secular identity. Under a secular regime, economic progress would have fueled national integration. As South Asia scholar Vali Nasr argues, a secular-economic approach would have required large-scale social reforms and a more equitable distribution of resources. For Nasr, the required reforms "ran counter to the class interests of the ruling elite, and defied the aim of their developmental agenda."[3] Political Islam emerged as a substitute.

Throughout its existence, Pakistan faced intense challenges from Muslim fundamentalists and a conservative ulema (clergy) who wanted to turn the country into a theocratic state. Since the 1980s, political discourse has been increasingly dominated by religious political parties with competing ideas about the role of Islam and the *Sunnah* (the Prophet Muhammad's words and deeds) in the state and the wider Muslim Ummah (brotherhood). Over the years, Pakistan has seen a reduction in the prominence of its limited but powerful tradition of Sufi Islam, which is generally more open and eclectic than Sunni Islam. Instead, Pakistan has become increasingly a Sunni-dominated society, and the status of minority Islamic denominations such as Shias, Ahmadis, and Sufis has become considerably more tenuous. Liberal civil society has remained weak and passive, even though some members have protested against particular ruling elites. They have not been strong enough to combat the menace of Islamist extremism that bedevils Pakistan, especially since the days of Zia-ul-Haq's military rule in the 1980s. Some even argue that strong elements within the Pakistani society, including the small middle class, harbor tendencies that support extremism.[4] A 2007 survey found that 54% of Pakistanis wanted strict application of Sharia law, while 25% wanted it in diluted forms. With a total of 79% in favor of Sharia law in some form, this was the highest percentage among Morocco, Egypt, Pakistan, and Indonesia, the four countries surveyed.[5]

In a sense, the use or misuse of political Islam has been a two-way street. The Pakistani elite's use of Islam for its strategic and tactical goals has reinforced extremist Islam, which in turn challenges the state's authority. Although most mainstream Pakistani politicians did not want to share power with the ulema or create an Islamic state, they have been unable or unwilling to state so unequivocally.[6] The Islamist clergy is able to pressure vulnerable political leaders even if they are secular in orientation. The state itself has opened up avenues for political Islam to exert that pressure as well. For example, the adoption of the Objectives Resolution in 1949, which "declared that sovereignty over the entire universe belongs to God, and the people of Pakistan are to exercise this sovereignty as God's legatees," provided a powerful rhetorical tool to the conservatives.[7] The Objectives Resolution, although initially viewed by the political class as an innocuous statement, subsequently generated conditions under which Islamists and the ulema could use it as an instrument for the disenfranchisement of minorities from the political process. Each constitution the country has adopted since the Objectives Resolution—in 1956, 1962, and 1973—has reaffirmed the religious character of the state. No political party can avoid offering deference to this logic, lest it becomes irrelevant. No civil society group has become powerful enough to question the religion-based logic of statehood, or the limitations to minority rights and religious freedom that have emerged over time.

This chapter traces the interplay of Islamism and politics through Pakistan's postindependence history. It considers the context of the divided polity within which political Islam operates.

Sectarian Differences

Increasingly, political Islamism has meant not just the dominance of Islam as such but the dominance of Sunni Islam, and in particular the Deobandi tradition, over every other sect. Over 95% of Pakistan's population adheres to Islam. However, it is largely a Sunni-dominated country, with nearly 75% of the total population following this branch. The Shia population comprises 20% while others, especially Christians,

Parsis, Buddhists, and Hindus, constitute about 5% of the population. The Shias are followers of Ali ibn Abu Talib, the Prophet Muhammad's cousin and son-in-law, whom they consider the legitimate successor to the Prophet. The Sunnis oppose this claim and do not regard him as "more righteous than his predecessors."[8] The Ahmadiyya minority, constituting some 2 million, venerate its founder Mirza Ghulam Ahmad as a messenger of God—a belief seen by many as rejecting Muhammad's status as the last Prophet. Pakistan also has a small Ismaili community. Ismailis belong to the Shia branch and regard Agha Khan, their imam in continuous succession since 1818, as their spiritual leader. They are community-oriented and focus on social services and development.

The Sunnis themselves are divided between the Barelvis and the Deobandis, 15% and 60% of Pakistan's population respectively. The Deobandis believe that the "Quran and Sunnah . . . provided a complete guide for life that needed no improvement by man." The Taliban movement in Afghanistan and Pakistan follow the fundamentalist ideas originating from the Deobandi madrassas. They have made every effort to impose their views on the state and society and have been partially successful.[9] Unlike the Deobandis, the Barelvis seem to hold to a more broader moderate and tolerant interpretation of Islamic teachings. They trace their origins from pre-partition Northern India, and have been known to draw from different religious practices of the subcontinent. This includes offering prayers to living or dead holymen or pirs, practices which the Deobandis view as paganist.[10]

The radicalization of Pakistani politics owes much to the divergent positions of Sunnis and Shias and the efforts by the Deobandi Sunnis to convert Pakistan into a "pure" Islamic state. These efforts have been resisted by the non-Deobandi Sunnis as well as the minority Shias. Both sides have engaged in violence to make their point. Pakistani domestic politics is interwoven with this conflict, and the efforts of politicians to use sectarianism for their objectives have only added to this conflictual relationship.[11]

Although some Shia Muslims like Zulfikar Ali Bhutto and Benazir Bhutto ruled Pakistan as prime ministers, their policies might have contributed to Sunni dominance over the years. Vali Nasr argues that the Shia-supported mix of secularism and populism of the former, coupled with corruption and authoritarianism, generated Sunni opposition, the military coup by the Sunni General Zia-ul-Haq, and the eventual hanging of the PPP leader. The military coup in 1977 basically ended the "Pakistani experiment with inclusive Muslim nationalism," and over the years, Shias lost much of their political power.[12] Benazir Bhutto attempted to appear to be Sunni,[13] and her father had already helped to further the cause of orthodoxy within Pakistan's Islamist politics by designating the Ahmadiyya minority un-Islamic in 1974.

Pakistan has also seen a profound marginalization of the Sufi Islamic tradition. This branch of Islam has perhaps been the closest to an ecumenical movement within the Islamic world, as it draws its inspiration from multiple sources such as Egyptian and Lebanese Christian hermits, Afghanistan's Buddhist monasticism, the devotionalist Bhakti movement of Hinduism and the mystical philosophy of Neoplatonism.[14] The sect believes in the direct experience of God through self-purification (*tasawwuf*) and renunciation, and that means intermediaries such as the ulema and legal and formal interpretations are not needed to obtain the divine experience.[15] The absence of ulema in religious practices makes Sufism unattractive to the traditionalists. Naturally, they opposed it and have been successful in undermining the influence of Sufism in Pakistan, especially since the time of Zia-ul-Haq.

The efforts to create a common Islamic identity failed to subsume the powerful sectarian distinctions within Pakistan. Whose Islam would the state follow: Shia, Sunni, Ahmadi, or Ismaili? The numerical predominance of Deobandi Sunni Islam has given it an advantage—but at the expense of other traditions. The struggle over the soul of Islam has thus been a continuing feature of Pakistani body politic ever since it came into being.

Ethnic Cleavages

From the days of Pakistan's creation, religion has not been able to bridge the different ethnic cleavages and different strands within the state. Ayesha Jalal puts it cogently:

> The Muslims of Sind, the N.W.F.P. and Baluchistan had one thing in common: a fierce attachment to their particularistic traditions, and a deep antipathy to any central control. The creation of Pakistan bundled them willy-nilly into a state dominated by their more

numerous co-religionists from western Punjab and placed them under the tight central control which Pakistan had to impose if it was to survive. The enthusiasm of these patriots of 'Pukhtunistan,' Sind and Balochistan for this union can be gauged by their efforts since independence to throw off the yoke of the Punjab.[16]

Even though the demands for provincial autonomy were temporarily shelved, they resurfaced in less than two decades. On the eastern side, the existence of Bengali as a distinct language and strong identification with coethnics in India helped to drive secession.[17] The new state on the western side had to find a way to integrate five main groups, the Sindhis, the Baloch, the Pashtuns, the Punjabis and the Mohajirs who migrated from India.[18] The Mohajirs, estimated at around 9 million in 1947, ended up in two major Pakistani cities, Karachi and Hyderabad, and their attitudes toward Pakistan underwent the most dramatic change of all groups. They were the most ardent supporters of Pakistan's creation but emerged as the country's sharpest critics as their economic and political status did not improve along the lines they had anticipated.[19]

Pakistan's largest city, Karachi, has witnessed much violence ever since the country came into being. The Mohajirs have been the main focal point of this conflict, as they displaced pre-existing groups in land, jobs and economic and political control. Often the violence has been generated by the feuding parties representing minority groups. In recent years, the Muttahida Qaumi Movement, representing the 45% of the city who are Urdu-speaking Mohajir settlers, and the Awami National Party, representing the city's Pashtun population (25%), have been at the forefront of violent clashes.[20] The Mohajirs came from the United Provinces, Rajasthan, and other Hindu-majority parts of northern India. They displaced the native Sindhi community in Karachi. By 1951, Karachi's Sindhi-speaking population was only 14% of the metropolitan population, while 58% spoke Urdu. At the same time, Mohajirs comprised 66% of Hyderabad, the second-largest city in Sindh.[21]

The alienation of minority Muslim ethnic groups has been occurring ever since the new state came into being. The general disaffection of ethnic minorities has been due to the economic and political policies that the successive Punjabi-dominated regimes have followed. For instance, in Sindh, the Mohajirs often complained of second-class treatment in economic opportunities. The transfer of the federal capital from Karachi to Islamabad, the imposition of Urdu at the cost of the Sindhi language, federal intervention in Sindhi provincial politics, and the absence of land distribution, are also all strongly held grievances, especially among the Sindhis.[22] Sindh has been plagued by violence because of the conflicts between different ethnic groups over these questions. A common religion has not helped in bridging these gaps, as they tend to arise from economic and political sources intertwined with ethnic political identities.

Balochistan has the most pronounced internal conflict of any of the provinces of Pakistan. The Balochi struggle is for autonomy and, more recently, for independence. The manner in which the province was integrated into Pakistan was the original source of discontentment. Of the four princely states constituting Balochistan, only three—Makran, Las Bela, and Kharan—willingly acceded to Pakistan. The fourth, Kalat, wanted independence, but eventually agreed to join Pakistan under the threat of military intervention. Pakistan's use of force to suppress the subsequent insurgency was the source of the Baloch discontentment. The Baloch have since complained, with justification, that their province is exploited by the Punjabi elite and that they have not received their due share of the national economic pie. The province is rich in mineral resources such as chromium, copper, iron, and coal, and in oil and gas, but they are not utilized for Balochi development.

Indeed, Pakistan's uneven modernization feeds the ethnic alienation of the province. The Baloch are highly aware that they are marginalized in comparison to other ethnic groups. The settlement of Balochistan by large number of Afghan refugees, the gradual erosion of the provincial autonomy offered by the 1973 constitution and the very low representation of Baloch in Pakistan's governing institutions (including the bureaucracy and the army) are the major challenges facing the Baloch. Many Baloch consider the mega infrastructure projects in the province as part of a colonization project by outsiders. They believe Punjabi bureaucrats and settlers are the beneficiaries, especially through their purchase of land adjacent to these projects. For instance, they claim the land around the Gwadar Coastal Highway that links the port city of Gwadar to Karachi has been acquired by people from the Punjab. Balochistan has the highest unemployment rate among all Pakistani provinces, despite the fact that it produces some 80% of the Pakistan's natural gas, which is consumed elsewhere. The province also has the highest illiteracy rate and the Baloch are denied their cultural rights, including the development and use of their language.[23]

The policies of General Ayub Khan alienated the Baloch, and violence erupted in the 1950s and 1960s.[24] Today it is called "Pakistan's Dirty War" (reminiscent of Argentina in the 1970s) because of the rising number of people who have either disappeared or been killed (on both sides). But the conflict has received little attention internationally, in part because most eyes are turned toward the fight against the Taliban and al-Qaeda in Pakistan's northwestern tribal areas.[25] Groups such as the Baloch National Front, the Balochistan Republican Army, and the Balochistan Liberation Army have carried out the struggle.

The Baloch nationalists have demanded a fair share of the wealth and improvements in living standards, especially with regard to education and health. Some groups go beyond this and want outright independence. The killing of popular leader Nawab Akbar Bugti in August 2006 only intensified the determination of the Baloch people for independence, which spurred a rise in Pakistani army's repression. The "kill and dump tactic" of the army, documented by Amnesty International, has targeted teachers, journalists, lawyers, and teenagers who allegedly participate in the insurgency. Groups like Human Rights Watch have documented the disappearance of hundreds of people and increased killings by non-Baloch settlers and the army. The Pakistani army wants to crush the insurgency, believing that it is supported by India. According to Bugti Brahumdagh Bugti (grandson of the assassinated leader Bugti and exiled leader of the Baloch Liberation Party), the repression has increased since the departure of the Musharraf regime in 2008.[26]

Pakistan's track record of treating non-Muslim minorities has been even worse. A study published in 1988 pointed out that Christians and Hindus are especially vulnerable to religious persecution. The social status of Hindus is particularly low as they are not "people of the book," members of Abrahamic religions such as Christianity and Judaism. Says Pakistani scholar Akbar Zaidi: "Even today as the 20th century comes to a close, most Muslims will not eat or drink with Hindus, and nor will they even touch their eating utensils. This intense discrimination is manifested at all levels and in all forms. Thus the Hindus form one of the poorest and most exploited communities of the country."[27] This discrimination is present despite the fact that a large number of Pakistanis trace their ancestry to Hinduism. Conversions were central to the spread of Islam in South Asia. The civilizational and cultural impact of Hinduism on Muslims and vice versa cannot be written off so easily.

The well-respected Karachi-based Jinnah Institute produced a sweeping report in 2011 that outlined the widespread institutional and structural discrimination that minorities face in Pakistan and the complicity of the state's judicial, executive, and legislative branches, as well as law enforcement agencies, in this state of affairs. Not only has the minorities' socioeconomic status declined over the years, but their low numbers also make it harder to have intercommunal dialog of any sort. Even progressive members of the ruling elite are afraid of offending the religious right, and hence condone the egregious violation of minority communities' human rights. The most visible example of this phenomenon was the case of a female Christian farmer from the Punjab, Aaasia Bibi. She was sentenced to death for breaking the blasphemy law for her alleged disrespect of the Prophet Muhammad in some arguments with her neighbors in June 2009. Despite evidence that the case was based on flimsy grounds, and the courts making contradictory verdicts, even President Asif Ali Zardari had to retreat from offering her a presidential pardon under intense pressure from Islamic parties and groups.[28]

Pakistan, thus, is a divided polity with many conflicts afflicting its multiethnic societal fabric. Ultimately, Islam could not bridge Pakistan's ethnic cleavages. An approach to national integration focused on economic development, equitable distribution of income, and democratic inclusiveness may well have done better. Pakistan's many communal conflicts have stemmed from a lack of economic and democratic inclusion of its diverse population. But rather than embrace reform, the Pakistani political elite has in general chosen to follow the path of Islamism.

Leaders and Islam

There is an argument that despite using religion to obtain a separate state, the Pakistani elite during the early years was not all that religious. The founding father of Pakistan, Mohammed Ali Jinnah, was anything but a staunch Islamist, although he did shift his position when he thought it necessary. He led the life of a Westerner: the way he practiced law, the way he dressed, and the way he engaged with Congress' leadership and the British were all Western in style. Interestingly, Jinnah himself belonged to the Khaja community—a minority Shia sect whose ancestors fled from Iran to western India between the tenth and sixteenth centuries because of religious persecution.[29] Ironically, his genius lay in mobilizing a whole people in the name of Islam, and then separating the state from India in an act that would make the Islamist coloration of Pakistan permanent.

Still, the creation of a secular Pakistan was the fear of some clergy and Islamist political leaders. In fact, clerical organizations such as the Ulama-i-Hind and politicians such as Jamaat-e-Islami (JI) founder Abdul Ala Mawdudi had opposed Pakistan's creation on this ground. Mawdudi argued that nationalism and Islam were incompatible. He feared that Pakistan would essentially be a Kemalist rather than Islamic state, while at the same time ensuring Hindu domination over Muslims in the rest of India.[30] Mawdudi, however, chose to settle in Pakistan. Through his JI party, he was the key intellectual figure pushing for an Islamic state in Pakistan until his death in 1979. Mawdudi believed that no earthly authority can claim sovereignty; it is God's alone. Political agencies created by human beings are supposed to reflect "divine ordinance." Indeed, all people hold responsibility as vice-regents of God's will, and this responsibility trumps the sovereignty claims of kings and presidents.[31] There is a strong sense of the hegemony of religion over civil authority in Mawdudi's preaching. If implemented, it would make a civil state extremely difficult to operate, especially in a society with multiple sects and ethnic groups.

Pakistan's formative years saw many debates between Jinnah's followers and Mawdudi. For Jinnah's followers, the state was simply meant to be a homeland for Muslims. The reason why the first constitution took 10 years to formulate was because of these competing positions. As noted above, the Objectives Resolution of 1949 affirmed that God alone was sovereign, and that Muslims ought to be "enabled" to live by the Quran and the Sunnah.[32] The negotiations to frame the first constitution also witnessed several other Islamist demands: a ban on the minority Ahmadi sect, the adoption of "Islamic Republic of Pakistan," as the country's official name, the creation of an Islamic research institute tasked with the Islamization of the country, and the "Repugnancy Clause," which declared that "no law could be adopted in contradiction to Islam."[33] Even if Jinnah's followers did not want to create an Islamic state, the challenge was that, without the twin cries, "Islam in Danger" and "Pakistan an Islamic state," Jinnah would not have been able to achieve the separation of Pakistan as an independent state.[34]

Ayub Khan's Secular Turn

The first military ruler of Pakistan, Ayub Khan, showed antipathy toward implementing Islamic laws. He was perhaps Pakistan's main hope for creating a state with some secular characteristics in the early stages. But he was not very successful in this endeavor. In the 1962 constitution he tried to drop the word "Islamic" from "Islamic Republic of Pakistan." A year earlier, he had tried via the Muslim Family Laws Ordinance to end polygamous marriages. Neither initiative succeeded.[35] Ayub Khan drew on the secular model created by Kemal Atatürk for Turkey, focusing on westernization and economic development and seeking the clergy's acquiescence. He attempted to give the state a role in defining the meaning of Islam in society, and that brought him into a major confrontation with the ulema. Ayub failed, partly due to societal resistance, partly due to increasing disenchantment with his rule (which collapsed by the end of the decade), and partly because of Islamism's continuing usefulness to the military as a weapon against India.[36]

Zulfikar Ali Bhutto's Political Gambling with Religion

Bhutto, a Western-educated leader, showed limited interest in Sharia laws. But his policies contributed greatly to the Islamization of Pakistan in later years. Even though he was considered a secularist and a socialist, Bhutto attempted to use Islam to achieve his political objectives. This attempt was not convincing to his Islamist opponents, who staged massive protests for his ouster. In order to gain their political support, he changed the PPP electoral platform to seek "Quranic social justice" and "Muhammad's egalitarianism." His opponents, however, were not convinced, and they formed the Pakistan National Alliance (PNA), which included the JI. Although Bhutto won the 1977 national elections, his opponents were agitated, alleging electoral fraud. Army chief

Zia-ul-Haq (appointed by Bhutto himself) exploited this to stage a successful coup in July 1977.[37]

Bhutto's contribution to turning Pakistan into an intolerant society, especially toward Islamic minority groups, is poignant. Bhutto was instrumental in designating the minority Ahmadiyya group an "un-Islamic" sect. This community, with some 2 million adherents, believes that their founder Mirza Ghulam Ahmad (1835 to 1908) was the last prophet sent by God. The Sunnis, on the other hand, believe that Ahmad "was an apostate who claimed for himself Khatm-e-Nubuwwat or, the status of the last divine prophet"—hence in contradiction to Muhammad's status.[38]

Clerics and Islamists wanted to ban the sect from the very beginning of the state. A powerful demand for the dismissal of Pakistan's first foreign minister, Muhammad Zafrullah Khan, a member of the Ahmadi community, led to riots in the Punjab in 1953. It was only in 1974, however, that Bhutto brought about a constitutional amendment to declare Ahmadis non-Muslim. This amendment took away the rights of the Ahmadis to call themselves "Muslims," to designate their places of worship "Mosques," and to use the call to prayer. It placed these restrictions under the Pakistani penal code.[39] The marginalization of this minority Muslim community was a major victory for Sunni zealots in Pakistan. This policy has plagued Pakistan since then, as Ahmadis have suffered periodic attacks from hard-core Islamist groups.

Bhutto's effort was to unite and stabilize the society in order to carry out his socialist economic reforms. He gave into the Islamists' demands to gain their support for his larger purposes. Among the major initiatives he took to appease the Islamists was imposing bans on drinking (despite being a drinker himself), gambling, and night clubs; declaring Friday the official holiday of the week instead of Sunday; and increasing the content of Islam in school syllabi.[40] These policies emboldened Islamic radicals and eventually the clergy and the military joined hands to overthrow him from power and execute him.[41]

Zia-ul-Haq and the Islamization of Pakistan

The major move toward Islamization occurred under the Zia-ul-Haq regime (1977–1988). Zia and his supporters were motivated not only by deep-rooted religious beliefs, but also a conviction that Islam was the only force that could unite Pakistan and prevent it from disintegrating.[42] Armed with money and weapons—partly a product of its geostrategic prominence in the war in Afghanistan—Zia began a major Islamization program in Pakistan. This program included reforms in politics, education, law, the economy, and the armed forces. More significantly, he increased the state's support to the madrassa education system, which would have a dramatic impact on subsequent generations of Pakistani children.

Islamist doctrine was now a much more fundamental part of politics and education. The Objectives Resolution of 1949 which reaffirmed the religious character of the state was made an integral part of the constitution and not just part of its preamble.[43] Zia appointed JI members to the cabinet and converted the Islamic Council to a direct advisory body of the government. He also made Islamic studies mandatory at all levels of education and reformed textbooks to remove content deemed un-Islamic. He created a new International Islamic University in Islamabad. Madrassa education was now equivalent to regular education, thereby making graduates eligible for jobs in the government and armed forces.[44] Indeed, Zia instituted confidential assessments of civil servants and awarded jobs based on knowledge of Islam and attendance at prayers. The reforms also gave tens of thousands of jobs in the judiciary and civil service to JI sympathizers.[45]

The anti-Ahmadi policies of the state continued and became more repressive under Zia's regime. In response to demands by various religious leaders, Zia agreed to promulgate an ordinance prohibiting Ahmadis from referring to themselves as Muslims (or "posing as such"). The law criminalized such acts, and even mandated the death penalty for some crimes. Since then, the community has been thoroughly marginalized in Pakistan, and it lives under constant fear of repression.[46]

Zia's implementation of blasphemy laws that made it a capital offense to "defile" the Prophet Muhammad was a major step. In accordance with these laws, a number of people have been sentenced to death, although not many of those sentences have been carried out. The presence of this law, with its vague language about what constitutes blasphemy, has generated considerable worry among Pakistan's minority communities—especially among Christians and Hindus—about Islamist vigilantism.[47]

Indeed, the legal system was an important arena for the promulgation of Islamism. In July 1977, Zia "declared that theft could be punished by amputation from the wrist of the left hand of a right-handed person and vice versa," while the 1979 Hudood ordinance stated that "punishments laid down in the Quran and Sunnah were now operative in Pakistan." According to the Zina ordinance, "rape was to be punished by the public flogging of the woman as well as the man," implying that the accused and the victim are both liable for the crime.[48] Zia granted further that legal evidence presented by women would have only half the value of that of men.[49]

In addition, the Zia regime introduced major judicial reforms, especially through the creation of a Federal Shariat Court in June 1980, which had the power to hear appeals resulting from the Hudood ordinances. This court was also given "powers to examine laws for 'repugnancy to Islam' and to entertain 'shariat petitions' filed by private citizens."[50] However, after realizing that all of these legal reforms might affect his own martial rule, Zia declared that "the Sharia court could not challenge any martial law regulation or order. The military, it seemed, was above Islamic law."[51] Further, Zia took several steps to Islamicize the economy. A 1981 declaration replaced interest payments with "profit and loss accounts." Another imposed the Zakat tax, taking out 2.5% annually from bank accounts on the first day of Ramadan.[52]

In entrenching the Islamic nature of the state, Zia undertook major policy initiatives that transformed the armed forces into the chief custodian and defender of the Islamic state. The regime embarked on a series of steps that solidified the Islamization of the Army. Among them were: the introduction of Islamic teachings into the curriculum of Army Command and Staff College; inclusion of Islamic education as part of the examination for promotions; the requirement for officers to read *The Quranic Concept of War*; the sidelining of secular officers and the promotion of conservative officers; the introduction of compulsory Friday prayers in regimental Mosques instead of by choice; and the appointment of Deobandi Mullahs to work among the troops as "regimental priests." In the previous era, most senior officers came from the upper class, including the landed aristocracy, and had English language education. Now, many were recruited from small towns and rural areas and were educated in state-run schools or madrassas. Large numbers of this new generation were Islamist adherents of the JI.[53]

Zia's policies also made the use of terror to achieve strategic objectives acceptable to the army. The soldiers were exhorted to believe that the Quranic conception of war sanctioned terrorism an acceptable weapon in the struggle for justice against materially superior enemies.[54] Religion could act as a "force multiplier" against more powerful opponents.[55] In many respects, Zia's role is akin to Aurangzeb, who transformed the somewhat tolerant Mughal India into a sectarian empire that was extremely intolerant toward other religions. The Pakistani army's close collaboration with Islamist extremist groups began under Zia's reign in the context of the Afghan conflict. Later, the collaboration continued through support for the separatist movement in Indian Kashmir. The victory in Afghanistan against a mighty Soviet empire reinforced the belief that Islam sanctioned asymmetric warfare and hence it should form part of the national military strategy.

Thousands of mujahid warriors were initially trained in Pakistan with the help of the United States and Saudi Arabia to fight the Soviet occupying forces, but once they left Afghanistan they moved on to other causes: global jihad and—more narrowly—wresting Kashmir from Indian control. Subsequently, many of them joined Osama bin Laden's al-Qaeda network. The Pakistani city of Peshawar became the epicenter for the training and dispatching of them to various terrorist missions. These warriors, coming from all over the world, were trained by the Pakistanis, especially the ISI. It is estimated that some 35,000 jihadists from 45 countries were trained in Pakistan prior to September 11, 2001.[56]

Political Islam in Pakistan after Zia

Zia-ul-Haq's Islamization policies did immense damage to whatever semblance of tolerant civil society Pakistan had developed, although their pernicious impact was evident even before his death. His immediate successors, the democratically elected Benazir Bhutto and Nawaz Sharif, did little to dismantle that legacy. Bhutto wanted to prove to Islamists that even though she was educated in the West, she could be trusted to protect and advance Pakistan's Islamic character.[57] Nawaz

Sharif was also religious. He came from a conservative family and proudly displayed his religious credentials. His main effort in this direction was the introduction of the 15th constitutional amendment in the National Assembly in October 1998. It would institute Sharia law as the supreme law of Pakistan, giving the prime minister the right to interpret the Quran and Sunnah anyways he pleased.[58] This amendment, however, was never passed, and was preempted by Sharif's overthrow by the military in a coup in October 1999.

General Pervez Musharraf came to power in October 1999. Evoking Ayub Khan in an earlier generation, Musharraf declared his intent to make Pakistan a moderate Islamic country like Turkey, somewhat similar to a previous effort by military ruler Ayub Khan in the early 1960s. General Musharraf's stated objective was to follow secularist Mustafa Kemal Atatürk, the founding father of modern Turkey. He attempted to repeal the blasphemy laws, but had to abandon the effort in May 2000 due to extreme opposition from religious groups.[59] This law was criticized for years by all minority groups because it allowed capital punishment for alleged desecration of the Prophet's name. In protest, a Catholic Bishop John Joseph committed suicide in May 1988. Musharraf's backtracking, however, emboldened Islamist forces within Pakistan.[60] Musharraf was able to obtain greater cooperation from Islamist parties for amending the constitution, which extended his rule, after these parties had initially opposed any further accumulation of power on the part of Musharraf. This was primarily owing to the fact that his regime itself had facilitated the Islamists' growth. In the 2002 elections, leaders of the more secular parties in Bhutto's PPP and Sharif's PML coalitions were barred from contesting elections. The alliance of Islamist parties, the Mutahhidah Majlis Amal (MMA), received the tacit support of the military.[61] Surprisingly, though, despite their increased activism, Islamist parties only received 11% of the electoral votes in the 2002 elections.[62]

The blasphemy law would become a crucial issue for Islamists once again in 2011. The governor of Punjab, Salmaan Taseer, was assassinated for commuting a Christian woman's death sentence for blasphemy. More ominously, several demonstrations, which included lawyers and middle-class groups, were held in support of the assassin, showing how deeply Zia's ideational influence had penetrated the Pakistani society. Even many of the peaceful Barelvis, who follow the Sufi tradition, supported the killer, Mumtaz Qadri, as did the young lawyers who had earlier organized massive pro-democracy demonstrations. Qadri was showered with rose petals during his court appearances.[63] The educated middle classes' support for the killer showed the increased influence of Islamists among them, although some believe it was a show of opposition to the liberal West and how Islam had been treated in the West in the Post-9/11 era.[64] In August 2012 this became a reality as a mentally challenged 14-year-old Christian girl, Rimsha Masih, was falsely accused of burning the Quran, leading to her detention and forcing her family to flee. It was subsequently proven that an anti-Christian cleric, Khalid Jadoon, did the burning himself to drive the Christians from his locality. The case against her was dismissed and she subsequently moved to Canada as a refugee.[65]

THE WAHHABI INFLUENCE

Among all the pernicious influences on Pakistan the worst has been that of the Wahhabi branch of Islam. Originating from Saudi Arabia in the eighteenth century, the Wahhabists are strict pietists with no tolerance for deviation from their medieval religious code. Its originator, Muhammad ibn Abd al-Wahhab (1703–1792), believed that the political weakness and moral decline of Muslims occurred because they deviated from the straight path of Islam. To reclaim their glory, Muslims must return to the community life enshrined in the Quran and the examples of Muhammad and the early Muslim community. In the Wahhabi worldview, other Muslim sects that deviated from the true teachings of the Prophet should be destroyed. In that spirit, Sufism became anathema to Wahhabism, and Sufi shrines and tombs became targets of destruction. To Wahhabists, through ijtihad (personal struggle) it was possible to return to purified Islam and weed out un-Islamic beliefs and practices among some Muslims.[66] Wahhabists are advocates of forceful conversion and the elimination of all varieties of religious syncretism. All forms of Western liberal influence, including science, music, art, and political ideology (e.g., liberal democracy), should be rejected in favor of pursuing the creation of a pure Islamic Caliphate.[67] According to Benazir Bhutto, Wahhabism is an austere and strict sect.

It rejects Christians, Jews, and even some Islamic sects as "apostates". Some Wahhabists claim that it is religious duty to kill Shias, which has led to civil war and bloodshed in the heart of Islam.[68] Moderate Muslims disagree with many of these Wahhabist propositions. However, the moderates are often unorganized and do not have the support of the state to project their views effectively.[69]

The Saudi regime has been one of the most prominent backers of radical Wahhabism in Pakistan and in Central Asia, although in the post-9/11 era it seems to have occasionally cracked down on radicals. Instead of focusing on trade and economic investment, Saudi Arabia has devoted its resources to religious propagation through missionary work, scholarships, and translations of the Quran into native languages.[70] Partly to placate domestic opponents of the monarchy's legitimacy, Saudi Arabia has supported extremist Wahhabi groups all through the region including the Taliban, although it later quarreled with them over bin Laden, who moved to Afghanistan to build his al-Qaeda network.[71] Today, even if Saudi official money has dried up for radical Islamic groups, private financial support from Saudi Arabia appears to be continuing.

THE MADRASSAS

The biggest impact of Wahhabism in Pakistan has been on its educational system. The retreat of the state and of private liberal educational institutions resulted in a major vacuum, one that has been filled by thousands of madrassas or religious schools, many of them operated or funded by Wahhabists. It should be noted that the different schools of Islam, such as Deobandi, Barelvi, and Ahl-I Hadith, all began introducing their madrassas in the mid-1970s. The majority of madrassas are affiliated to five educational boards (wafaqs) controlled by either Sunnis or Shias. Students are taught to defend their theological viewpoint (maslaks) against other traditions, heretical beliefs, and Western-oriented worldviews.[72] The Persian Gulf monarchies, such as Saudi Arabia and the United Arab Emirates, provided financial support to many such schools in order to stem the leftward turn in Pakistani politics during the late 1960s and early 1970s.[73] Although some madrassas have attempted to adjust their curriculum to modern times, many still base it on premedieval Islam. That precludes any teaching of modern mathematics, science, and the liberal arts, or of religions and philosophies other than Islam. Even where such subjects are taught, as one scholar has put it, "most of the books taught in this curriculum are very old. Books used in philosophy and logic, for example, were written in the thirteenth and fourteenth centuries. Medicine is taught through an eleventh-century text that is still considered an authentic study of human anatomy and pathology. In what we have described as purely religious subjects, the books used date back to the seventeenth century at the latest and the eleventh century at the earliest. Books prescribed for astronomy, mathematics, and grammar are more than five- to seven-hundred-year-old texts."[74]

The relative absence of critical thinking means that students are highly susceptible to propaganda and hyperbole. Every other religion becomes an enemy of Islam, and the killing of infidels is allowed if deemed necessary. Non-Abrahamic religions like Hinduism receive the worst treatment. Furthermore, Wahhabi madrassas teach that Muslims who do not agree with Wahabbism can be eliminated in the name of religious piety. In that sense, the Wahhabi philosophy is like any absolutist ideology which preaches the annihilation of the nonbeliever in pursuit of societal hegemony.[75]

The role of the madrassas in fomenting militant sectarianism is well documented. They are the breeding grounds of young fanatics who are willing to carry out suicide missions. Many of these schools teach that modern civil society is evil and have fostered intolerant and antidemocratic views among their students.[76] School textbooks in Pakistan have been especially guilty of spreading intolerance toward minorities, especially Hindus and, to a certain extent, Christians. The US Commission on International Religious Freedom studied over 100 school textbooks from grade 1 to 10. In its November 2011 report, the commission contended that these textbooks put forth an image of Hindus as enemies of Islam, preaching a religion of injustice.[77]

The most significant aspect of the tragedy for Pakistan is the inability and unwillingness of the Pakistani state to put an end to radically oriented madrassas, reform them, or provide a serious alternative. This is largely because of the absence of a viable public educational system that can offer free or affordable education to the general public, a void which the madrassas fill. According to one study, in 2009 Pakistan spent only 2.6% of its GDP on education. This has resulted in both weak educational opportunity and very low standards. Accordingly, 45% of children drop out before completing elementary education, one-fourth of the elementary teachers are untrained, and 7 million children in the five–to-nine-year-old group do not attend school. Moreover, 9% of primary schools do not have blackboards, 24% no textbooks, 46% no desks, and 36% no electricity.[78] According to one estimate, in 2009 some 12,000 "ghost schools" existed in Pakistan where teachers did not show up regularly but drew salaries. Between 2008 and 2013 radical Islamists have destroyed some 995 schools and 35 colleges in the Khyber Pakhtunkhwa province alone. Fear keeps many children, especially girls, from attending schools.[79] According to a UNICEF report in April 2012 some 7 million primary school age children were not attending schools.[80] The civilians and military rulers alike, even when they acted to curtail Wahhabism, did very little to transform the Pakistani educational system. Instead, they typically make contradictory policy statements that on the one hand praise madrassas and on the other promise reform.

The efforts by different governments of Pakistan to reform madrassas have failed for two reasons: strong opposition from the seminaries and the government's own lack of interest. Under a reform process initiated by the government in 2003, the madrassas, estimated at between 20,000 and 25,000 in number, have been required to register and reveal their financial records. In addition, they are supposed to offer courses on secular subjects. In the forefront of opposition to madrassa reform has been the Wafq-ul-Madaris, which controls over 8,200 madrassas, along with the Tanzeemaat Madaris Deeniya and Tanzim-ul-Madaris Ahle Sunnat. Since these madrassas are mostly funded by local businesses, overseas-based religious foundations, charities, and the Pakistani diaspora, they have been able to retain their independence.[81]

To be clear, madrassas are not the only culprits in the radicalization of Pakistan. The poorest sections of the society are the ones generally getting educated in the madrassas. The political and economic elites manage to enroll their children into private schools while many in the middle class send theirs to government schools. However, despite this, it is also clear that more and more of the middle class has been radicalized. One survey in July 2011 found that "poor Pakistanis nationwide disliked the militant groups about two times more than middle class Pakistanis, who were mildly positive toward the groups." The authors hypothesized that "this is because much of Pakistan's militant violence is concentrated in poorer areas and in the bazaars and mosques where less affluent people sell goods, shop, and pray. In addition to being in more physical danger than the rich, the poor are at more of an economic risk from attacks, and income losses are more consequential for them."[82] In fact several studies show that a majority of suicide terrorists tend to come from those educated outside madrassas and whose income levels are significantly above the poverty level.[83]

One important consequence of the shift toward Islamist politics in Pakistan has been an increasingly Islamist tint to foreign and security policy. No less than other segments of society, the armed forces have become increasingly indoctrinated by Islamist ideology. As the state extolls religion, Islamic discourse has become popular among the soldiers (especially since the time of Zia-ul-Haq). Some soldiers even supported militants that the Pakistani army itself was fighting in places like Waziristan.[84] The blasphemy law has strong support in the top echelons of the military, the so-called "jihadist generals" who are opposed to making any major amendments to the law. From the wars on Pakistan's borders has come a self-conception of the military as "soldiers of Islam."[85]

The military's intelligence branch—the ISI—has been a major player in the radicalization of the country. Because of its support for terrorists in neighboring countries, especially Indian-controlled Kashmir and Afghanistan, it has offered Islamist forces a huge space in the country to operate without opposition.[86] The ISI has actively promoted groups like LeT and JeM, two of the leading extremist groups. Both have engaged in terrorist strikes in India, including the Mumbai attacks of November 2008. The ISI has also collaborated with the Pakistan Taliban, whose most prominent faction, the Haqqani Network, has emerged as the most potent insurgent group in Afghanistan. Led by Jalaluddin Haqqani, their group consist of between 5,000 and 15,000 fighters spread around the mountainous terrain saddling Afghanistan and Pakistan. They reportedly obtain money from sympathizers in the Gulf as well as from extortion, smuggling, and kidnapping. (The network was also an ally of the CIA during the war against the Soviet Union in the 1980s.)[87]

The interplay between a warrior state and fundamentalist Islam is nowhere more evident than in Pakistan's policy toward Afghanistan. The geopolitical role of Pakistan in waging the war on the Soviet Union in Afghanistan was discussed in Chapter 4. However, the most pernicious aspect of the policy occurred in 1996 when Pakistan, under Benazir Bhutto, sided with the Taliban in the civil war in Afghanistan. This was justified as a necessary step to prevent the victory of the pro-India alliance of non-Pasthun forces in Afghanistan.

Conclusions

The use—and misuse—of religion by the state and its military has not only weakened Pakistan, it has undermined its potential to emerge as a strong, tolerant, and democratic state. Many of the tendencies that radical Islamist movements hold are undemocratic and antithetical to a society built around democracy, tolerance, and pluralism. They espouse extreme versions of Sharia law and generally ignore the peaceful and tolerant aspects of Islam.

The more liberal traditions within Islam, for instance in the Sufi and Barelvi lines, are not sufficiently valued in Pakistan today. This is because of the proclivity of the elite—civilian and military—to employ strategies of asymmetric warfare that include terror. The ruling elite is also perfectly willing to use hundreds and even thousands of youth, especially those from foreign countries, who are willing to die for their cause. The inclination on the part of the Pakistani civilian and military elite to affiliate with extremist Islamists arises from the deep-rooted hyper-realpolitik ideas they carry. Extremism has proven a useful tool in the asymmetric war against India (in Kashmir) and previously the Soviet Union (in Afghanistan), and for the maintenance of Pakistani interests in Afghanistan since the 1990s. The Taliban became attractive because they would give Pakistan some form of hegemonic control over Afghanistan. Keeping Afghanistan as a vassal state was viewed as essential for national security purposes: to preclude the influence of India in that country and, more importantly, to reduce the chance of a unified Pushtun nation emerging.

The chances of Pakistan emerging anytime soon as a tolerant Islamic state have faded as the twenty-first century advances. The proclivity of the national security elite to use Islam for waging asymmetric wars also implies that they will not abandon it easily. The core of Pakistani military and civilian political elite, even if it does not want to do so, has to pay homage to extremist Islamic values. Much of the post-Zia-ul-Haq generation has been brought up under these ethos. When the electorate votes against Islamist political parties, observers often cite it as a sign that Pakistan in on the path toward liberalism. But this is a chimera as long as the so-called non-religious political parties also support policies of intolerance and the promotion of a single-core religious line. The only way Pakistan can remain a moderate Islamic state is to strengthen its liberal space and the values that syncretic branches of Islam, such as Sufism, hold. But that also remains unlikely given the powerful hold that the hardcore Sunni-Deobandi-Wahhabi coalition has over Pakistan today. The geopolitics of the region vis-à-vis India, Afghanistan, and US military involvement have also only helped to deepen this orientation.

A leading South Asian analyst, M. J. Akbar, argues that "the 'Islamization' of the Constitution preceded Zia, and efforts to reverse his legacy have not succeeded, because a strain of theocracy runs through the DNA of the idea of Pakistan. The effort to convert Pakistan into a Taliban-style Islamic emirate will continue in one form or the other, at a slow or faster pace."[88] Although these efforts may not fully succeed, the likelihood of reversing the course appears to be dim for the foreseeable future.

7

Comparing Pakistan

AFTER COMPLETING BARELY a month of independence, the founding father of Pakistan Mohammad Ali Jinnah expressed his belief that Pakistan had a pivotal role to play in the Cold War competition just beginning to emerge between the United States and the USSR and that it could extract rents for the services to Washington. In a conversation with renowned American photographer and wartime correspondent Margaret Bourke-White at his new residence in Karachi in September 1947 Jinnah declared: "America needs Pakistan more than Pakistan needs America." To Jinnah, Pakistan was "the pivot of the world, as we are placed . . . the frontier on which the future position of the world revolves." His logic, deriving from a realpolitik understanding, was that if the United States was willing to defend Turkey and Greece against Russia, it would be "much more interested in pouring money and arms into Pakistan" because "if Russia walks in here, he concluded, the whole world is menaced." Bourke-White recalls this argument being repeated by government officials throughout Pakistan. They would tell her: "Surely America will build up our Army . . . Surely America will give us loans to keep Russia from walking in."[1]

Jinnah and his bureaucrats' predictions came true as Pakistan would emerge as a pivotal player in the Cold War conflict until the mid-1960s and then again after the Soviet invasion of Afghanistan in 1979, receiving substantial military and economic aid from the United States. Pakistan provided bases for espionage of Soviet military facilities and in May 1960 the Soviet Union announced the shooting down of a U2 spy plane and the capture of its pilot, Gary Powers, who had taken off from Peshawar.[2] Pakistan played a key intermediary role in secret negotiations establishing diplomatic links between China and the United States by the Nixon-Kissinger team during the early 1970s. In July 1971, US National Security Advisor Henry Kissinger used a Pakistani air force plane to travel to Beijing from Islamabad after claiming he had a stomach flu and was going to rest at a Pakistani hill station. During this secret trip, arrangements were made for President Richard Nixon's successful visit to Beijing in February 1972, eventually producing the United States–China rapprochement and full diplomatic relations in January 1979.[3]

Pakistan's success in tapping the geopolitical dividend proved to be a curse as it prevented the elite from launching deep reforms or seeking a more sustainable developmental path, including international trade. The lack of domestic reforms, especially land reforms, and the inattention to education at all levels crippled Pakistan's ability to progress. Pakistan became a war-making state without the capacity to build a modern state. Its top-down coercive approach to national integration only worsened the situation. The elite's use of religion for sectarian political goals widened the chasm among its various ethnic communities. The strategic approach of getting involved in great power geopolitical conflicts as well as taking on a larger India, often by resorting to asymmetric means, only helped to weaken Pakistan as violent nonstate forces now have turned against the state itself. Yet the temptation is very high for the Pakistani elite to tread the same path. How have other countries that received American support fared? How have other Muslim majority countries dealt with war and development in the contemporary era?

War was pivotal to the solidification of many European nations in the modern age. But this has not been uniformly the case in the developing world. Warrior states in the developing world have ranged from strong to desperately weak. And this includes states that receive enormous external assistance because of their geostrategic location. Some countries, like Israel, South Korea and Taiwan, have developed strong and effective states in the face of continuous existential security threats. These are, of course, outliers. Many other warrior states, like Egypt, Indonesia, and Turkey, are weaker than the East Asian tigers—Egypt and Indonesia considerably so. However, Indonesia has, over time, ridden itself of military rule and has become, in recent years, a more inclusive democracy. It also pulled out of East Timor and has managed to pacify some of its simmering separatist movements, such as in Aceh. Egypt has, since the 1970s, pursued its national security with considerably greater restraint. In doing so it eschewed foreign policy adventurism as a source of legitimacy. Turkey has devoted substantial attention to war-making over the years, whether in Cyprus or against its Kurdish population. But some important incidents aside, Turkey's foreign policy has not had the same element of adventurism that Pakistan's has had; instead, since Ataturk, Ankara has focused on keeping its foreign commitments in line with its capabilities, and in expanding its economic base. As in Pakistan, Turkey's military has actively intervened in politics on numerous occasions. But it has used its dominant power position to protect the secular state from falling to religious control, a trajectory opposite of what Pakistan followed. During the past decade or so, the Turkish army has loosened its control over the political system and a soft Islamic party has been in control, with civilian rule stronger than ever.

All of these countries have a strong focus on national security. All are in important geostrategic locations and all have received substantial American assistance.[4] However, to varying degrees, they have not suffered from the geostrategic curse to the extent that Pakistan has. While focusing on national security, they have generally adopted much more restrained security policies. South Korea and Taiwan have not let their security focus get in the way of rapid and sustained economic growth. Nor have they dismissed the importance of democratic legitimacy. Indeed, they turned their strategic location into an economic benefit by using it as an entry into world markets rather than merely as a source of direct revenue. This chapter presents these cases to put Pakistan in comparative perspective.

The first section of this chapter looks at larger Muslim-majority states—Turkey, Indonesia, and Egypt. It also exposes, by way of contrast, how intertwined the twin problems of Pakistan's hyper-realpolitik approach and its embrace of Islamist extremism are. The second section discusses South Korea and Taiwan, developmental states par excellence.

Muslim-Majority States

Turkey

Turkey shares several features in common with Pakistan. A longstanding US ally situated in a crucial geostrategic location, it has had a clear preoccupation with national security and a military that has actively engaged in political life. Turkey's security environment is different and it is a member of NATO, but Ankara still has had an intense military-security focus that is somewhat similar to Pakistan's. However, whereas these conditions have generated continuous political instability, state weakness, and economic stagnation in Pakistan, Turkey has managed to maintain economic development and a fairly strong state from its founding in 1923 by Mustafa Kemal Atatürk. It has done so through a more restrained foreign policy, an awareness of the importance of economic development, and a secular resistance to Islamist extremism.

Atatürk focused on developing a strong, secular, modernizing state, and in doing so achieved an enormous shift away from Ottoman politics.[5] Kemalist guidelines for Turkey included secular, republican nationalism and statism.[6] The Kemalist success in changing the orientation of Turkey was an unparalleled feat in an Islamic country, and for that matter in any country in the world, except probably Japan following the Meiji restoration (1866–1868). It was a top-down transformative project, a "revolution from above" like in its Japanese antecedent.[7] It was meant to change not only the way people perceived society and religion, but how they acted in their daily lives. In that sense it called for a far-reaching evolution from a deeply Islamic conservatism to secularism.[8] The result was a highly centralized state that largely directed economic development from the top down. The military was the guardian of the secular state, which created the potential for the emergence of a garrison state. Since Atatürk, successive governments maintained a fair degree of consensus around Kemalist principles, with the military standing mostly in the background—but sometimes in the foreground—as their guarantor. Recently, there have been some major changes under the Justice and Development Party (AKP): an opening up to Islam, continued trade liberalization, and the retreat of the armed forces. But throughout its post-1923 history, with some important exceptions, Turkey has retained a much stronger, more stable state with a considerably more restrained foreign policy than has Pakistan, despite much in common with the latter.

At the junction of two continents and close to a third, bordering the former Soviet Union and several key Middle Eastern states, and commanding the Bosphorus and Dardanelles Straits, Turkey is in one of the most vital geostrategic locations in the world, possibly even more so than Pakistan. Yet its elite has not played double games—that is, by seeking to convert this importance to the advantage of the corporatist interests of the army—at least not to the same degree as in Pakistan. Like Pakistan, Turkey is one of the leading recipients of US economic and military aid. During the Cold War, Turkey offered major bases to NATO that strengthened Western deterrent capabilities against the Soviet Union. In return, the Turks received $4.5 billion in economic assistance and $9.6 billion in military assistance. During the Persian Gulf War of 1991, the regular outlay of US security assistance was raised from $553.4 million to $635.4 million, and Turkey imported $1.8 billion in arms from the United States in 1990–1991.[9] In the post-9/11 world, US bases and transport corridors on Turkish territory took on renewed importance, for example in the campaign in Afghanistan.[10] Indeed, Turkey commanded NATO's International Security Assistance Force mission in Afghanistan from July 2002 to January 2003.[11] At the same time, it received an enormous spike in economic and military assistance from the United States, from below $25 million in each year from 1999 to 2001 to $276 million in 2002. However, the Iraq war was a different matter: Turkey believed it was not adequately compensated for losses incurred in the 1990–1991 Gulf War, and was worried about the effects of a possible Kurdish state in Iraq after a US invasion, and antiwar sentiment in Turkey was strong.[12] During the 2003 invasion of Iraq by the United States, Turkey did not permit the use of its border as a front for the invasion.[13] It did allow US overflights of Turkish territory for military operations in Iraq as of March 2004 but did not permit the use of Turkish airbases. A large majority of Turks condemned the American invasion and began to regard the United States as Turkey's single largest threat. Thus anti-Americanism has become more rife in Turkey, similar to Pakistan.[14] However, since 2003, Turkey has continued to receive some $31.6 million per year, on average, in economic and military assistance from the United States.

The similarity to Pakistan does not stop with external aid. Turkey also approaches its regional environment with a strong sense of insecurity. Mustafa Aydın calls this a "perennial insecurity complex."[15] However, in several respects, Turkey's conflicts are much more restrained than Pakistan's. It is one of the few powerful states in the multipolar Middle East, rather than a revisionist challenger to a dominant regional power as with Pakistan in South Asia. Its engagement with Europe, through NATO and the European Union (EU) accession process, has helped to induce restraint in its foreign policy. Turkey's secular approach precludes a fear among its neighbors that it will embrace religious extremism. Nor is it continuously seeking to redeem lost territory, as with Pakistan and Kashmir.

Turkey's most important local rivalry has been with Greece. The war between the two countries in 1920–1923 set the stage for ongoing tensions and conflict in subsequent decades. The 1923 Treaty of Lausanne demarcated the borders, with major population transfers to both sides. After a period of relative peace, tensions began to mount in the 1950s over Cyprus, divided between Turkish and Greek Cypriots. In July 1974, this reached a boiling point when a right-wing Greek faction, with the support of Athens, staged a coup to overthrow Archbishop Makarios's biethnic government, prompting Turkey to invade northern Cyprus. The Turkish military presence generated international condemnation, including from the UN Security Council. However, Cyprus is far from being Turkey's Kashmir. The population of the island is today divided on ethnic lines, with a UN force interposed between the two sides.[16] Rather than ongoing insurgency and violence, a cold peace has prevailed over the island. That the conflict has not been more violent had to do in part with the possibility, long hinted at but highly doubtful, of Turkish accession to the EU.[17] Greece has also pursued policies that have effectively reduced the potential for the remilitarization of the conflict.[18]

Like Pakistan, Turkey has had to face a major separatist conflict in its Kurdish territory. In total, there are about 25 million Kurds, and about half of them live in Turkey. The rest are spread among neighboring states, from Syria to Iran. The Kurds represent around 18% of the population of Turkey.[19] They have been denied an independent state, and have been subject to political and social repression. They have responded with guerilla war and insurgency, with the Kurdistan Workers' Party (PKK) leading a violent revolt in Turkey from 1984 through the late 1990s. The Turkish military responded with intense suppression, including the recruitment of local paramilitaries or "Village Guards."

The conflict has spilled over to neighboring countries, with the PKK frequently seeking cross-border safe havens and Turkey attempting to deny them. Turkish troops have frequently conducted raids into northern Iraq in "hot pursuit" of PKK units, including a six-week operation in March 1995 involving 40,000 Turkish troops.[20] Commando operations and bombing raids in Iranian territory in July 1999 led to a serious dispute between Ankara and Tehran.[21] In October 1998 Turkey massed troops on its border with Syria in an effort to compel Damascus to arrest PKK's exiled leader, Abdullah Öcalan. Syria expelled Öcalan, and after searching for a safe harbor across Russia, Italy, and Greece, he was arrested in Nairobi by Turkish agents in February 1999.[22] By successfully imprisoning the PKK's paramount leader, severely weakening its opportunities for external bases, and increasing its effective control over its southeastern territory, Turkey has indicated a clear advantage over Pakistan in its ability to deal with a major insurgency. Thus, despite some similarities in the nature of the problem that Turkey faced vis-à-vis its minority Kurds and Pakistan with its minorities in Balochistan and the Pashtuns, Turkey appears to be more successful in dealing with the separatist issue.

Turkey's security environment is less intense than Pakistan's. Underlying this less intense conflict environment is a more restrained approach to foreign policy. Not that Turkish leaders have shied away from military security as a dominant state goal. Turkey is similar to Pakistan in terms of some of the assumptions the elite holds on security as well as the intentions of neighboring states. They both share a realpolitik worldview. Turkish society in general has also been socialized, largely through the compulsory military service of all adult male members, to unconditionally support military values.[23] The military has traditionally considered itself the guardian of the Turkish nation, with a moral and legal obligation to protect it against both internal and external threats. It has treated military threats with challenges to Kemalist values as equivalent.[24] However, this dominance has been mellowed by several factors. It has generally not implied much foreign policy aggression. And

Turkey's long institutional membership in NATO and its desire to join the EU has encouraged the elite toward moderating their security policies and pursuing less ambitious geopolitical agendas than Pakistan.

Indeed, one crucial area where Atatürk and the Pakistani elite differ is the pragmatism of the former and the ideologically based ambitious grand strategy of the latter. Dankwart Rustow summarized Turkey's pragmatic restraint back in 1968: "Kemal's central tenet, moreover, works both ways: Force must back Right, but no rights must be claimed beyond what force can hold; and it was this type of realistic, even pessimistic, appraisal of the situation that had repeatedly put him at odds with his superiors during World War I. Realistic self-limitation, a readiness to fit ends to means, remains one of his lasting contributions to Turkish statecraft."[25] There indeed is a major difference between the Pakistani elite's worldview and Kemalist pragmatism. The relationship between means and ends and capabilities and ambition has been more pragmatic, realistic, and in sync in the Turkish case as compared to that of the Pakistani elite.

Unlike Pakistan's generally offensive military doctrine, Turkey has adopted a defensive doctrine for a long period of time. Ali Karaosmanoğlu suggests this has been the case since the eighteenth century, as a result of the Ottoman Empire's failures in wars with the Western neighbors and the introduction of liberal and internationalist elements in its foreign policy.[26] In a subsequent era, Turkish foreign policy added further elements of restraint, with the pursuit of liberal, internationalist policies in trade and multilateralism in the 1990s.[27] Turkey's influential AKP foreign minister, Ahmet Davutoğlu, has attempted to pursue a "zero problem policy" to avoid confrontation with Turkey's neighbors,[28] though disputes with Israel over the blockade of Gaza and with Syria over the latter's uprising since 2011 has certainly posed challenges to this policy. In the summer of 2012, Syrian refugees began to put tremendous pressure on Turkey to engage in some form of military action to prevent the Assad regime from conducting mass killings and allowing starvation to spread. This is unlikely to lead to a major war between Turkey and Syria as the Syrian regime is simply incapable of sustaining such a conflict. In general, Turkey's restraint in security matters is a far cry from Pakistan's hard realpolitik and its use of extremist forces in the pursuit of revisionist foreign policy ends.

In addition, Turkish governments since Atatürk have balanced security concerns with the need for economic development. Turkey has achieved moderate economic growth over time, with average annual growth rates since 1960 of 4.6%, though it has occasionally experienced severe recessions. Adjusted for inflation, Turkey's per capita income has more than tripled over that period. Poverty has declined somewhat, with none of the population living on less than $1 per day as of 2008, and the percentage on less than $2 per day declining from almost 10% in 2002 to 4.16% by 2008. However, income inequalities remain high and the per capita income is still of a middle-range level. Nearly 20% of the Turkish population is believed to live below the poverty line as of 2009, with a rural poverty rate of almost 40%.[29]

Unlike Pakistan, Turkey introduced land reforms early on. Various political efforts toward reform began in the mid-1930s, with a land reform law instituted in 1945. The reasons for introducing such a law were fear of rural unrest from landless peasants and agricultural laborers, a desire to strengthen nationalism and hence support for the regime in the countryside, and diverting peasants away from leftist ideologies.[30] However, political interference in land reforms and a lack of publicity for the new law meant that the law was only moderately successful. Between 1947 and 1962, 1.8 million hectares were distributed from out of a total cultivated area of almost 20 million hectares. Most of this was public land rather than redistributed from large landholdings.[31]

In terms of the larger economic policy, Turkey pursued a partial developmental state agenda. Initially in the 1930s, it followed state-centered economic development. In the 1960s, it followed import substitution strategies, and after the 1980s it shifted to export-oriented policies.[32] The discouragement of foreign investment and international trade in the "developmentalist" era did slow Turkey's overall economic development.[33] It was only after the end of the Cold War that Turkey started to liberalize its trade position. Under the AKP, Turkey has maintained solid economic growth. As Kemal Kirişci argues, the increasing focus on international trade has directly contributed to moderation in Turkish foreign policy, such that a narrow national security focus has been diminishing. Indeed, Ankara has reached rapprochements with its neighbors in order to improve economic relations.[34]

In the religious sphere, Atatürk's reforms were designed to prevent Turkey from falling into the trap of Islamist politics. Political Islam could certainly have served as a basis for a state in a country that had a 99% Muslim population and was the inheritor of the legacy of Ottoman rule over much of the Muslim world more generally. Moreover, as a state on the edge of Europe, Islam provided a clear identity. However, Atatürk instituted reforms that limited the possibilities for religious influence in politics and made the Turkish military the vanguard of protecting the secular state. Placing religion under state control and translating the Quran into Turkish to make it available to ordinary people weakened the power of the ulema as the sole interpreters of Islam. At the same time, the state focused on nationalism rather than Islam: Islam was not the state religion under the constitution, Islamic teachings were removed from the primary school curriculum, and Turkish nationalism built instead on pre-Islamic roots.[35]

Still, Islam was not totally removed from political life. Kemalists used Islam more pragmatically. They deployed Islam first in their war against Ottoman and Western forces. Later, "without changing its basic secularist stance, the Turkish state adopted a double discourse: on the one hand, establishing rigid segregation between Islam and the public political realm; on the other, accommodating and incorporating Islamic politics into the system in various ways."[36] But the use of Islam contrasts sharply with its use in Pakistan. Perhaps nothing is as illustrative of the difference as how two generals used political Islam after launching military coups in the two countries. After Turkey's coup of 1960, the leader of the military junta, General Cemal Gürsel, declared that Islam was a "constructive," "dynamic" force, which he contrasted with a reactionary vision of Islam. The regime then trained forward-looking imams to promote the state's modernizing views.[37] Gürsel's use of Islam offers a clear contrast to how Zia-ul-Haq, after his own coup in Pakistan in 1977, promoted a fundamentalist line.

Both Turkey and Pakistan have had difficulties in accommodating religious minorities, although for different reasons. Turkey, despite being secular, has seen a decline of its Christian population partly because of the state policy of not allowing any new building or property acquisition by the Christian churches beyond what they held before the revolution in 1923. Although there is more religious freedom for minorities in

Turkey than in Pakistan, the minority religions have not been encouraged to propagate their faith to the general public.[38] A mere 1% of Turkey is non-Muslim, unlike Pakistan, where the number is closer to 5%. This is despite the fact that, under the Ottoman Empire, the millet system allowed each minority religious community, including Christians and Jews, to follow its unique legal system, with courts, judges, and legal principles for its community members. Secular Turkey discouraged religious education for both Muslims and non-Muslims and all educational institutions have been under state control.[39] The deeply conservative nature of Turkish society, despite its secular credentials, may have been the reason why non-Muslims have not made many inroads in society. However, unlike in Pakistan, non-Muslims do not face laws like the ones related to "blasphemy" or threats to their lives as documented in Chapter 6.

The military has regarded itself as the guardian of this secular order, and has intervened in politics with this agenda in mind. Most notably, since the 1920s Turkey has experienced four military coups either in defense of the secular state or in opposition to the perceived weaknesses of the civilian regime in upholding Kemalist values. The 1960 and 1980 coups were direct military takeovers. In the other two, in 1971 and 1977, the military's threat of takeover compelled elected governments to cede power. After these coups, the military eventually retreated to the barracks, paving the way for civilian government to return. The 600,000-strong military also retained its strong reputation and popular support as the protector of Turkey's secular order.[40] In particular, it has exercised greater authority when there has been political instability and weak civilian governments in power.[41] In this respect, both the Turkish and the Pakistani military showed a top-down approach as guardians of their country's respective sociopolitical order.

However, since the 1980s, the Turkish military has been playing a less prominent role in society than it used to. Over time, the military elite seemed to have realized that when it intervenes, it damages its own internal cohesion, and undermines its public image as an institution above the political fray. It also has avenues for behind-the-scenes influence, such as its monthly National Security Council meetings.[42] But such a change has been much less pronounced in the Pakistani context. The Pakistani military's willingness to directly control the state may have been temporarily diminished after the collapse of the Musharraf regime in August 2008, but it has not resulted in a substantial weakening of power of the military.

In the early 2000s Turkey began to allow moderate Islam to flourish. As a result, some changes have occurred in Turkish attitudes. The Islam-rooted Justice and Development Party (AKP) won the elections in November 2002. Political debate has emerged around the increasing number of women wearing the traditional veil. At the same time, Turkey moderated several of its policies in an effort to enter the European Union. These included reforms in constitutional, legal, and economic arenas, involving fundamental freedoms of expression and of religion as well as some efforts toward the settlement of the Cyprus and Kurdish conflicts. However, the huge potential migration from Turkey to other parts of Europe such as Germany, which is already home to a massive number of Turkish migrants, and an aversion to admitting a Muslim-majority country, have both played a significant role in EU reluctance to admit Turkey as a full-fledged member. The negotiations on EU accession have been stalled since 2008, despite a commitment to begin the process of admitting Turkey at various EU summits. It is unlikely that the EU will expand anytime soon to include Turkey, given the financial and political crisis that Europe has been facing since 2008.[43]

Civil-military relations have been under serious stress under the AKP government, with occasional rumors of possible military intervention to prevent the AKP's limited Islamization policies. However, the trend seems to favor the civilian government. The charismatic and somewhat authoritarian prime minister, Recep Tayyip Erdoğan, has been able to transform Turkey both economically and politically. The military is a much tamed institution today. Under Erdoğan's leadership, Turkey has become a leading regional power in the Middle East, emerging as a significant trading state with exports increasing to $114 billion in 2011 from $36 billion in 2002.[44] Turkey's economic prosperity has helped to solidify Erdoğan's position. In August 2007, he weathered the opposition of the military and the Kemalist Republican People's Party (CHP) to the candidacy of Abdullah Gül, an Islamist sympathizer, for the post of President of Turkey.[45] In September 2010, in successful amendments ratified through a popular referendum, Erdoğan's government managed to modify the constitution to make the military more accountable to parliament and the executive. The 26-article amendment was in tune with EU demands and included the expansion of civil liberties, abolition of immunity for military personnel who engaged in coups, and provisions for the protection of the children, the elderly, and the disabled.[46] The referendum received over 58% of the electorate's support and was approved on the 30th anniversary of a military coup, altering the very constitution that the military, in 1982, had framed in the aftermath of that coup.[47]

The military seems to have resigned itself to this new order, however grudgingly. In July 2011, the top Turkish generals and admirals from the navy, army and the air force resigned en masse in opposition to the prime minister's policies toward the military. In particular, they were aggrieved by the trial of 40 generals and the fresh arrest warrants for 22 generals who were accused of conspiring to overthrow the Erdoğan government. The prime minister then appointed his own choice, General Necdet Ozel, as the military commander, marking a major event in civilian control over the military.[48] In earlier times, this would have led to a coup, but today it seems the military has learned to live under a civilian government even when it may have some Islamic slant in its policies. Interestingly, in September 2012 some 330 officers were found guilty of a coup attempt and were sentenced to 20-years prison terms.[49]

Turkey's changes under the AKP show that a national security state can avoid the extremes that Pakistan has suffered through. The military can be placed under civilian control, and such a state can adopt policies that can reduce the chances of intolerance and extremism, while allowing religion a space in the public domain. Also, the Turkish example shows that democracy can be made compatible with Islamic values.[50] However, fissures have been developing in Turkey because of the efforts of the AKP government to introduce more Islamist ideas into the political system and the growing disenchantment of the secular middle class at Erdoğan's authoritarian policies which have targeted his opponents as well as journalists. Mass protests erupted in the summer of 2013 against Erdoğan, although the protestors were subsequently pacified.[51] Only time can tell whether Turkey will abandon its secular principles and whether the divisions between the religious and secular forces will become unbridgeable. Some Pakistani leaders occasionally speak of a desire to become like Turkey, but these expressions have been proclamations only. For instance, General Pervez Musharraf wanted to become the Atatürk of Pakistan, only to back away in the end, fearing an Islamist backlash. General Ayub Khan also had some interest in the Turkish model, but did not live up to this hope.

Indonesia

Indonesia has much in common with Pakistan. They are, respectively, the largest and second-largest Muslim-majority countries in the world by population. Both are in geostrategically important locations, with Indonesia a giant in Southeast Asia and sitting astride some of the world's most important shipping lanes. Like Pakistan, it received considerable material assistance from the United States: $3.8 billion in economic assistance and $659 million in military assistance during the Cold War, and $3.5 billion in economic assistance and $117.5 million in military assistance since then.[52] Indonesia's geopolitical importance is likely to increase with China's rise and the United States' Asian shift in foreign policy. Both Indonesia and Pakistan have faced several serious internal conflicts, both in major cities and in the periphery. And in both cases, the armed forces have had a vital role to play in politics. It is true that Indonesia, unlike Pakistan, does not have an intense rivalry with a larger neighbor. However, Indonesia has pursued development more consistently and, in recent years, has shifted toward a democratic system with civilian control over the military.

Indonesia became free in August 1949 after a bloody war of independence with the Dutch colonial rulers. For the next half-century it labored under authoritarian rule, first by President Sukarno (1945–1967) and then by Suharto (1967–1998). The founding fathers of Indonesia adopted the doctrine of "*pancasila,*" or "five principles" to serve as the guiding posts of state policy. These principles have evolved since 1945, and their meaning and content have been open to interpretation and debate among various groups. For instance, the first principle—"belief in One Almighty God"—might be seen as making Indonesia an Islamic state. However, it has been clarified by Indonesian governments that the concept encompasses all officially recognized religions—Islam, Christianity, Hinduism, and Buddhism—and that it, in doing so, gives Indonesia a "mild secular character" by not privileging any single religion as the state religion.[53] The second principle commits the state to treat all in a fair manner, while the third is the unity of Indonesia, a vast chain of over 13,000 islands and comprising 350-odd different ethnic groups. The fourth principle emphasizes governance of the country through consultation and consensus, and the final principle expresses a commitment to social justice for all Indonesians.[54]

During the 1940s, the Indonesian military emerged as a revolutionary force fighting against the Dutch colonial rulers. After independence, it initially gave civilian leaders a chance to run democratic governments. While Sukarno served as a president with limited powers, parliamentary governments were not able to achieve stability. Military leaders pushed for a stronger role in governing the country. In 1957, the charismatic founding father of Indonesia, Sukarno, proclaimed martial law. The armed forces were a core component of his "Guided Democracy" approach, taking an important role in political and social life.[55] In a sort of gradual coup over 1965–1967, General Suharto took power. The military legitimized its power by adopting the doctrine called "dual function" (*dwifungsi*), giving it a direct role in national security and political governance of the country. The strategy of "people's defense" facilitated the military's direct coordination with the civilian population and the right to intervene in all aspects of Indonesia's politics, society, and economy.[56] The territorial organization of the Army made its presence felt in every part of the country down to the village level.[57]

In May 1998, army rule ended when President Suharto was overthrown and a civilian political system emerged. General Wiranto, army chief as of February 1998, did not reassert military rule when Suharto left office. The first free elections since 1957, on June 7, 1999, saw a new Parliament elected. Along with representatives appointed by the national elections commission and by provincial governments, Parliament formed a People's Consultative Assembly that elected Abdurrahman Wahid president.[58] Wahid was able to reduce the powers of the military over time. The withdrawal of Indonesian troops from East Timor in 1999 and the winding-down of the conflict in Aceh have both reduced the obsession with internal security and thus the role of the military in politics. Indonesia has held two general elections since 1998 and the military's role has been progressively reduced. In 2007 the Freedom House called Indonesia fully "free."[59]

In both Indonesia and Pakistan, then, the army has been a core player and has viewed itself as the guardian of the country's security and political order. In the Indonesian case, the army had revolutionary roots in the struggle for independence against the Dutch, whereas the Pakistani army was a postindependence creation, drawing from the remnants of the British Indian army. The Indonesian army focused more on internal enemies, including communists, Islamists, and regional secessionist movements. In Pakistan the army also faces numerous internal challengers, but its primary function since independence has been its external conflict with India. In the governance of the country, both the Indonesian and the Pakistani armies have played a key role, often more powerful than the civilian authorities. However, since 1998, the Indonesian army has lost that role while Pakistan's army continues to enjoy the dominant status in the country's political and economic order.

The Indonesian army also appeared not to have hobnobbed with Islamist extremists. Ultimately, as Kikue Hamayotsu explains, "despite some superficial readjustment from the 1990s on, Islam remained largely in an off-side position in the state's project of nation-building."[60] In fact, in the early decades the army fought intense battles against doctrinaire Islamists who wanted to turn Indonesia into an Islamic state, by siding with President Sukarno's *pancasila* doctrine.[61]

This antipathy of the Indonesian army toward Islamic doctrines may have something to do with the fact that the Indonesian Army has been dominated by an officer corps heavily influenced by the syncretic Javanese culture.[62] Indonesia in general has been impacted by various civilizations and religions, including Hinduism, Buddhism, and Christianity, thereby creating a more plural and tolerant polity and society than Pakistan. Islam also spread to the Indonesian islands largely through peaceful means, brought mostly by traders from Arabia and India, returning Indonesian traders, and traveling Sufi mystics, and then spread from the top down by rulers who were the first to convert.[63]

But there is a compelling political logic to the lack of cooperation with extremists. Even though Suharto had alliances with Muslim parties, when he came to power he sidelined those parties and drew on political support from many different communities.[64] As an archipelago, Indonesia is considerably more secure from external threat than Pakistan, despite the historical occupation by the Dutch and the Japanese.

Lacking really strong and enduring international conflicts with stronger powers, Indonesia has had no real reason to cooperate with asymmetric forces such as jihadist groups. Instead, the Indonesian army and political elite sought to contain internal enemies.

Indeed, Indonesia has not lacked for internal conflicts. Initial troubles were in Java (one of the main islands)—in the east between communists and their opponents and in the west after the proclamations of Darul Islam groups that wanted to convert Indonesia to an Islamic state, strictly following Sharia laws.[65] In addition, Indonesia had several incidents of communal violence involving Muslim and Christian populations in Moluccas and Central Sulawesi, and these flare up occasionally even today.[66] Secessionist movements in Aceh, Irian Jaya, and East Timor were a response to the repressive policies of the Suharto government. Similar to Pakistan, these movements had genuine grievances which the central government either could not or would not address. In the name of nation-building, the Indonesian state engaged in policies that alienated these provinces for a long period of time. Its 1975 annexation of East Timor—formerly a Portuguese colony—led to a brutal occupation. It relocated upwards of 100,000 people from East Timor to depopulate the region, exploited its oil and natural gas resources without returning much benefit to the local population, and in the course of counterinsurgency against the Fretilin independence movement, killed around 200,000 civilians—one third of the pre-1975 population.[67] Elsewhere, Jakarta enjoyed the fruits of exploiting Aceh's considerable natural resources wealth without distributing the gains to the local population. In response to the Aceh uprising of the early 1990s, the government declared a military operations area that enabled the Indonesian armed forces to conduct severe human rights abuses.[68] After Suharto's resignation in 1998, these liberation movements experienced a resurgence, with new uprisings in both Aceh and East Timor.[69] Eventually, the latter gained its independence in May 2002. As for Aceh, the Indian Ocean Tsunami of 2004—resulting from an earthquake just off of Aceh's coast and devastating the region—eventually helped lead to a peace agreement with the Gerakan Aceh Merdeka secessionist group. The agreement included considerable autonomy for the province and a democratic transition in which the former rebels now hold political power.[70]

Since the Bali bombings of 2002, which killed 202 people, Indonesia has also adopted a strong policy of suppressing Islamic terrorism, especially by its most violent group, Jamaat-e-Islami (JI). It has cooperated with the United States in its War on Terror.[71] Unlike Pakistan, the leaders of Indonesia realized the pitfalls of playing with terrorism and Islamic extremism. They suppressed Islamists and also made efforts to deny them political opportunities in conflicts like in Aceh. Today, Indonesia is touted as a rising middle power and a country where tolerant democratic values are fostered. Indonesia's membership in the Association of Southeast Asian Nations helped to ease its tensions with neighbors and its leaders abandoned a hyper-realpolitik approach to national security even when the military was in control.

The military rulers of Indonesia, though they did not pursue a full-fledged developmental state approach, still did adopt certain progrowth policies unlike their Pakistani counterparts. They opened up the country's economy with the aim of receiving foreign capital, and made significant investments in infrastructure, agriculture, and export industries.[72] Crucially, the Indonesian state has not fallen prey to the "resource curse" to nearly the extent that other oil- and gas-rich countries have. Andrew Rosser argues that this curse was avoided because Suharto's conservative social and economic base led to more focus on assorted private-sector development and the diversification of Indonesia's economy, while his shift toward the West in the Cold War granted access to export markets and foreign investment.[73] The effect was moderate to high rates of economic growth. However, corruption has been a very important economic obstacle. The main beneficiaries of the economic growth have been the armed forces themselves and their bureaucratic allies.[74] Worse, Indonesia has experienced low growth rates since the Asian financial crisis of 1997–1998.[75]

The Pakistani elite, both military and civilian, can take some cues from the Indonesian experience and transform their society as well if they wish to do so. The Indonesian army decided to give up power after decades of direct rule, and the newly ascendant civilians were able to assert themselves. Indonesian society in general has supported the civilian enterprise, although the military still has preeminent social status. It was in fact the civil society of Indonesia that stood by the elected leaders, especially when President Wahid stripped the military of its dominant role and placed it under civilian control.[76] Pakistan's civil society did play an important role in forcing General Musharraf to abdicate power in 2008; however, the military still remains the final arbiter of power in Pakistan. In Pakistan, progressive civil society organizations have not been nearly as effective as in Indonesia. The Indonesian decision to withdraw from East Timor and to settle the Aceh conflict facilitated the diminution of the military's *raison d'être* in Indonesian society. Strong-willed civilian leaders, with the support of civil society, have been essential for this outcome.

Egypt

Egypt has many similarities and several differences with Pakistan. Its history is shaped by its pivotal location on the globe, and like Pakistan it is at a crossroad of imperial and great power conflicts and invasions. Egypt has retained the composite culture left behind by various empires, including the Pharaonic, Persian, Hellenistic, Roman, and Byzantine. Egypt has since then been ruled by the Arabs (639–1250), Turkish Mamuluks (1250–1516), the Ottomans (1517–1867), interrupted briefly by Napoleon's France 1798–1801. Like Pakistan, it was also a British colony. From 1882 until 1922 the British maintained an occupation and then a protectorate in Egypt. London retained substantial influence in the country after its nominal independence under a new monarchy, until 1952. That year, the Free Officers Movement, led by Gamal Abdel Nasser, successfully overthrew the king, ended foreign influence, and created an authoritarian state.[77]

In foreign policy terms, Nasser's rule was dominated by three themes: conflict with Israel, an assertion of Egyptian independence from external influence, and obtaining leadership in the Arab world and the developing world more generally. Nationalizing the Suez Canal to help fund development projects brought Egypt to war with a coalition of Britain, France, and Israel in 1956. In 1967, Nasser's belligerence—including demanding the removal of the UN peacekeepers that had patrolled the border since the previous war and blockading Israel's access to the Red Sea—helped to provoke war with Israel. The result was a humiliating defeat. Egypt lost almost all of its military aircraft, and, more importantly, the Sinai Peninsula. The canal that Nasser had fought to control 11 years prior was closed. Nasser offered to resign, only to take back the offer under public pressure, and then engaged in a purge of military officers whom he suspected of plotting his ouster and whom he blamed for the military disaster.[78] Rejecting recognition of and negotiation with Israel, Nasser instead pursued a "War of Attrition," engaging Israeli artillery in duels across the canal and commando raids into occupied territory.

During his rule, Nasser also created a semiwelfare state, but income inequalities and mass poverty continued unabated. His regime had some limited successes in instituting land reforms in a country in which one-third of the fertile land was owned by .05% of the population. The 1952 land reforms law, modified in 1958 and 1961, put a ceiling of 100 acres on land that a single family could hold, ended absentee owner-ship, capped rent on leased lands, strengthened the legal rights of peas-ants, and forcefully confiscated and distributed excess land to millions of poor peasants.[79] However, the land reforms were undercut by the rich and middle-income peasants who dominated the administrative bodies created to carry out the reforms by selling land to friends and family. Ultimately Nasser himself undermined some of his own tools for administering land reforms.

Nasser was successful in receiving allegiance from the ulema, despite the much greater emphasis placed on Arab nationalism and socialism in Nasser's rule. The constitutional charter he created, for example, had limited references to Islam. However, the clergy was eager to show that the values of Islam and socialism were similar, values such as equality, social justice, and brotherhood.[80] This was far from the only religious response to Nasser's rule. Members of the Muslim Brotherhood, which originated in 1928, attempted to assassinate the president and take over the country in 1954, but failed in the effort. What distinguished the brotherhood was its opposition to Western notions of secularism and rationalism, and it also had a strong program for social welfare and reli-gious revitalization.[81]

The regimes of both Nasser and his successor Anwar Sadat were highly authoritarian. Their political parties rubber-stamped the leader's deci-sions. The mass media was a close ally of the regime. Large-scale corrup-tion existed as the regime attempted to gain favors from powerful interest groups. The military was the key to the regime's survival and the intel-ligence apparatus "dominated other agents of repression."[82] However, the military was never as dominant as in Pakistan or even akin to the guardianship role that the Turkish military enjoyed. The president remained the most powerful decision-maker in Egypt. The military's role was instead well captured by Tarek Osman: it "enjoyed a detached, exceptional status—ahead of and superior to any other organization in the country."[83]

Upon Nasser's death in 1970, Anwar Sadat succeeded as president. Sadat presided over a profound shift in Egypt's orientation. He attempted to rectify Nasser's legacy of socialism, his close ties with the Soviet Union, and the economic decline and territorial loss to Israel that his rule had witnessed. First, he proposed a confederation with Libya and Syria, using the proposal to draw his internal opponents to the forefront. He then successfully purged them in 1971, with Vice-Premier Ali Sabri the most significant victim.[84] But more important was the shift to come. Sadat attempted to distance Egypt from the Soviet Union and turn instead to an American alignment, with the understanding that the United States could deliver to Egypt the Sinai and provide more substantial economic aid. After some embarrassing dithering about regaining Sinai, Sadat achieved a dramatic coup in October 1973. With a sudden assault on Israeli positions in Sinai, Sadat was able to both reestablish military credibility and give himself a reputation as the "Hero of the Crossing," even though the Egyptian forces were eventually turned back. Inflicting a psychological shock on Israel and reestablishing his own reputation at home paved the way for negotiations over the Sinai and for Egyptian recognition of Israel. The result, ultimately, was the Camp David Agreements of 1978–1979.[85]

This agreements, which returned the Sinai to Egypt in exchange for recognition of Israel and a peace treaty, led to massive American assistance to Cairo. Indeed, Egypt since 1979 is an especially interesting case of a country suffering from the "geostrategic curse." Having enjoyed considerable Soviet assistance until the 1970s, since 1979 Egypt has received nearly $2 billion every year from the US. It has made Egypt the number two recipient of American aid, after Israel. Since 1979, Cairo has received about $66 billion from the United States: $26.4 billion in economic aid, and $39.5 billion in military aid.[86] Saudi Arabia has also offered substantial aid to Egypt. Beyond aid, Egypt also received huge sums in remittances (totaling $2.9 billion in 2001 alone) from expatriates working mainly in the Gulf.[87] The assistance has meant that the Egyptian government has not had to establish a long-term, sustainable vision for stability and legitimate rule. As long as the aid was flowing, the government could fund itself quite handsomely and distribute revenues to wealthy officers as well as other regime cronies.

However, in a major difference from Pakistan, the aid has meant a profound moderation in foreign policy. American assistance has come with a major condition: peace with Israel. In contrast, the United States offered crucial backing in Pakistan's war with India in 1971 and did not oppose its adventurism in Afghanistan in the 1990s. Washington has not tried or was not able to impose such conditionalities for peace on Pakistan for the various reasons discussed in Chapter 5. But the Camp David Accords ended Egypt's continuous preoccupation with external security. By diverting attention away from an obsessive focus with external security, Camp David could have heralded much more of a shift away from the garrison state and toward economic development than actually occurred. The power of the national security state has declined, although the military continued to be the dominant institution for another three decades and retains a stronghold in post-Mubarak Egypt. The Egyptian leadership, however, has failed in developing the country economically. Economic liberalization and a degree of economic growth came with continued poverty and inequality.

Despite the potential represented by Camp David, in some respects it contributed to instability. Along with repression and the economic dislocation associated with the decline of the Egyptian welfare state, peace with Israel helped to strengthen support for the Muslim Brotherhood. First Sadat supported Muslim parties by freeing arrested members of the Muslim Brotherhood, and sought an alliance in order to aid his retreat from Nasserite ideology. Despite his efforts to use them for his political purposes, he could not control their growth or political trajectories. Members of a Muslim extremist group would eventually assassinate him for making peace with Israel and other unpopular policies his regime pursued.[88] Indeed, Sadat's open-door economic policy, partial democratization, alliance with the West, and conciliation with Israel all generated opportunities for different social forces to emerge, many in strong opposition to Sadat's rule.[89] Unlike Pakistan, the state did not try to give the Islamists much space—with the exception of Sadat's limited opening—nor did it use them for its geopolitical purposes, something it could have pursued in its struggle against Israel and in support of the Palestinian cause. Here the influence of the United States has been more effective in preventing the ruling elite from using nonstate actors for broader strategic goals (unlike the Pakistan case).

Hosni Mubarak assumed power upon Sadat's assassination in October 1981. His regime lasted 30 years, deposed by the army amid a popular uprising in January and February 2011. Mubarak's was an authoritarian regime which relied on the army for its support base. Although he allowed a very limited degree of political contestation from 1984 onward, his party controlled the political system through a variety of means. Indeed, scholars have argued that Mubarak's flexibility—granting some political openings while holding power at a deep level—was one reason he survived for so long.[90] Although opposition parties gained a respectable number of seats in parliament in the 1980s, Mubarak dominated the legislature through procedures such as the strategic use of removing parliamentary immunity from any independent, well-financed legislators who emerged.[91] Mubarak held four presidential elections, and in all of them except for one, he was the only candidate who was allowed to run. The last election saw massive vote rigging, generating major discontent among the population. He also attempted to suppress the Muslim Brotherhood by imprisoning many of its key members and denying it official status as a political party. This failed to prevent the spread of the influence of the party. The economy grew during the 1990s and 2000s, but severe economic inequalities persisted.

Protests and labor action began to emerge in the late 2000s. In January 2011 the simmering discontent among the people burst open in several Arab states. It was dubbed the "Arab Spring." Amid a popular uprising and initial fierce repression, Mubarak abdicated power and an interim arrangement was created, with an eventual election to frame a new constitution. What is impressive was the rise of an Egyptian civil society using modern Internet technology and social media to spread its message. Initial post-Mubarak politics were manipulated quite strongly from behind the scenes by the Supreme Council for the Armed Forces (SCAF). From June 14 to 17, 2012, SCAF embarked on a series of moves to consolidate its power, dissolving the newly elected parliament and passing a constitutional amendment maintaining the full autonomy of the military from civilian rule, all while Mohamed Morsi, the Muslim Brotherhood candidate, won Egypt's presidential election.[92] However, in August, Morsi replaced Field Marshal Mohamed Hussein Tantawi, the head of SCAF, and General Sami Enan, the military chief of staff, ordered the retirement of several other senior officers, and overturned the June 2012 constitutional declaration.[93] This move, possibly occurring with the support of junior members of SCAF and with the apparent acquiescence of Tantawi and Enan, appeared to have constituted a new assertion of civilian control over the military, but it did not.[94] Morsi's subsequent crackdowns on journalists and other political opponents, his attempt to wield extraordinary powers above judicial review, and his effort to adopt a quickly drafted constitution through a referendum did not bode well for the nascent democratic order. In view of the dramatic decline of liberties, economic collapse, and resultant violent protests, on July 3, 2013 the commander-in-chief of the armed forces, General Abdul al-Sisi, deposed Morsi and established an interim government under Adli Mansour while promising elections by early 2014. Egypt, it appears, has become somewhat similar to Pakistan in terms of the fragility of democracy, military control, and Islamist onslaught. The Army's move received strong support from secular parties and their electoral base, but strong disapproval from the Muslim Brotherhood which continued its struggle for reinstatement of Morsi who was in power only for a year.[95] It is not clear what will happen if the Brotherhood wins the next presidential election. The inability of the Muslim Brotherhood to govern as an inclusive party and its effort to consolidate power through authoritarian means offer important lessons for the Arab world as well as countries such as Pakistan.[96]

Thus, Egypt resembles Pakistan in many important respects. The Egyptian elite refused to innovate the country to become a developmental state. In both countries, this had much to do with the power of a landed aristocracy, but more importantly with the geostrategic curse of massive assistance from outside. Similar to Pakistan's successive rulers, none of the Egyptian leaders—Nasser, Sadat, and Mubarak—left any strong democratic institutions. Both countries have had strong militaries; in the case of Egypt, however, the leaders were able to control the military and intelligence institutions, unlike the veto power enjoyed by the

Pakistani military whenever civilians ruled the country. This was partly because all Egyptian leaders from Nasser onward came from the military and possessed few democratic credentials. The similarities between Pakistan and Egypt include a 20–30% support base for Islamic parties. But in the latter, Islamist extremists have been given very little space to operate. This may be changing slowly; Egypt is poised to more closely resemble Pakistan if the Muslim Brotherhood is successful in its battle with secular groups for control over the country once again.

Despite the strong influence of the armed forces, which in Pakistan led to foreign policy adventurism, Egypt did show pragmatism in ending its rivalries. It has refrained from acquiring nuclear weapons and competing with Israel beyond a point. This pragmatism is an important potential asset for Egypt's future. It means that an obsession with national security and a hyper-awareness of threats may not stand in the way of Egypt's development. If the military's role in politics and society can be reduced, Islamist forces represented by the Muslim Brotherhood tamed, and proper democratic institutions installed, then this potential can, hopefully, be realized.

The cases of Turkey, Indonesia and Egypt show Muslim countries can focus on national security without it becoming an obsession or bringing it into alignment with extremist networks. None of these countries has felt the need to make use of non-state actors for their foreign policy ambitions, and so none has embarked upon the dangerous game that Pakistan has played. The revolutionary changes taking place in several Arab states since January 2011 show that democratic changes are possible through popular revolts in Muslim countries, even though some of them are electing Islamist parties to power.

Closer to home, Pakistan's former eastern half, Bangladesh, has made major strides toward greater democracy in 2010 after years of military rule, occasional democracy and internecine party warfare. Today, Bangladesh, despite its crushing poverty, has adopted several progressive policies, including promoting the education of women, and has a better record than many northern states of India in addressing poverty and malnutrition. In spite of several structural and environmental challenges it faces, Bangladesh also has been increasing its trading focus and has witnessed sustained economic growth. Despite a major contentious relationship between the two countries over issues such as border demarcation, migration and sharing the Ganges River waters, an attitudinal change with respect to India is also evident as Bangladesh has reduced its opposition to trading with India and using the Indian market for meeting its growth potential. A nonconfrontational approach toward India helps to create the geopolitical space needed for Bangladesh to build friendly relations with other leading states, especially China. The result of this change has been a substantial improvement in relations and a settlement of all border disputes through a far-reaching agreement signed during Indian prime minister Manmohan Singh's visit to Dhaka in September 2011.[97] It is, however, difficult to predict if the opposition party will follow through on these policies in the volatile arena of Bangladesh politics given its past proclivity toward a confrontationist attitude toward India.

Non-Muslim National-Security States

South Korea and Taiwan

A strong focus on national security and a garrison state need not produce weakness, perpetual conflict, and economic stagnation. Far from it: such conditions can actually assist in development and state strength. South Korea and Taiwan turned these conditions into economic development's biggest success stories, and changed course toward democracy in the 1990s. Even when they were national security states, their ruling elite adopted a trading state strategy. They are aptly called "developmental states," defined as "organizational complexes in which expert and coherent bureaucratic agencies collaborate with organized private sectors to spur national economic transformation."[98]

In fact, in stark contrast to Pakistan, the conventional wisdom about South Korea and Taiwan is that external threats and a focus on national security actually helped in this process. Scholars argue that South Korea and Taiwan adopted a developmental state strategy due to powerful systemic pressures and vulnerabilities. The basic story is that they needed foreign exchange to arm in order to confront their adversaries, but had little revenue of their own. At the same time, they feared that a decline in living standards would generate popular protest.[99] Confronting these problems, South Korea and Taiwan focused on developing export economies. Several other factors—like a relatively well-developed bureaucracy under Japanese colonialism, the lack of a strong rural elite that would have stood in the way of industrialization, and a leadership with development priorities—helped as well. Pakistan, in contrast, lacked a strong bureaucracy, had a very powerful rural landed aristocracy, and has hardly had far-sighted leadership in the economic realm.

South Korea and Taiwan thus offer fascinating case studies for a comparative analysis with Pakistan. Both have been active allies of the United States, recipients of considerable aid from Washington, and participants in the American-led alliance structures during much of the Cold War. South Korea and Taiwan also experienced wars and crises after their formation, faced enduring rivalries with their neighbors, and have been targets of great power politics.

As a consequence, both have been warrior states. Both states have assigned huge importance to military security and have created elaborate institutions for the provision of security. Interestingly, both also share with Pakistan a moment of creation in violent separation from states that became long-term rivals: North Korea and the People's Republic of China. And both have maintained, with regard to these states, a sense of hypervigilance and an ongoing confrontation with communism. For Hagen Koo, these circumstances "provided the state with a permanent excuse for violence and repression. They also led to hypermilitarization and the maintenance of an extensive security system of police and intelligence."[100] But the two countries' elites approached their security and economic policies differently from Pakistan, focusing on export-oriented industrialization as a way to build up capacity over the long term. Both started off as weak states, but over a period of time, they acquired more state capacity than Pakistan did.

After decades of continuous fast growth, these East Asian tigers transitioned from dictatorship to democracy. Similar to Pakistan, both South Korea and Taiwan had authoritarian regimes for much of their early period. In South Korea, the initial change happened in 1983–1984. Civil society groups such as students, trade unions, and church groups mobilized along with the opposition political party, and the authoritarian regime had to make concessions, even abandoning some repressive policies. The presidential elections in 1987 and the National Assembly elections in 1988 consolidated the democratic transition in South Korea.[101] In Taiwan, the military came under civilian control in 1987, and since then Taiwan has had several elections and the civilians are in firm control of the political scene. One scholar attributes this to the use of robust strategies by the civilians to enhance their control over the military.[102] Along with a democratic transition, Taiwan also became a welfare state with a number of reforms undertaken in their social security system.[103]

In both of these countries, economic development strategy emerged in several stages. In the early 1950s, they began by trying to substitute local industry for imports, and to promote rural development. But by the late 1950s, they started to shift to export-oriented industrial development in labor-intensive goods. A further shift led them to upgrades in productivity during the 1970s.[104] During this decade, the Park Chung-hee regime in Seoul offered substantial support from the state to the industrial conglomerates (chaebol) in order to promote expansion and economies of scale.[105] They also changed their economic strategy in the latter half of the 1980s and increasingly adopted neoliberal policies, and their major industries are world leaders. This form of adaptation became a necessity with the end of the Cold War and in particular in the post-Asian financial crisis economic environment. By 2000, they had to compete for foreign capital with an ever-expanding number of nations, most notably the BRIC countries (Brazil, Russia, India, and China). Regardless, growth in both Taiwan and South Korea was quite rapid over this entire period.

What differed between Pakistan and these two states? One theory focuses on the existential nature of the threats that the latter faced. It was existential threat that encouraged states like Israel, South Korea, and Taiwan to forge ahead with policies to increase the power of the state vis-à-vis their societies, and the pursuit of specific industrialization and export-driven strategies to face these threats. Countries like Syria and Egypt did not face such existential threats, but were mired in protracted conflicts with their neighbors that, while violent, never really raised the specter of complete defeat. The conflicts thus did not require these states to become overwhelmingly powerful vis-à-vis different civil society groups that challenged the state.[106] It is interesting to consider why the perceived existential threat from India did not produce a similar result in Pakistan.

To confront the threat that they faced, South Korea and Taiwan turned to American assistance. However, the aid came with much greater pressure to embrace market economy policies. USAID disbursed $1.5 billion in economic aid for 15 years from 1950 on. In 1965, though, it stopped, declaring that Taiwan was the first country to "graduate" from US foreign aid.[107] South Korea also received substantial US economic and military aid. Between 1953 and 1958 it received an annual inflow of $270 million, which was 15% of South Korea's gross national product. This US assistance allowed the regimes of Syngman Rhee in South Korea and Chiang Kai-shek in Taiwan to maintain basic economic and social order as well as invest in education. USAID focused on the private sector, and pressured these countries to adopt free market economies with the private sector as a leading player. In fact, USAID pushed the governments of these allies to *reduce* military expenditures and to focus on development.[108] In this context, the active United States armed presence in both countries—troops in South Korea and a naval presence in the Taiwan Strait—helped take the defense burden off Seoul and Taipei. Pakistan, on the other hand, received aid but little similar pressure from the United States or other donors. They concurred with the Pakistani elite's view of raising private savings by maintaining inequality among various groups and redistributing profits to the higher income groups, whereas South Korea and Taiwan followed a strategy of "inclusive capitalism" by investing in education, health care, and social welfare.[109]

Thus international conditions, though similar in many respects to Pakistan's, had subtle differences that helped to drive the developmental state. The two countries also had favorable domestic conditions. Japanese colonialism—1910 to 1945 in Korea, 1895 to 1945 in Taiwan—had helped to create the preconditions for the developmental state to emerge.[110] Brutal though it was, Japanese colonialism did leave both countries with relatively coherent bureaucracies. In Korea, for example, there were 87,552 bureaucratic officials by 1937, some 35,000 of whom were Korean. This civil service was very large relative to colonial bureaucracies in European colonies that were more distant from the colonial metropole. Korean officials trained under bureaucratic tutelage imported from Japan's Meiji modernization experience, such that even though they occupied only junior positions in the colonial bureaucracy, they were ready to assume state administration after Japan's departure in 1945.[111] Further, in both countries the political elite was able to reform the civil services to carry out their developmental agendas by instilling meritocracy in segments of the bureaucracy.[112] These bureaucracies played a key role in helping to set developmental priorities. They also managed businesses access to loans in such a way to reward growth-promoting and well-performing enterprises. It has been argued that these states were able to achieve success not due to their coercive capacity—though it was quite high[113]— but due to their ability to negotiate and cooperate with key domestic actors while maintaining their own autonomy, they were able to coordinate viable responses and achieve positive results.[114]

Japanese colonialism also helped create the conditions for reduced pressure to redistribute income. With very high literacy rates and unusually low economic inequality after colonialism, both South Korea and Taiwan faced less risk that either their political systems or their economies would only serve the interests of a few.[115] Crucially, as well, the Japanese steadily eroded the power of the landed elite—in sharp contrast to British rule in colonial India, which often reinforced the power of local landed princes and zamindars. The Japanese introduced limited land reforms and new farming practices.[116] The two states were able to implement further successful land reforms between 1948 and 1950. By the 1960s, they both obtained some degree of power over the top echelon of the agrarian class and did not face any serious class opposition to their policies of externally oriented industrialization. The rise of the middle class followed, with small entrepreneurs and highly qualified workforces facilitating this process.[117] Moreover, these countries assigned considerable importance to education, especially technical education, something Pakistan failed to do. Ethnic homogeneity also facilitated growth: governments could focus on growth-promoting policies while others had to deal with interethnic distribution of wealth.[118] The South Korean state in particular was able to insulate itself from social classes that would have constrained the ability of the state to make economic progress.[119] The end of the Syngman Rhee regime, which had depended on private-sector help for its political success, and its replacement in 1961–1962 by a cohesive, united, reformist group of military officers under Park Chung-hee, enabled the state to regain its autonomy from various social forces that sought to control power. It was at this moment that South Korea's export-led industrialization took off.[120] However, this success in achieving development would later strengthen working and middle classes. Ultimately this helped to produce a democratic transition in the country.[121]

In Pakistan, barring the somewhat higher growth rates of the Ayub Khan period between 1958 and 1965, economic growth did not keep pace with the rise in population. Nor did Pakistan adopt a trading state strategy that emphasized a diversified industrial base. Moreover, Pakistan also faced structural constraints such as increasing global trade liberalization. By the 1990s its major export—textiles—faced immense competition from other emerging economies like Bangladesh and China. Pakistan was certainly under threat, and would have been better able to face this threat with greater prosperity. But the state was under no pressure to seek export-driven growth as there were sufficient payments coming from abroad for maintaining its garrison state. This aid came without any strong conditions for the development of a vibrant industrial sector. The geostrategic curse did not afflict the East Asian cases as much as Pakistan and most other cases (except Egypt) discussed before. This is partly because elites in those other nations consciously adopted a trading and developmental state strategy and used geostrategic salience as a market opening device. Moreover, in order to engage in trade they had to improve domestic production capacities. They also were lucky not to have the same kind of feudal structure that Pakistan has been endowed with: an elite and landed aristocracy that would be willing to sacrifice their countries' long-term prosperity for the sake of their own continued dominance.

In addition, the Pakistani state, instead of suppressing or gaining the cooperation of civil society groups in the direction of economic development, fostered and nurtured them for geopolitical projects. Once they became too strong, the state could neither take them on nor abandon them. An additional problem has been the religious character of many civil society groups in question. Their priorities have been far from political stability and export-led growth. The state has tried to ride the tiger of political Islam. While it has been an ally in some respects, it is a profound threat to stability and economic prosperity as well.

Conclusions

A variety of states discussed here show different pathways through which warrior states have evolved and transformed themselves in the contemporary period. The Muslim states of Turkey, Indonesia, and Egypt all experienced military dominance, but they transformed themselves over time at least to some extent. Even Bangladesh has managed to tame the military. In Pakistan, however, the military retains ultimate authority, and its hypervigilance on national security issues dominates policy and politics. The non-Muslim states of South Korea and Taiwan also are quintessential warrior states, but they avoided many of the drawbacks from which Pakistan continues to suffer. They transformed from authoritarian regimes to democracies even when the security situation remained precarious. The rise of democratic rule in these countries was the result of middle class mobilization, international pressures, and the emulation of other successful democratic transitions. But they also relied on leaders who took the pivotal conscious steps toward democracy. In South Korea, for example, President Roh Tae-woo, who came to power in 1988, oversaw crucial political reforms, instituting practices like tolerance of the opposition, freedom of the press, and decentralization of government. His successor, Kim Young-sam (1993–1998) expanded the scope for civil society organizations.[122]

In some respects, the warrior state in Pakistan is different from Taiwan and South Korea. They faced existential wars, whereas Pakistan's wars have been limited in nature. However, war (and the threat of war) was never utilized by the Pakistani elite to transform the country's economic policies as the East Asians states did. It is in fact useful to compare the larger wars involving great powers that both Pakistan and the East Asian states sat alongside. The East Asian states exploited the opportunities presented by the Vietnam War to trade more intensely with the United States. The Afghan war offered such an opportunity to Pakistan, but the elite failed to implement a trading state strategy with the United States. Of course, Washington's exclusive focus on the military relationship did not help much in this regard. The Pakistani elite also lacked the orientation toward developmental state policies. Although war can provide the original impetus, a country still needs human agency (i.e., effective leadership) to make use of it. In East Asia, for instance, the Philippines had just as good an opportunity to grow as South Korea and Taiwan during the Vietnam War, but it did not transform itself into a developmental state. Traditional elites continued to dominate the Philippines, weakening its ability to generate or implement effective developmental state policies.

The cases in this chapter suggest that Pakistan was not doomed by geopolitics to continued instability and poverty. Rather, Pakistan's geostrategic location has proven to be a curse because domestic actors took advantage of both the external support provided by the United States and others and the threats it faced for their own narrow ends. But if Pakistan had leaders with developmental priorities and pragmatic ideas, its history may have been much different.

8

The Warrior State Today

ON MAY 21, 2013, Pakistan's caretaker Prime Minister Mir Hazar Khan Khoso placed a dress code for government officials which included an optional provision for them to avoid wearing socks because air conditioners in government offices were not working for the most part. Since the winter months of 2012, Pakistan has been beset by an acute shortage of electricity and power outages lasting 12 to 18 hours a day became the norm for many parts of the country. The power crisis has been looming for several years partly due to increasing demand and undersupply caused by lack of payment to suppliers.[1] The Pakistani economy has not made much progress during the past several years and the international debt repayment became an urgent issue requiring a bailout by the International Monetary Fund in July 2013. As a silver lining, a very weak civilian government was allowed to stay in power and completed its five-year term in May 2013. The May elections produced a clear winner in Nawaz Sharif's Pakistan Muslim League-Nawaz (PML-N) in the National Assembly and the Army stayed away from manipulating the electoral process. Despite this positive outcome, Pakistan faces an uncertain future, with its economy in shambles, its civil society in disarray, and its future trajectory with Afghanistan and India in question. Some 5,000 security personnel and over 40,000 civilians have already been killed by the Taliban-inflicted violence in recent years alone.[2] The fundamental question then is how has Pakistan become such an insecure, weak state and what does this case tell us about the relationship between war-making and state building in view of the analyses contained in the previous chapters?

The Trap of the Warrior State

One thing is certain; Pakistan's ongoing war-making efforts have deeply affected its prospects for emerging as a tolerant, prosperous and unified nation-state. This has major implications not only for Pakistan, but also for global and regional security orders. The Pakistani case is an exemplar for an unfortunate outcome in the contemporary world: intense war-making activity leading to the creation of a weak, insecurity-generating state. It also shows the capacity of the warrior state to survive, with its institutions deeply entrenched. In order to remain in power, the national security establishment in a warrior state refuses to make the necessary changes for transformation, fearing that it will lose control of the society it is supposed to protect.

The warrior state thus makes its own trap from which it cannot easily escape. Reform requires powerful external and internal forces demanding change, usually the result of a dramatic failure of the state in a war or a deep economic crisis. The rise to power of a reformist coalition is crucial for meaningful changes to occur. However, such a coalition's emergence can be stifled by the national security idiom—in its own way as powerful a symbolic force as intense nationalism. A warrior state's search for security can lead to higher levels of insecurity, and in order to counter those insecurities, it will resort to additional military and realpolitik means—leading, in a vicious cycle, to further insecurity. This insecurity dilemma of the warrior state is both its staple challenge and its own creation, even as outside forces assist the process. A warrior state thus can create self-fulfilling prophecies that it hopes to avoid.

Charles Tilly offers a powerful explanation for why war-making has become a "protection racket" in many instances. States Tilly:

> Governments' provision of protection . . . often qualifies as racke-teering. To the extent that the threats against which a government protects its citizens are imaginary or are consequences of its own activities, the government has organized a protection racket. Since governments themselves commonly simulate, stimulate or even fabri-cate threats of external war and since the repressive and extractive activities of governments often constitute the largest current threats to the livelihoods of their own citizens, many governments operate in

essentially the same ways as racketeers. There is, of course, a difference: Racketeers, by the conventional definition, operate without the
sanctity of governments.[3]

The Pakistani military indeed shows how a protector can become a
protection racketeer. The military has assumed the protector's role quite
intensely. This role comes from twin fears for the future in its immediate neighborhood. One is the fear of India, with which Pakistan seeks
strategic parity. The other is the fear of losing control over Afghanistan,
which has a majority Pashtun population whose brethren also live on
the Pakistani side and whose allegiance to the Pakistani state is suspect.
But in that role, the protector often generates policies or behavior that
makes insecurity a reality. It also encourages or closes its eyes to nonstate actors who wage its many battles, be it in Kashmir or in Afghanistan, and these forces have become a potent source of insecurity to the
general Pakistani public. The army once again is called to assume the
protector's role from the threats that it has partially created in the first
place. This conundrum has also been driven by a desire on the part of
the generals to maintain their dominant social, political and economic
status internally. Without the need for its protection, the pivotal role
of the armed forces in the Pakistani society would be in question. Insecurity in this case has the element of strong corporatist interests of the
military elite attached to the warrior state.

Internally, the tendency on the part of the Pakistani state to engage in
coercion to achieve domination over social forces has not worked either.
This is partly because, like many contemporary states and unlike various
European examples, the organization of society into multiple ethnic
groups, religious identities, and class interests makes it virtually impossible to knit together a unified country, even through coercion. The
capacity of groups to resist has increased from the modern European era,
when it was easier to repress oppositional groups. The Europeans also did
not have to worry about the issue of legitimacy, unlike the contemporary
era when people are more aware of their rights. The Pakistani state elite
is indeed trying the European top-down approach in a different historical era and has failed to elicit cooperation from the disparate groups
that constitute the country. This is because it has little to offer to the

general public by way of meaningful public goods that would generate sustained loyalty from all sections of the society. The war-making state faces the "state-strength dilemma" that Kal Holsti has identified: in order to suppress dissident forces, the state engages in coercive methods, which then encourage opponents to intensify their efforts at resisting the state. The central government thus becomes less powerful as years pass because coercion does not bring the legitimacy that is needed.[4]

What the Pakistani state elite has been unable to do is to engage in state-society bargaining and to make the compromises and arrangements that are necessary for proper state formation and consolidation. In the European context, despite the immense pain and suffering caused by war, the bargain between the state and society produced a variety of rights to the general population.[5] Tilly himself recognizes that this bargaining with domestic actors is missing in most developing countries.[6] Many contemporary developing states acquired their military capabilities from outside "without the internal forging of mutual constraints between rulers and ruled." The outside supply of goods and expertise through military alliances produced low incentives for the civilianization of these countries.[7]

In the Pakistani case, the wherewithal for war-making has come from outside through the financial and military support of the United States, its Western allies, China, Saudi Arabia, and financial institutions such as the IMF and the World Bank. It is therefore unnecessary for the elite to make the necessary bargains with its own society for internal development. This rentier economy has also allowed the Pakistani elite to avoid either a developmental state strategy or a trading state strategy and instead privilege external security (defined in purely military terms). In the army's view, internal reforms mean losing control of the warrior state, the *raison d'être* of the elite's privileged position in the Pakistani society. The geostrategic curse in this case is therefore almost similar to the resource curse that analysts employ when explaining the uneven development of many petro states in the Middle East and elsewhere.

War-Making and State-Building Today

Charles Tilly's original dictum, "war made the state and the state made war" is a powerful statement. Critics do point out the highly contextual nature of the theory and find that there are problems with the empirical examples of Europe itself. Some have argued that the logic of the sequence that Tilly and other protagonists of the theory propose need not be applicable to all war-making states. The idea that greater need for revenue inevitably encourages states to tax and become efficient need not always be the case. Similarly, the state elite may not learn the right lessons from previous wars and reform and rebuild, as assumed in the original Tilly logic. Some states may be more vulnerable than others to the dysfunctionalities that war can generate. In some cases, learning may occur in a dysfunctional and negative way.[8]

We should also keep in mind that constant war made many European states weaker and dysfunctional. The prominent examples include Spain, Portugal, the Balkan states, Poland, Burgundy, and Austria-Hungary. It is worth looking at the reasons for these states' failure to progress in the direction that Tilly attributes to state formation in Europe in his earlier works. Other examples include Bulgaria in 1913 and Serbia, Greece and Montenegro, the winners of the Balkan wars in 1912/13 that became weak. A more prominent example has been the British case—the victory in World War II proved to be a disaster for Britain as it subsequently lost its empire.[9] Japan and Germany after World War II probably benefited from their defeat: the states in the two countries acquired new forms of strength and vitality and adopted a trading state strategy to development, much different from the warrior state approach they held historically. The Cold War alliance with the US and competition with the Soviet bloc helped them significantly in that endeavor. Among winners of wars, only some have successfully consolidated their national power. There may be other factors and conditions operating side by side to make the war-making and state-building correlation possible.

Sociologist Michael Mann has argued that even those European states that became strong through war-making began, by the mid-nineteenth century, to allocate resources to civilian progress and infrastructure development. By the twentieth century, education and healthcare assumed larger portions of the state's budget and, in some instances, more than defense during peacetime.[10] It has also been argued that rulers such as Prussia's Otto von Bismarck laid the foundations of a welfare state by arguing that the soldiers needed to be literate and well-fed in order to achieve greater mobility.[11] Since much of the adult population had to be ready for war-fighting the general population had to be educated and fed. It is interesting to know why a warrior state like Pakistan does not seem pressured to educate or feed its general population on a mass scale. It may well be that a volunteer army like Pakistan's needs only a small fraction of the large population and that segment is well taken care of by the state. Much has changed in military technology since the nineteenth century, and a mass army is less useful today than an elite, technologically capable force. European states, on the other hand, needed to draw from their smaller population bases more regularly for the constant wars they were waging.

In modern times, it is very clear that warrior states needed to adopt a trading and developmental state approach to become stronger. South Korea, Taiwan and China became strong states after they embraced a developmental state strategy along with war-making. Without Deng Xiaoping's economic reforms, China would have been an unstable and poor country today despite waging several wars with its neighboring countries and the US-led UN coalition in Korea. Pakistan has not benefited from war-making because it never became a developmental state. Its elite learned different lessons from the wars it fought and the security threats it faced, and used war and war preparation to advance its own position within a divided society rather than the general welfare of the country at large. War could be an initial condition for state development, but countries need other conditions for adaptation and consolidation.

Is the typical war-making state, then, anachronistic today? Is it possible to provide security and welfare by instituting proper reforms and encouraging the general population to become literate and successful? In fact, a state that encounters intense conflict with its rivals could devote its attention to welfare as well as military preparation. Security is no longer border security alone, and even when the potential for a military dispute exists, it can be reduced by mechanisms such as trade and engagement—through institutions and civil society—with the adversaries. States do not need to constantly prepare for war to ensure their security.

A problem is that the kind of large-scale war-making that the European states engaged in is no longer available as a mechanism to transform a society. Playing with war-making is a very risky strategy for a developing country today. Examples of warrior countries that have destroyed themselves include African states such as Congo, Ethiopia, Eritrea, Somalia, and in Asia, North Korea. White-ruled South Africa was a war-making state that could not achieve inclusive progress, beyond the facade of developing its infrastructure. The key way a warrior state can progress is through a simultaneous pursuit of trading and internal development. In an age of deepened economic globalization, this has become all the more important. A state focused on military planning and narrow security may not attract finance and capital from the international market.[12] It is states such as South Korea and Taiwan—which have pursued war preparation hand in hand with trade and internal development—that are the exceptions in the developing world, able to bridge the gap between war and economic globalization.

Pakistan's experience shows that the war-making state may bring neither economic development nor political cohesion. If anything can bring prosperity in the globalized world of the twenty-first century, it is likely to be a state that reduces the role of military and war-making efforts. A strong commitment to developmentalism and participatory democracy is a necessary feature of strong, cohesive states. Today, Brazil, which was ruled by the military not so long ago, has emerged as a strong developmental state with a vibrant democratic order. Despite all its weaknesses, India shows that the forces that are making it an emerging power are largely economic, propelling the rise of a globalized middle class that also strongly supports democratic institutions. Where India has failed is in its ability to redistribute some of its new wealth to the poor. Far too easily, corrupt political and bureaucratic elites are able to siphon it off for themselves. Even so, India's poverty has declined in many parts of the large country, especially in the South and the West. This has been achieved largely through a high rate of economic growth and the efforts of a young but dynamic globalized workforce in areas like information technology and pharmaceuticals, which has used the tools of globalization to its advantage.

Unlike China and India, the warrior state in Pakistan has neither allowed nor encouraged its younger generation to globalize and benefit from economic liberalization. They are not given the necessary education, especially in science and technology. Instead, generations of Pakistanis, especially the poor, are taught in archaic religious seminaries. This has helped to associated Pakistan, perilously, with the negative forces of globalization. Pakistan's youth, unlike its counterparts in India or in other Muslim-majority countries like Indonesia, Malaysia, and Bangladesh, are deprived of modern education and the choice of joining the global workforce where their skills would have value, Pakistan has therefore missed out on the benefits of economic globalization associated with greater international trade, investment, and workforce mobility. In 2012–2013, Pakistan's position in the Global Competitiveness Index stood at 124 among 144 countries. According to this report, Pakistan is exceptionally weak on infrastructure, macroeconomic environment, health and primary education, higher education and training, labor market efficiency, financial market development, technological readiness, innovation, and market sophistication.[13]

Pakistan also has a major demographic challenge at hand. Pakistan's population has been growing exponentially since 1947. In 2010, it had an estimated population of 185 million, and it is poised to grow to 300 million or so by 2050, at which point Pakistan will be the world's fourth most populous nation.[14] It also has a so-called youth bulge, with some 60% of the population below the age of 25. Many of these youths have been educated in madrassas and have few qualifications for gainful employment in the service or manufacturing sectors, the major growth areas of other South Asian economies such as India. A majority of them also tend to strongly support an Islamic state and do not view terrorism as a leading problem facing Pakistan.[15] Since Pakistan has not economically globalized, its economy cannot absorb these young people into good jobs. Their ability to migrate is also constrained by severe visa restrictions, especially from the industrialized world. A substantial percentage of Pakistan's population is concentrated in urban centers that have emerged as major hubs of extremism and recruitment bases for radical groups.

The Muslim-majority countries that have prospered in recent years have all shied away from an emphasis on war-making. Indonesia is a good example of a state that has (despite ups and downs) succeeded in becoming a moderate state and achieving a reasonable amount of progress and unity, in contrast to Pakistan. Even Bangladesh is slowly emerging out of its earlier pathologies, which were similar to Pakistan's own. South Korea and Taiwan have adopted simultaneous trading state and national security state strategies for some time. In addition, they have powerful middle classes that are now able to preserve their demo-cratic structures. They also have developed economic interdependence with other states—including, in the Taiwanese case, with its arch enemy, China.

As the state system evolves, war is unlikely to be the means to achieve strength, partly because of the difficulties of waging wars or of mobilizing populations toward that purpose.[16] Further, in a nucle-arized region like South Asia, war may be unthinkable. But rivalry is the core of war-making activity today. Does intense rivalry with an outside power generate state-building as war did in the past? Political scientists Karen Rasler and William Thompson have found that rivalry encouraged increases in military spending, but the latter does not neces-sarily contribute to nation-building. Instead, it diverts investment from genuine economic and social development.[17] Thus enduring rivalries and protracted conflicts, similar to that Pakistan has been engaging in, have little chance of making the country a stronger entity in the world system.

Will Pakistan Transform?

By 2009, Pakistan had shown some signs of change. It held elections in 2008 that resulted in a civilian government emerging. Due to an intense campaign by the United States and the internal strengthening of Taliban forces, the Pakistani elite reluctantly decided to take on the Taliban. The civilian government led by the PPP lasted its full term, exiting office in May 2013 while the elected president Asif Ali Zardari remained in power for the full term until September 2013. The army outwardly gave up power, even if it retained many aspects of state control, most notably in the areas of national security and relations with the United States and India. In the May 2013 elections, the Pakistan Muslim League led by Nawaz Sharif won a majority and subsequently managed to form a government. The army, to its credit, stayed away from electoral politics during the campaign. However, several factors impeded a true progression toward democracy in Pakistan. First, the warrior state still dominates the power structure. The army and the ISI are somewhat parallel authority points, and they can challenge and veto the weak civilian government at any time. Second, the political parties remain weak. They are often unable to agree on societal or economic transformation and are afraid of military retribution were they to undertake meaningful reforms. Third, the Pakistani Taliban has strengthened its position over the years, engaging in random killings and political violence, and members of the civilian political parties are increasingly afraid of taking them on in an attempt to defeat them. Other acts of the Taliban include killing of health workers distributing polio vaccines and destruction of schools to prevent girls from getting an education. Instead of taking them on, the Pakistani leaders, especially Nawaz Sharif, the current prime minister, are talking of negotiating with the Taliban, the success of which would depend conceding some of their demands such as imposing more Islamic laws in Pakistan.

Fourth, the temptation on the part of the military and the ISI to play "double games" continues. They maintain an outward alliance with the United States but covertly support its enemies. The question is why they continue to do so. It might well be that American financial support can be preserved only by playing such double games. Once the source of the threat is removed, the United States would perhaps abandon Pakistan as it had done in the past. To the Pakistani national security establishment, it is clear that the American forces are bound to leave Afghanistan. When that happens, Pakistan will need the same Taliban forces to gain control of that country and keep it as a vassal state. However, this strategy of controlling Afghanistan is counterproductive, as a weak Afghanistan creates blowback effects on Pakistan. Also, this policy precludes a grand reconciliation of different ethnic groups in Afghanistan. Rather, it encourages such groups to continue their violent opposition to one another, variously obtaining support from Pakistan, India, Russia, and the Central Asian republics. The probable result is a continuation of the vicious cycle of violence. Pakistan's expectation that these ethnic groups and their supporters will simply give up their fight and allow Pakistan's hold on a Taliban-style regime in Afghanistan once again is based on false assumptions. A Taliban-led Afghanistan will immensely hurt Pakistan's security and economic interests. Taliban's victory in Afghanistan, therefore, while tactically useful for the Pakistani military in the short term, is sure to be a strategic disaster in the long run. Pakistan, however, appears to have no inclination to prevent the Taliban from degenerating into extremism and gaining control of Afghanistan or a major part of it once again.

If a Taliban-dominated government does emerge in Afghanistan, it will only embolden the war-making state of Pakistan and magnify the conflict with India. Such a geopolitical victory will enhance the role of the army and improve its position vis-à-vis the civilian government. Moreover, it is likely that Taliban rule will be challenged by non-Pashtun minority groups with the help of countries like India, ensuring that Afghanistan remains weak and embattled.

Much bleaker is the chance for a peace settlement with India, given the tendency of the military and ISI to act as spoilers in any peace process started by civilian leaders. Relations with India, although they have improved slightly through talks in 2011, and an agreement to increase mutual trade are unlikely to reach a permanent solution. This is because Pakistan still seeks strategic parity with a much larger entity. As India's economic strength increases, this becomes more difficult and the Pakistani elite gets more frustrated. A prominent US historian Walter Russell Mead has accurately captured the problem of Pakistan competing militarily with India. In his view, Pakistan can become an economically powerful country if it transforms its military competition with India to a developmental competition. The security conflict is preventing the military from severing its ties to the extremist groups. He puts it correctly: "To say that without a resolution to the Kashmir issue Pakistan cannot prosper is to say that India has a veto power over the future of Pakistan, that India must give permission before Pakistan can launch its projects of development."[18]

Unfortunately, for Pakistan, the current balance-of-power dynamics in Asia is once again likely to fuel an intense competitive relationship with India. The intensifying power rivalry between China and India increases the importance of Pakistan as an ally for China. This would mean that, despite efforts to the contrary, the Indo-Pakistan rivalry and the war-making efforts of Pakistan will likely continue for the foreseeable future.

There are many who believe that if the Kashmir problem is solved, Pakistan can then focus on economic development. The challenge is the manner in which it will be solved. It may go either way in terms of Pakistan's internal development. There is no guarantee that territorial gains in Kashmir in favor of Pakistan will automatically lead in a positive direction. The military elite may in fact conclude that its coercive strategy worked and that it now needs more security to protect Kashmir against potential Indian intrusions. It will also depend on whether the Kashmiris want to live under Pakistani control. If not, Kashmir will remain a perpetual source of three-way conflict between India, Pakistan, and the Kashmiris. The acquisition of Kashmir will likely increase the legitimacy of the military, and civil authority will be unlikely to benefit. It may only intensify the appetite of the Pakistani military to strengthen its hyper-realpolitik policies in an effort to achieve power parity with India. The possibility of an independent, secular Kashmir emerging is very low given the theocratic nature of the major liberation movements there, and this would mean potentially another Afghanistan in the cross-border region of India, Pakistan, and China. None of this is to suggest that the Kashmir conflict should not be settled, but without a major change in the attitudes of the protagonists on how these territories should be governed, a change in borders is likely to cause more harm than good to the regional security order and Pakistan's internal development itself. It might well be advisable for Pakistan (as General Musharraf figured out) and India to give maximum autonomy to the Kashmiris but without radically revising territorial boundaries.

In sum, any potential geopolitical victories may not necessarily provide Pakistanis security, democracy, or development because the warrior state is unlikely to be transformed into a benign state after such triumphs. The warrior state as constituted now is unlikely to be able to provide economic opportunity or genuine security for the Pakistani people. International investors are unlikely to come to Pakistan without a safe and secure environment. Radical transformation is necessary in the way the Pakistani elite and civil society think of security and development. Pakistan's key allies, especially the United States and China, need to rethink their strategy toward this beleaguered nation.

Some have argued that the peculiar cultural context of Pakistan is the source of its difficulties in creating a proper national sense or political order. This argument has problems as Pakistanis in general, like their Indian counterparts, are more successful outside their country than inside. This indicates that it is hardly the case that Pakistan simply cannot prosper. Instead, it is government policy that makes the difference here. That is abundantly clear in the cases of countries such as China and India which did not change their cultures during the 1980s and 1990s.[19] Reputed studies on development show that it is human-made institutions and policies that determine the fate of nations, whether they became prosperous or homogeneous. One such study concludes convincingly that if society creates proper institutions, incentives, and reward structures and allows all its members to participate in economic opportunities, it can escape from poverty and become strong.[20]

The sources of change are important—major crises that the elite cannot cope with, other than through reforms, may be the kind of incentive required to propel the changes in the way things are done presently. Pakistan's misfortune is that none of the crises it faced has been strong enough to move its society into a different pathway. Its elite seems to have learned perverse lessons from crises and wars, which has indeed emboldened the hyper-realpolitik orientation that it has been imbued with. The several economic crises that the country has faced during the past decades have not been catalysts for change because the United States, its Western allies, China, Saudi Arabia, the Gulf States, and the international financial institutions were there to help out whenever there was a crisis. Often, these crises happened in the context of geopolitical conflicts and as a result, keeping the Pakistani elite on their side was the primary strategy of the United States and other Western powers. When assured of such support, the elite decided to pursue strategies of "double games" by pretending to support US objectives, while actually doing very little to make radical changes that would transform Pakistani society or bring regional peace and order. Easy money through strategic entanglements meant less incentives to engage in taxation or societal innovation, the routes through which European war-making states became strong and innovative and enacted democratic reforms. Thus the "geostrategic curse" operates as a debilitating force on Pakistan's proper development.

It does not have to be always this way. Military regimes have been engines of change in different countries from East Asia to South America. The Pakistani military elite similarly has a choice. But demand for democratic transition and its supply have to be synchronized. In this case, this synchronization has been largely absent or skewed. The geopolitical circumstances appear to be the source of this predicament of Pakistan, but if we are waiting for other countries to make concessions so that the military will change its position (an oft-stated argument of

Pakistani scholars and generals) it may never happen. Victories in geopolitical conflicts may simply embolden the military's inflated societal position and lead to the expansion of its grand ambitions. Much democratic change that occurred in Chile, Brazil, Argentina, South Korea, Taiwan, and Indonesia, and more recently in Turkey was due to the discrediting of the military as the lead societal actor.

What Needs to be Done

Pakistan's transformation will only take place if both its strategic circumstances and the ideas and assumptions that the elite hold change fundamentally. Although some of the strategic circumstances are beyond Pakistan's control, its neighboring states and the great powers can at best minimally help guide them in a positive direction. Internally, the Pakistani elite has to adopt a semisecular or at least tolerant quasi-Islamic state model and begin considering development as its core mission. Education, health care, and good infrastructure have to be key sources of national strength. Meaningful land reforms must take place. Pakistani rulers also have to regard that an immersion in the world economic system as necessary for survival, and to do that they need to reform the nation's economic and political systems and land rights. Externally, Pakistan needs to abandon many of the tactics that it pursues in conflict with India and Afghanistan, although this may require assistance from these countries.

Changing the ideas and assumptions that the Pakistani establishment and security elites hold is crucial to implementing a meaningful transformation of Pakistan. Currently, these assumptions are based on hyper-realpolitik—indeed Hobbesian—ideas grounded in religious ideology, but without the realist canon of "prudence," which advocates congruence and compatibility between capabilities and objectives. Ultimately, the choice for change should come from within Pakistan itself. International pressure helped to reduce the power of the military in Turkey, Indonesia, Egypt, and South Korea, but it was the rise of a liberal civil society (except in Egypt) that reined in the military and that established democratic regimes in those countries. Similarly, the Pakistani civil society, as well as political parties, should rein in the military and intelligence apparatuses that have driven their country in the direction of a geopolitical competition that has produced few positive results for either the security or the development that the Pakistani people deserve. If the military and its intelligence agency persist in "double games" and keep supporting terrorism, Pakistan will eventually fall apart, causing unimaginable damage to itself and to the world. A fundamental democratic structure, a developmental state founded on trade and economic progress, rather than an intense warrior state, should become the motto of Pakistan's middle class and civil society. A strategy that precludes hyper-realpolitik tendencies is necessary for Pakistan to emerge as a strong, equitable and moderate state even while retaining its core Islamic identity. Pakistan needs to transform itself into a tolerant state where minority rights are protected and differences among diverse ethnic groups are respected and managed through nonviolent democratic and judicial processes.

In a highly globalized world, a traditional warrior state built around an intolerant religious or political ideology is fast becoming an anachronism. It not only promotes ideas and values that are archaic, but is plainly dangerous to its society and the rest of the world. A pragmatic-minded elite and a tolerant and liberal civil society are essential for transformational change. Without such a change, the purpose of the Pakistani state will remain narrow and out of date. In this sense, Pakistan has some crucial choices to make as the twenty-first century advances.

NOTES

Chapter 1

1. On German militarism, see Martin Kitchen, *The German Officer Corps: 1890–1914* (Oxford: Clarendon Press, 1968); Gordon A. Craig, *The Politics of the Prussian Army: 1640–1945* (Oxford: Clarendon Press, 1964); General Friedrich Von Bernhardi, *Germany and the Next War*, trans. Allen H. Powles (New York: Longmans, Green, 1914). The difference is that unlike Pakistan, Germany did become a strong state through its war-making efforts, only to engage in many self-destructive wars and eventually transform as a state that underplay war as an instrument of national policy.

2. For more on this, see T. V. Paul, "Why Has the India-Pakistan Rivalry Been So Enduring? Power Asymmetry and an Intractable Conflict," *Security Studies* 15, no. 4 (October–December 2006): 600–30.

3. Scholars have identified the concept of "geostrategic rents" in key US allies like Turkey. See Andrew J.A. Mango, "Testing Time in Turkey," *The Washington Quarterly* 20, no. 1 (1997): 3–20. See also Jennifer N. Brass, "Djibouti's Unusual Resource Curse," *Journal of Modern African Studies* 46, no. 4 (2008): 523–45.

4. For the data, see "About Those Billions," *Newsweek*, October 20, 2009, accessed November 29, 2012, http://www.thedailybeast.com/newsweek/2009/10/21/about-those-billions.html.

5. Charles Tilly, "Reflections on the History of European State-Making," in *The Formation of National States in Western Europe*, ed. Charles Tilly (Princeton: Princeton University Press, 1975), 3–83; Charles Tilly, "War Making and State Making as Organized Crime," in *Bringing the State Back In*, ed. Peter Evans *et al.* (Cambridge: Cambridge University Press, 1985), 169–91; Bruce D. Porter, *War and the Rise of the State* (New York: The Free Press, 1994). The pioneering arguments to this effect were made by Otto Hintze and Max Weber. See Hintze, *The Historical Essays of Otto Hintze*, ed. Felix Gilbert (New York: Oxford University Press, 1975), chapter 4; Randall

Collins, *Weberian Sociological Theory* (Cambridge: Cambridge University Press, 1986). See also Gianfranco Poggi, *The Development of the Modern State: A Sociological Introduction* (Palo Alto: Stanford University Press, 1978).

6. Tilly, "Reflections"; Porter, *War.*

7. For these, see Porter, *War*, 11–18.

8. Cameron G. Thies, "State Building, Interstate and Intra-state Rivalry: A Study of Post-Colonial Developing Country Extractive Efforts, 1975–2000," *International Studies Quarterly*, 48, no. 1 (March 2004), 55.

9. Tilly, "Reflections."

10. See for instance, Paul Kennedy, *The Rise and Fall of the Great Powers* (New York: Random House, 1987). This synthesis of coercion and capital in European state formation was expressed most clearly by Charles Tilly in his *Coercion, Capital and European States, AD 990–1992* (Oxford: Blackwell, 1992).

11. Tilly, "Reflections," 42.

12. Porter, *War*, 15–16. Other historical sociologists offer different mechanisms that generated conditions for the creation of strong states in Europe. For instance, Gorski believes religious faiths such as Calvinism might have contributed to the strengthening of states in Europe by creating "more obedient and industrious subjects with less coercion and violence," and this helped to increase "not only the regulatory power of the state, but its extractive and coercive capacities as well." Philip S. Gorski, *The Disciplinary Revolution: Calvinism and the Rise of the State in Early Modern Europe* (Chicago: University of Chicago Press, 2003), xvi.

13. Norman Davies, *Vanished Kingdoms: The Rise and Fall of States and Nations* (New York: Viking, 2011). See also, Les Harding, *Dead Countries of the Nineteenth and Twentieth Centuries: Aden to Zululand* (Lanham: Scarecrow Press, 1998) for an exhaustive list of independent or semi-independent states that went into extinction.

14. Theda Skocpol, *State and Social Revolutions* (Cambridge: Cambridge University Press, 1979).

15. On these options, see Albert O. Hirschman, *Exit, Voice, and Loyalty* (Cambridge: Harvard University Press, 1970).

16. Georg Sørensen, "War and State Making—Why Doesn't it Work in the Third World?" (Paper Presented at the International Studies Association (ISA) Annual Convention, New Orleans, March 24–27, 2002). See also, Michael C. Desch, "War and Strong States, Peace and Weak States?," *International Organization* 50, no. 2 (Spring 1996), 237–268; Brian D. Taylor and Roxana Botea, "Tilly Tally: War-Making and State-Making in the Contemporary Third World," *International Studies Review*, 10, no. 1 (March 2008), 27–56.

17. Jeffrey Herbst, *States and Power in Africa* (Princeton, NJ: Princeton University Press, 2000).

18. Miguel Angel Centeno, *Blood and Debt: War and the Nation-State in Latin America* (University Park: Pennsylvania State University Press, 2002);

Mary P. Callahan, *Making Enemies: War and State building in Burma* (Ithaca: Cornell University Press, 2003).

19. Mancur Olson, *The Rise and Decline of Nations* (New Haven: Yale University Press; 1984); Kennedy, *Rise and Fall.*

20. Robert I. Rotberg, ed., *State Failure and State Weakness in a Time of Terror* (Washington, DC: Brookings Institution Press, 2003).

21. Skocpol, *State and Social Revolutions,* 29.

22. Joel S. Migdal, *Strong Societies and Weak States* (Princeton: Princeton University Press, 1988), 4–5.

23. Kalevi J. Holsti, *The State, War, and the State of War* (Cambridge: Cambridge University Press, 1996), 104, 106.

24. Karl Deutsch *et al.*, *Political Community and the North Atlantic Area: International Organization in the Light of Historical Experience* (Princeton: Princeton University Press, 1957); Emanuel Adler and Michael N. Barnett, ed., *Security Communities* (Cambridge: Cambridge University Press, 1998); Bruce Russett and John R. Oneal, *Triangulating Peace: Democracy, Interdependence, and International Organizations* (New York: W.W. Norton, 2001).

25. For example, see the discussion of England in Douglass C. North and Barry R. Weingast. "Constitutions and Commitment: The Evolution of Institutions Governing Public Choice in Seventeenth-Century England," *The Journal of Economic History* 49, no. 4 (December 1989): 803–832; and Daron Acemoğlu and James A. Robinson, *Why Nations Fail* (New York: Crown, 2012), 182–212.

26. Richard N. Rosecrance, *The Rise of the Trading State* (New York: Basic Books, 1986). War-ravaged Japan adopted economic development as its first priority guided by the state and its "developmental state." Chalmers A. Johnson, *MITI and the Japanese Miracle: The Growth of Industrial Policy, 1925–1975* (Palo Alto: Stanford University Press, 1982).

27. Adrian Leftwich, "Bringing Politics Back in: Towards a Model of the Developmental State," *The Journal of Development Studies* 31, no. 3 (February 1995): 400.

28. T. V. Paul, "State Capacity and South Asia's Perennial Insecurity Problems," in *South Asia's Weak States: Understanding Regional Insecurity*, ed. T. V. Paul (Palo Alto: Stanford University Press, 2010), 5. See also Migdal, *Strong Societies and Weak States*, 4–5; Joel S. Migdal, *State in Society* (Cambridge: Cambridge University Press, 2001); Peter Evans, *Embedded Autonomy* (Princeton: Princeton University Press, 1995).

29. See "The Failed State Index 2011," *Foreign Policy Magazine*, accessed November 29, 2012, http://www.foreignpolicy.com/articles/2011/06/17/2011_failed_states_index_interactive_map_and_rankings.

30. Benjamin Miller, *States, Nations, and the Great Powers: The Sources of Regional War and Peace* (Cambridge: Cambridge University Press, 2007), 18.

31. Owen Bennett Jones, *Pakistan: Eye of the Storm* (New Haven: Yale University Press, 2002). Population data from *CIA World Factbook*, accessed November

29, 2012. https://www.cia.gov/library/publications/the-world-factbook/geos/pk.htm.l.

32. World Economic Forum, *Global Competitiveness Report, 2012–13*, 284, accessed November 29, 2012, http://www3.weforum.org/docs/WEF_GlobalCompetitivenessReport_2012-13.pdf.

33. United Nations Development Program (UNDP), *UN Development Report-2013* (New York, 2013), 146, accessed May 30, 2013, http://www.undp.org/content/dam/undp/library/corporate/HDR/2013GlobalHDR/English/HDR2013%20Report%20English.pdf.

34. Barring a few studies, the literature on the subject of Pakistan's development is rather descriptive. There are hardly any works that apply the war and state literature to Pakistan. Partial exceptions include, Hussain Haqqani, *Pakistan: Between Mosque and Military* (Washington, DC: Brookings Institution Press, 2005); Stephen P. Cohen, *The Idea of Pakistan* (Washington, D.C: Brookings Institution Press, 2004); Ayesha Jalal, *Democracy and Authoritarianism in South Asia: A Comparative and Historical Perspective* (Cambridge: Cambridge University Press, 1995); Farzana Shaikh, *Making Sense of Pakistan* (New York: Columbia University Press, 2009); Anatol Lieven, *Pakistan: A Hard Country* (London: Allen Lane, 2011); and Ishtiaq Ahmed, *The Pakistan Garrison State: Origins, Evolution, Consequences, (1947–2011)* (New York: Oxford University Press, 2013).

35. David E. Sanger and Eric Schmitt, "Pakistani Nuclear Arms Pose Challenge to U.S. Policy," *New York Times*, January 31, 2011, accessed November 29, 2012, http://www.nytimes.com/2011/02/01/world/asia/01policy.html?pagewanted=all.

36. It must be stated that Tilly himself recognized the difficulties of the European experience being repeated in the developing world. See Tilly, "Reflections," 81.

Chapter 2

1. Panorama: The Nuclear Wal Mart, BBC One, November 12, 2006, accessed May 30, 2013, <http://www.youtube.com/watch?v=_E4OHWL79xQ>

2. Huma Khan, "U.S. Slaps Sanctions on AQ Khan and Others," *ABC News*, January 12, 2009, accessed May 30, 2013, http://abcnews.go.com/blogs/politics/2009/01/us-slaps-sancti/.

3. "Why is the U.S. Hampering a Swiss Investigation into A. Q. Khan's International Nuclear Arms Smuggling Ring?" *Democracy Now*, June 2, 2006. Accessed May 30, 2013, http://www.democracynow.org/2006/6/2/why_is_the_u_s_hampering.

4. Joby Warrick, "Nuclear Scientist A.Q. Khan Is Freed From House Arrest," *The Washington Post*, February 7, 2009, accessed May 30, 2013, http://articles.washingtonpost.com/2009-02-07/world/36929757_1_nuclear-weapons-abdul-qadeer-khan-david-albright.

5. Husain Haqqani, *Pakistan: Between Mosque and Military* (Washington, DC: Carnegie Endowment for International Peace, 2005).

6. Tim Harford and Michael Klein, "Aid and Resource Curse," *Public Policy for the Private Sector*, note number 291 (April 2005); Deborah A. Brautigam and Stephen Knack, "Foreign Aid, Institutions and Governance in Sub-Saharan Africa," *Economic Development and Cultural Change* 52, no. 2 (January 2004): 255–85; Michael Klein and Tim Harford, *The Market for Aid* (Washington, DC: International Finance Corporation, 2005).

7. Leonard Wantchekon, "Why do Resource Abundant Countries have Authoritarian Governments?" *Journal of African Finance and Economic Development* 5, no. 2 (2002): 57–77; Michael d Ross, "Does Oil Hinder Democracy?" *World Politics* 53, no. 3 (April 2001): 327–328; Terry Lynn Karl, *The Paradox of Plenty: Oil Booms and Petro-States* (Berkeley: University of California Press, 1997), 7.

8. Michael L. Ross, *The Oil Curse* (Princeton: Princeton University Press, 2012).

9. Nathan Jensen and Leonard Wantchekon, "Resource Wealth and Political Regimes in Africa," *Comparative Political Studies* 37, no. 7 (September 2004): 816–841.

10. Sabrina Tavernise, "Pakistan's Elite Pay Few Taxes, Widening Gap," *New York Times,* July 18, 2010, accessed November 9, 2011, http://www.nytimes.com/2010/07/19/world/asia/19taxes.html?pagewanted=all.

11. For instance, between July 2011 and March 2012 Pakistan received 9.73 billion dollars in overseas remittances. *Pakistan Observer*, April 16, 2012, accessed April 17, 2012, http://pakobserver.net/detailnews.asp?id=150455.

12. Fareed Zakaria, *The Future of Freedom* (New York: W.W. Norton, 2003), 75–76.

13. S. Akbar Zaidi, "Who Benefits from U.S. Aid to Pakistan?" *Carnegie Policy Outlook*, September 21, 2011: 3, 5, accessed November 30, 2012, http://carnegieendowment.org/2011/09/21/who-benefits-from-u.s.-aid-to-pakistan/8kg7.

14. Muhammad Arshad Khan and Ayaz Ahmed, "Foreign Aid—Blessing or Curse: Evidence from Pakistan," The *Pakistan Development Review* 46, no. 3 (Autumn 2007): 215–216, 223.

15. Ghulam Mohey-ud-din, "Impact of Foreign Aid on Economic Development in Pakistan [1960–2002]," MPRA Paper No. 1211 (June 2005): 5, accessed November 30, 2012, http://mpra.ub.uni-muenchen.de/1211/.

16. Omar Noman, *Economic and Social Progress in Asia: Why Pakistan did not Become a Tiger* (Karachi: Oxford University Press, 1997), 136, 177.

17. For these wider benefits, see Baldev Raj Nayar, *The Geopolitics of Globalization: The Consequences for Development* (New Delhi: Oxford University Press, 2005), 241; Noman, *Economic and Social Progress in Asia*, 135–7.

18. Azeem Ibrahim, "U.S. Aid to Pakistan—U.S. Taxpayers have Funded Pakistani Corruption," Belfer Center Discussion paper 2009–06, Harvard Kennedy School (July 2009):21, accessed November 30, 2012, http://belfercenter.ksg.harvard.edu/files/Final_DP_2009_06_08092009.pdf.

19. Reeta Chaudhuri Tremblay and Julian Schofield, "Institutional Causes of the India-Pakistan Enduring Rivalry," in *The India-Pakistan Conflict: An Enduring Rivalry*, ed. T. V. Paul (Cambridge: Cambridge University Press, 2005), chapter 10.

20. On this, see Ayesha Siddiqa-Agha, *Military Inc. Inside Pakistan's Military Economy* (London: Pluto Press, 2007).

21. Haqqani, *Between Mosque and Military*, 2.

22. Judith Goldstein and Robert O. Keohane, "Ideas and Foreign Policy: An Analytical Framework," in Goldstein and Keohane, eds., *Ideas and Foreign Policy* (Ithaca: Cornell University Press, 1993): 8, 12. On the role of ideas, see also Judith Goldstein, *Ideas, Interests, and American Trade Policy* (Ithaca: Cornell University Press, 1993); John M. Owen, *The Clash of Ideas in World Politics* (Princeton: Princeton University Press, 2010).

23. Some of these ideas shape into normative beliefs which are guideposts on how to act and how not to act with "prescriptions with justifications attached to them." Neta C. Crawford, *Arguments and Change in World Politics* (Cambridge: Cambridge University Press, 2002), 40.

24. Alexander Wendt, *Social Theory of International Politics* (Cambridge: Cambridge University Press, 1999), 260.

25. Hedley Bull, *The Anarchical Society: A Study of Order in World Politics* (New York: Columbia University Press, 1977), 24–5.

26. Wendt, *Social Theory*, 297–299.

27. Stephen P. Cohen, *The Idea of Pakistan* (Washington D.C.: Brookings Institution Press, 2004), 72.

28. Two Pakistani scholars state the nostalgia of sections of the society: "Pakistanis live in the ruins of the defeat of the Muslim Mughal Empire in India by British colonial power in the mid-nineteenth century. Their version of history is nostalgic for a time when Muslims ruled over India and were carriers of a great civilization." Pervez Hoodbhoy and Zia Mian, "Pakistan, the Army and the Conflict Within," Middle East Research and Information Project (MERIP), July 12, 2011, accessed November 20, 2012, http://www.merip.org/mero/mero071211. For the successor state to the Mughal empire idea, see M. J. Akbar, *TinderBox: The Past and Future of Pakistan* (New Delhi: Harper Collins, 2011), xi.

29. Iqbal Akhund, *Trial and Error: The Advent and Eclipse of Benazir Bhutto* (Karachi: Oxford University Press, 2000), 116.

30. Tahir Kamran, *Democracy and Governance in Pakistan* (Lahore: South Asia Partnership Pakistan, 2008), 26. Cohen argues that there are some hardline elements in Pakistani military that believe in the breakup of India, and the restoration of a larger Muslim political order along the lines of a grand Mughal empire, is feasible by force if necessary and "if martial Muslims assumed their rightful place in the vanguard of an Indian revolution that would unite all Muslims of the subcontinent." Stephen P. Cohen, *Shooting for a Century: The India-Pakistan Conundrum* (Washington DC: Brookings Institution Press, 2013), 114.

31. General M. Zia-Ul-Haq, foreword to *The Quaranic Concept of War*, by S. K. Malik (Lahore: Wajidalis, 1979), ii.

32. To Victoria Schofield, Bhutto strengthened Pakistan's relations with the Arab and Muslim world in order to partially cure Pakistan's "inferiority complex" with India. See her *Bhutto: Trial and Execution* (London: Caswell, 1979), 9.

33. Stephen P. Cohen, "Pakistan: Arrival and Departure," in *The Future of Pakistan*, ed., Stephen P. Cohen (Washington, DC: Brookings Institution Press, 2011), 25.

34. Cited in Ahmed Rashid, *Taliban: Islam, Oil and the New Great Game in Central Asia* (London: I. B. Tauris, 2000), 195.

35. The historical claim to parity with India rested on "the idea of power as a Muslim prerogative. . . . For Pakistan has sought also to emulate India by aspiring to the status of a regional power—a status it associates with India—and to realize it through control over subordinate powers, most notably Afghanistan, and through the possession of nuclear weapons." Farzana Shaikh, *Making Sense of Pakistan* (New York: Columbia University Press, 2009), 9.

36. Major General M. Amin Khan Burki, foreword to *India: A Study in Profile*, by Javed Hassan (Rawalpindi: Army Education Press, 1990), ii.

37. Hassan, *India*, 51.

38. Haqqani, *Pakistan*, 269; Hassan, *India*, 111, 125–8, 139.

39. Cohen, *Shooting for a Century*, 113.

40. Ibid.

41. Malik, *The Quranic Concept of War*, 66.

42. Zulfikar Ali Bhutto, *The Myth of Independence* (London: Oxford University Press, 1969), 180.

43. On the garrison state and its origins see Tan Tai Yong, *The Garrison State: The Military, Government and Society in Colonial Punjab 1849–1947* (New Delhi: Sage Publications, 2005); Ayesha Jalal, *The State of Martial Rule: The Origins of Pakistan's Political Economy of Defence* (Cambridge: Cambridge University Press, 2007). See also Ishtiaq Ahmed, *The Pakistan Garrison State Origins, Evolution, Consequences (1947-2011)* (New York: Oxford University Press, 2013).

44. As Samuel Huntington states: intentions are "political in nature, inherently fickle and changeable, and virtually impossible to evaluate and predict." *The Soldier and the State: The Theory and Politics of Civil-Military Relations* (Cambridge, MA: Belknap Press, 1981), 66. Barry Posen, *Sources of Military Doctrine* (Ithaca, NY: Cornell University Press, 1986), 48–9.

45. Mohammad Ayub Khan, *Friends Not Masters: A Political Autobiography* (London: Oxford University Press, 1967), 122.

46. The security dilemma arises from states' arms race behavior. When a state attempts to obtain security though arms acquisition, it reduces the security of the other and as that state attempts to catch up a spiraling arms race results, making both sides less secure than they originally started. For this,

see John H. Herz, "Idealist Internationalism and the Security Dilemma," *World Politics* 2, no. 2 (January 1950): 157–80; Robert Jervis, "Cooperation under the Security Dilemma," *World Politics* 30, no. 2, (January 1978): 167–214.

47. Cohen cites the example of the presentation of India in the curriculum of the Military Staff College at Quetta. "Indian strategic objectives are said to be fixed, rooted in communal attitudes and illusions of great-power status. The syllabus is often factually inaccurate, and instructors do not encourage debate or discussion on the subject. The analysis drives home one important point: Indian intentions are subject to rapid change; hence the Pakistani military planner must focus only on the already substantial (and growing) Indian capability and not on the fluid nature of Indian intentions. Pakistan does have a real security problem in relation to India, but the Staff College and the National Defense College offer their students a stereotyped, reductionist theory of Indian motives and strategy." Cohen, *The Idea of Pakistan*, 107. Cohen uses the example of the book by Hassan, *India*.

48. For these pathologies, see Stephen Van Evera, *Causes of War: Power and Roots of Conflict* (Ithaca: Cornell University Press, 1999), 14–34.

49. Francis Fukuyama, *State-Building: Governance and World Order in the 21st Century* (Ithaca: Cornell University Press, 2004), 35–6.

50. Theda Skocpol, *States and Social Revolutions* (Cambridge: Cambridge University Press, 1979), 4.

51. Atul Kohli, *State-Directed Development* (Cambridge: Cambridge University Press, 2004), 18; Stephen Haggard, *Pathways from the Periphery: The Politics of Growth in the Newly Industrializing Countries* (Ithaca: Cornell University Press, 1990), 23–50; Bruce Cumings, *Korea's Place in the Sun* (New York: W. W. Norton, 1997).

52. Andrew Mango, *Atatürk* (London: John Murray, 1999); Stephen Kinzer, *Crescent and Star: Turkey between Two Worlds* (New York: Farrar, Straus and Giroux, 2001).

53. For instance, see Mohammed Ayoob, *The Many Faces of Political Islam: Religion and Politics in the Muslim World* (Ann Arbor: The University of Michigan Press, 2008), 93. The problem with this argument is that it assumes more time will produce democratic outcomes. Pakistan's trajectory over the past 60 years does not offer any consolation to this logic. Moreover, Ayoob himself explores the cases of Indonesia, Malaysia, and Turkey to show that democracy can develop in postcolonial Muslim states even without the luxury of time. Further, the example of India shows that democratic institutions in a postcolonial society can develop without a long period of gestation.

54. Sørensen, "War and State Making."

55. Stephen Graham, "Pakistan Agrees to $7.6 billion IMF Bailout," *Huffington Post*, November 15, 2008, accessed May 30, 2013, http://www.huffingtonpost.com/2008/11/15/pakistan-agrees-to-76-bil_n_144080.html.

Chapter 3

1. Shuja Nawaz, *Crossed Swords: Pakistan, Its Army, and the Wars within* (Karachi: Oxford University Press, 2008), 156–69; Rasul Baksh Rais, "Introduction," in *State, Society and Democratic Change in Pakistan*, ed., Rais (Karachi: Oxford University Press, 1997), xv.

2. Myron Weiner, "Political Integration and Political Development," *The Annals of the American Academy of Political and Social Science*, vol. 358 (March 1965): 52–64.

3. Khalid Bin Sayeed, "Some Reflections on the Democratization process," in *State, Society, and Democratic Change in Pakistan*, ed., Rais, 2.

4. For this logic, see Alfred Stepan, Juan J. Linz, and Yogendra Yadav, *Crafting-State-Nations: India and Other Multinational Democracies* (Baltimore: Johns Hopkins University Press, 2011), 4–6.

5. According to one study, the number may actually be closer to 17.9 million. Prashant Bharadwaj, Asim Khwaja, and Atif Mian, "The Big March: Migratory Flows after the Partition of India," *Economic and Political Weekly* (August 30, 2008): 39–40.

6. Ravinder Kaur, "India and Pakistan: Partition Lessons," *Open Democracy*, August 16, 2007, accessed November 30, 2012, http://www.opendemocracy.net/article/india.

7. Paul R. Brass, "The Partition of India and the Retributive Genocide in the Punjab, 1946–47: Means, Methods, and Purposes," *Journal of Genocide Research* 5, no. 1 (2003): 71–101; Swarna Aiyar, "'August Anarchy': The Partition Massacres in Punjab, 1947," *South Asia: Journal of South Asian Studies*, 18, no. 1 (1995): 13–36. For an excellent account of the partition of Punjab, see Ishtiq Ahmed, *The Punjab Bloodied, Partitioned and Cleansed* (Karachi: Oxford University Press, 2012).

8. According to Noman, the "Muslim elite of these provinces was well represented in state governments formed after the 1937 provincial elections," which made them relatively unenthusiastic about the idea of Pakistan. Omar Noman, *The Political Economy of Pakistan, 1947–1985* (London: KPI, 1988), 4. See also Ian Talbot, *Provincial Politics and the Pakistan Movement* (Karachi: Oxford University Press, 1988). In Bengal, the movement was stronger than Punjab as Muslims wanted to eliminate the Hindu landlords and moneylenders who they felt were exploiting them. Salahuddin Ahmed, *Bangladesh: Past and Present* (New Delhi: A.P.H. Publishing, 2004), 129.

9. Talbot, *Provincial Politics*, xiii.

10. See Stanley A. Wolpert, *Jinnah of Pakistan* (New York: Oxford University Press, 1984); Jaswant Singh, *Jinnah: India, Partition, Independence* (New York, Oxford University Press, 2010); Ayesha Jalal, *The Sole Spokesman: Jinnah, the Muslim League and the Demand for Pakistan* (Cambridge: Cambridge University Press, 1985).

11. For some of these causes, see Akbar S. Ahmed, *Jinnah, Pakistan and Islamic Identity* (London: Routledge, 1997), 66–93.

12. Ayesha Jalal, *Democracy and Authoritarianism in South Asia: A Comparative and Historical Perspective* (Cambridge: Cambridge University Press, 1995), 25.

13. Ahmad, *Jinnah, Pakistan and Islamic Identity*, 25.

14. Talbott, *Provincial Politics,* xiii.

15. Chaudhri Muhammad Ali, *The Emergence of Pakistan* (New York: Columbia University Press, 1967), 27–29.

16. Penderel Moon, *Divide and Quit* (Berkeley: University of California Press, 1962), 15.

17. For this argument, see Narendra Singh Sarila, *The Shadow of the Great Game: The Untold Story of India's Partition* (New York: Carroll & Graf, 2006). Singh, an aide to Lord Louis Mountbatten (the last viceroy of British India), reveals that the British leaders, realizing that the Indian National Congress would not support their strategic interests vis-à-vis the Soviet Union, decided to side with Jinnah and the Muslim League as a better partner for the great game in South and Southwest Asia. Although not in power in 1947, former Prime Minister Winston Churchill was totally opposed to Indian independence and had much disdain for Congress leaders, especially Gandhi. See Arthur Herman, *Gandhi and Churchill: The Epic Rivalry that Destroyed an Empire and Forged our Age* (New York: Bantam Books, 2008).

18. Moon, *Divide and Quit*, 21.

19. Ibid., 43.

20. On the various causes and consequence of this rivalry, see T. V. Paul ed., *The India-Pakistan Conflict: An Enduring Rivalry* (Cambridge: Cambridge University Press, 2005).

21. Jinnah's desire for protecting the rights of religious minorities is captured in his speech in August 1947 at the Constituent Assembly when he said: "You are free; you are free to go to your temples, you are free to go to your mosques or to any other place of worship in this State of Pakistan . . . You may belong to any religion or cast or creed—that has nothing to do with the business of the State. . . . We are starting in the days when there is no discrimination, no distinction between one community and another, no discrimination between one caste or creed and another. We are starting with this fundamental principle that we are all citizens and equal citizens of one State." Mohammed Ali Jinnah, *Speeches of Quaid-i-Azam Mohammed Ali Jinnah as Governor General of Pakistan* (Karachi: Sind Observer Press, 1948), 10, quoted in Ahmed, *Jinnah, Pakistan and Islamic Identity*, 175.

22. Ahmed, *Jinnah, Pakistan and Islamic Identity*, 176–8.

23. Rizwan Ahmed, *Sayings of Quaid-i-Azam Mohammed Ali Jinnah* (Karachi: Quaidi Foundation and Pakistan Movement Center, 1993), quoted in Ahmed, *Jinnah, Pakistan and Islamic Identity*, 194.

24. Ahmed *Sayings of Quaid-i-Azam*, 153, cited in Ahmed, *Jinnah, Pakistan and Islamic Identity*, 195.

25. Wolpert, *Jinnah of Pakistan*, 261.

26. Ahmed, *Jinnah, Pakistan and Islamic Identity*, 195. Jinnah chose ambiguity in his views on secularism, because he wanted to build "a coalition of zamindars, pirs and parts of the Indian Muslim elite," who would not have supported a secular party in competition with Nehru's Congress. Pervez Hoodbhoy, "Jinnah and the Islamic State: Setting the Record Straight," *Economic and Political Weekly* 42, no. 32 (August 11–17, 2007): 3301–2.

27. On this see Ralph Braibanti, "Public Bureaucracy and Judiciary in Pakistan," in *Bureaucracy and Political Development*, ed. Joseph LaPalombara (Princeton: Princeton University Press, 1963), 360–440.

28. Based on the 1950 estimates from United Nations Department of Economic and Social Affairs, *World Population Prospects, the 2010 Revision* (New York: United Nations, 2011).

29. Peter R. Blood, ed., *Pakistan: A Country Study* (Washington D.C.: Library of Congress, Federal Research Division, 1995), 37.

30. Jalal, *The State of Martial Rule*, 42.

31. Shuja Nawaz, *Crossed Swords: Pakistan, Its Army and the Wars within* (Karachi: Oxford University Press, 2008), 32.

32. Tahir Kamran, *Democracy and Governance in Pakistan* (Lahore: South Asia Partnership Pakistan, 2008), 37.

33. Hamza Alavi, "Class and State," in *Pakistan: The Roots of Dictatorship*, ed. Hassan Gardezi and Jamil Rashid (London: Zed Press, 1983), 78.

34. Kamran, *Democracy and Governance*, 26.

35. On this, see Nawaz, *Crossed Swords*, 42–73. On the origins of the Kashmir dispute, see Michael Brecher, *The Struggle for Kashmir* (New York: Oxford University Press, 1953); Sisir Gupta, *Kashmir: A Study in India-Pakistan Relations* (Bombay: Indian Council of World Affairs, 1967); Victoria Schofield, *Kashmir in Conflict: India, Pakistan and the Unending War* (London: I.B. Tauris, 2010); Raju G.C.Thomas, ed., *Perspectives on Kashmir: Roots of Conflict in South Asia* (Boulder, CO: Westview Press, 1992). See also Amitabh Mattoo, Kapil Kak, and Happymon Jacob, eds., *India & Pakistan: Pathways Ahead* (New Delhi: KW Publishers, 2007) on various efforts to settle the conflict.

36. Mahesh Shankar, "Insuring the Future: The Reputational Imperative and Territorial Disputes in South Asia, 1949–1965," (PhD dissertation., McGill University, 2012).

37. Alavi, "Class and State," 79.

38. Ibid., 81.

39. Hassan Askari Rizvi, *Military and Politics in Pakistan* (Lahore: Progressive Publishers, 1974) 56.

40. The *Dawn*, August 17, 1953, cited in Rizvi, *The Military and Politics*, 55.

41. Robert J. McMahon, *The Cold War on the Periphery: The United States, India and Pakistan* (New York: Columbia University Press, 1994).

42. Alavi, "Class and State," 78.

43. Rais, "Introduction," xv.

44. This general sense of regret is present in his discussion of the Sino-India war in Khan, *Friends Not Masters*, 140–53.

45. Shirin Tahir-Kheli, *The United States and Pakistan: The Evolution of an Influence Relationship* (New York: Praeger, 1982), 18.

46. John Fricker, *Battle for Pakistan: the Air War of 1965* (London: Ian Allan, 1979), 11, 13.

47. Salmaan Taseer, *Bhutto: A Political Biography* (New Delhi: Vikas Publishing, 1980), 60.

48. Abdul Ali Malik, "Operation Gibraltar: A General's View," *Muslim* (October 14, 1986); Mohammed Musa, *My Version: India-Pakistan War 1965* (New Delhi: ABC Publishing House, 1983), 2.

49. Mohammed Asghar Khan, *The First Round: Indo-Pakistan War 1965* (London: Islamic Information Services, 1979), 76; T. V. Paul, *Asymmetric Conflicts: War Initiation by Weaker Powers* (Cambridge: Cambridge University Press, 1994), 110–114. Several Pakistani generals who participated in the War have written on Pakistan's role in initiating the incursions into Kashmir and thereby precipitating a war. Major general retd. Mahmud Ali Durrani, a participant in the war and later military secretary to President Zia-ul-Haq, has conceded that "we started the intrusions on the border" and that Pakistan did not achieve anything by going to wars with India. "Pak Intrusion on Borders Triggered 1965 War: Durrani," accessed November 14, 2011, http://www.defence.pk/forums/military-history/34055-paks-intrusions-borders-triggered-1965-war-durrani.html.

50. S. M. Zafar, "Constitutional Development," in *Pakistan: Founders' Aspirations and Today's Realities*, ed. Hafeez Malik (Karachi: Oxford University Press, 2001), 40.

51. Hassan Abbas, *Pakistan's Drift into Extremism: Allah, the Army, and America's War on Terror* (Armonk, NY: M.E. Sharpe, 2005), 51.

52. Rounaq Jahan, *Pakistan: A Failure in National Integration* (New York: Columbia University Press, 1972), 6.

53. Ibid., 28.

54. Robert LaPorte Jr., "Succession in Pakistan: Continuity and Change in a Garrison State," *Asian Survey* 9, no. 11 (November 1969): 848.

55. Shahid Javed Burki, *Pakistan Under Bhutto, 1971–1977* (New York: St. Martin's Press, 1980), 45. See also, S. Akbar Zaidi, *Pakistan's Economic and Social Development* (New Delhi: Rupa & Co., 2004), 16–9.

56. Zaidi, *Pakistan's Economic and Social Development*, 17.

57. Kamran, *Democracy and Governance*, 59.

58. Zafar, "Constitutional Development," 41.

59. See Richard Sisson and Leo E. Rose, *War and Secession: Pakistan, India, and the Creation of Bangladesh* (Berkeley, CA: University of California Press, 1990), 23–34; 54–90.

60. On this see Sisson and Rose, *War and Secession*.

61. Nawaz, *Crossed Swords*, 310–315. According to a former Pakistani Defence Secretary Tariq Waseem Ghazi, the 1971 war has been considered as an embarrassment by the Pakistani military and officers prefer not to talk about it. They do not consider it as a military defeat but a political defeat caused by the rift between Bhutto and Mujibur Rahman which coincided with the strategic ambitions of India. Interview with the Author, Copenhagen, June 19, 2013.

62. Christopher Van Hollen, "The Tilt Policy Revisited: Nixon-Kissinger Geopolitics and South Asia," *Asian Survey* 20, no. 4 (April 1980): 339–61; William Burr, ed., *The Kissinger Transcripts* (New York: The New Press, 1998), 46–57.

63. Quoted in Mike Moore, "Eating Grass," *The Bulletin of the Atomic Scientists* 49, no. 5 (June 1993), 2.

64. Quoted in Feroz Hassan Khan, *Eating Grass: The Making of the Pakistani Bomb* (Palo Alto: Stanford University Press, 2012), 87.

65. Anwar H. Syed, *The Discourse and Politics of Zulfikar Ali Bhutto* (New York: St. Martin's Press, 1992), 21.

66. Russell J. Leng, *Bargaining and Learning in Recurring Crises* (Ann Arbor: University of Michigan Press, 2000), 260; Russell J. Leng, "Realpolitik and Learning in the India-Pakistan Rivalry," in *The India Pakistan-Conflict*, ed., Paul, 112.

67. Stephen P. Cohen, *The Idea of Pakistan* (Washington, DC: Brookings Institution Press, 2004), 77.

68. Jamil Rashid and Hassan N. Gardezi, "Independent Pakistan: Its Political Economy," in *Pakistan: the Roots of Dictatorship*, ed., Gardezi and Rashid, 12.

69. Ibid., 12.

70. Ibid.

71. Burki, *Pakistan under Bhutto*, 4.

72. Raju G.C. Thomas, "The South Asian Security Balance in a Western Dominant World," in *Balance of Power: Theory and Practice in the 21st Century*, eds., T. V. Paul, James J. Wirtz, and Michel Fortmann (Palo Alto: Stanford University Press, 2004), 317.

73. Victoria Schofield, *Bhutto: Trial and Execution* (London: Caswell, 1979).

74. Shahid Javed Burki, "Pakistan under Zia, 1977–1988," *Asian Survey* 28, no. 10 (October 1988), 1087.

75. Thomas Taylor Hammond, *Red Flag Over Afghanistan: The Communist Coup, the Soviet Invasion, and the Consequences* (Boulder, CO: Westview Press, 1984), 49–102.

76. Steve Coll, *Ghost Wars: The Secret History of the CIA, Afghanistan, and Bin Laden, from the Soviet Invasion to September 10, 2011* (New York: Penguin Press, 2004), 38–50.

77. Hammond, *Red Flag*, 120–124; A. Z. Hilali, *US-Pakistan Relationship: Soviet Invasion of Afghanistan* (Aldershot, UK: Ashgate Publishing, 2005), 139–58.

78. For more details see Hilali, *US-Pakistan Relationship*, 139–230.

79. Coll, *Ghost Wars,* 63–8.

80. Ahmed Rashid, *Jihad: The Rise of Militant Islam in Central Asia* (New Haven: Yale University, 2002), 215.

81. Deepa M. Ollapally, *The Politics of Extremism in South Asia* (Cambridge: Cambridge University Press, 2008), 138.

82. Bruno Tertrais, "Khan's Nuclear Exports: Was there a State Strategy?" in *Pakistan's Nuclear Future: Worries Beyond War*, ed., Henry D. Sokoloski (Carlisle Barracks, PA: Strategic Studies Institute, US Army War College, 2008), 13–57.

83. Shyam Bhatia, *Goodbye Shahzadi: A Political Biography of Benazir Bhutto* (New Delhi: Roli Books, 2008), 41–2.

84. In a secret letter to a *Sunday Times* reporter Khan revealed the Chinese support to Pakistan by way of natural and enriched uranium, and uranium hexafluoride, and the supply of drawings and components of nuclear weapons to Iran and North Korea. Simon Henderson, "Investigation: Nuclear Scandal-Dr. Abdul Qadeer Khan," *The Sunday Times*, September 20, 2009, accessed November 30, 2012, http://www.defence.pk/forums/pakistan-strategic-forces/34705-investigation-nuclear-scandal-dr-abdul-qadeer-khan.html.

85. For the Kargil story, see Peter R. Lavoy, ed., *Asymmetric War in South Asia: The Causes and Consequences of the Kargil Conflict* (Cambridge: Cambridge University Press, 2009); Bruce Riedel, "American Diplomacy and the 1999 Kargil Summit at Blair House," in *Asymmetric War in South Asia*, 130–43.

86. Deputy Secretary of State Richard Armitage is said to have carried the tough message to Pakistan that it would be bombed to the stone age if it refuses to support the war on al-Queda and the Taliban in Afghanistan. "US 'threatened to bomb' Pakistan," *BBC News*, September 22, 2006, accessed November 30, 2012, http://news.bbc.co.uk/2/hi/south_asia/5369198.stm.

87. Owen Bennett Jones, *Pakistan: Eye of the Storm* (New Haven, CT: Yale University Press, 2002), 3.

88. Mark Mazzetti, Jane Perlez, Eric Schmitt and Andrew W. Lehren, "Pakistan Aids Insurgency in Afghanistan, Reports Assert," *New York Times*, July 25, 2010, accessed November 30, 2012, http://www.nytimes.com/2010/07/26/world/asia/26isi.html?pagewanted=all; see also Rob Crilly and Alex Spillius, "Wikileaks: Pakistan Accused of Helping Taliban in Afghanistan Attacks," *The Telegraph,* July 26, 2010, accessed November 30, 2012, http://www.telegraph.co.uk/news/worldnews/asia/afghanistan/7910687/Wikileaks-Pakistan-accused-of-helping-Taliban-in-Afghanistan-attacks.html.

89. "A senior al-Qaeda commander in Kunar province said: 'Pakistan knows everything. They control everything. I can't [expletive] on tree in Kunar [province] without them watching. The Taliban are not Islam. The Taliban are Islamabad.'" "In Quotes: Excerpts from Nato Report on Taliban", *BBC News Asia*, February 1, 2012, accessed November 30, 2012, http://www.bbc.co.uk/news/world-asia-16829368.

90. "Pakistan Minorities Minister Shahbaz Bhatti Shot Dead," *BBC News*, March 2, 2011, accessed November 30, 2012, http://www.bbc.co.uk/news/world-south-asia-12617562.

91. See Ashley J. Tellis, "Pakistan's Army Rule," *The National Interest*, June 28, 2011, accessed November 30, 2012, http://nationalinterest.org/commentary/pakistans-army-rule-5536; See also Ahmed Rashid, *Pakistan on the Brink* (New York: Viking, 2012); Ian Talbot, *Pakistan: A New History* (New York: Columbia University Press, 2012), chapter 8.

92. Ajit Kumar Singh, "Pakistan: Sinking State," *South Asia Intelligence Review*, 11, no. 36 (March 11, 2013), 2.

93. Manan Ahmed Asif, "Pakistan's Tyrannical Majority," *The New York Times*, May 10, 2013, accessed May 30, 2013, http://wap.nytimes.com/2013/05/11/opinion/pakistans-tyrannical-majority.html.

94. On various dimensions of this withdrawal, see Hy S. Rothstein and John Arquilla, eds., *The Afghan Endgames* (Washington, DC: Georgetown University Press, 2012).

95. "Pakistan Army Sees 'Internal Threats' as Greatest Security Risk," *The Dawn*, January 2, 2013, accessed May 30, 2013, http://dawn.com/2013/01/03/pakistan-army-sees-internal-threats-as-greatest-security-risk/.

96. "Hopes Fade for 135 Feared Dead in Pakistan Avalanche," *The Dawn*, April 8, 2012, accessed November 30, 2012, http://dawn.com/2012/04/08/army-hopes-miracle-will-save-avalanche-victims/.

97. "India says Pakistan 'Beheaded' Kashmir Soldier," *BBC News*, January 9, 2013, accessed February 4, 2013, http://www.bbc.co.uk/news/world-asia-india-20954975.

98. "SC Orders Arrest of PM Ashraf in RPP Case," *The Dawn*, January 15, 2013, accessed on February 4, 2013, http://dawn.com/news/778965/sc-orders-arrest-of-pm-ashraf-reports.

99. "Qadri Announces End to Protest after Government Deal," *The Dawn*, January 17, 2013, accessed February 4, 2013, http://dawn.com/2013/01/17/talks-between-govt-qadri-concluded-successfully/.

100. Dr. Moeed Pirzada and Fahd Husain, "Policy Brief—Pakistani Media: Achievements, Failures & Way Forward?," Jinnah Institute, March 30, 2012, accessed on December 13, 2012, http://www.jinnah-institute.org/images/b0312-18%20pdf.pdf.

101. Iftekharul Bashar, "Pakistan, Social Networking and the Facebook Jihad Phenomenon," *East Asia Forum*, March 15, 2011, accessed on December 12, 2012, http://www.eastasiaforum.org/2011/03/15/pakistan-social-networking-and-the-facebook-jihad-phenomenon/.

102. For the statistics on the casualties, see "PIPS Report: Awami National Party Bore the Brunt of Pre-election Violence," *The Express Tribune*, May 25, 2013, accessed May 30, 2013, http://tribune.com.pk/story/554140/pips-report-awami-national-party-bore-the-brunt-of-pre-election-violence/?print=true.

103. Salman Masood, "Musharraf Under Arrest on Charges in Bhutto Assassination," *New York Times*, April 26, 2013, accessed May 30, 2013, http://www.nytimes.com/2013/04/27/world/asia/musharraf-under-arrest-on-charges-in-bhutto-assassination.html.

104. Zofeen Ebrahim, "Groaning under Power Cuts, Scorching Temps in Pakistan" *Inter Press Service*, May 23, 2013.

Chapter 4

1. Quoted in Shuja Nawaz, *Crossed Swords: Pakistan, Its Army and the Wars Within* (Karachi: Oxford University Press, 2008), 511. Lieuenant-General Tariq Waseem Ghazi, who attended this meeting told this author that Musharaff was visibly upset over Mrs. Bhutto's rebuffing, especially the repeated questioning of the political and military repercussions of such an invasion and this incident affected his subsequent relationship with the prime minister. Interview with the Author, Copenhagen, June 19, 2013.

2. "Army Rejects Sharif Claim," *BBC News* June 13, 2000, accessed May 30, 2013, http://news.bbc.co.uk/2/hi/south_asia/787795.stm.

3. Zulfikar Ali Bhutto, Interviewed by Kuldip Nayar, *Sunday Magazine*, (Calcutta, July 10–16, 1983), reprinted in *Strategic Digest* (New Delhi, July 1984), 745–746.

4. Ahmed Rashid, "The Anarchic Republic of Pakistan," *National Interest* 109 (September/October 2010): 23.

5. Stephen P. Cohen, *The Idea of Pakistan* (Washington DC: Brookings Institution Press, 2004), 56.

6. Harold D. Lasswell, *The Analysis of Political Behavior* (London: Routledge and Kegan Paul, 1948), 146, 149, 153, 154.

7. For this, see Amos Perlmutter, "The Praetorian State and the Praetorian Army: Toward a Taxonomy of Civilian-Military Relations in Developing Polities," *Comparative Politics* 1, no. 3 (April 1969): 382–404.

8. Hendrik Spruyt, *Ending Empire: Contested Sovereignty and Territorial Partition* (Ithaca: Cornell University Press, 2005), 9.

9. Harold D. Lasswell, "Sino-Japanese Crisis: The Garrison State versus the Civilian State," in *Essays on the Garrison State*, eds., Harold D. Lasswell and Jay Stanley (New Brunswick: Transaction Publishers, 1997) 43.

10. Michael Mann, *States, War and Capitalism: Studies in Political Sociology* (Oxford: Basil Blackwell, 1988), 124. See also Alfred Vagts, *A History of Militarism: Civilian and Military* (New York: The Free Press, 1959), 13, 15; Stanislav Andreski, *Military Organization and Society* (Berkeley: University of California Press, 1968), 185.

11. Jay Stanley and David R. Segal, "Conclusion: Landmarks in Defense Literature," in *Essays on the Garrison State*, 132.

12. Harold D. Lasswell, "The Universal Peril: Perpetual Crisis and the Garrison-Prison State," in *Essays on the Garrison State*, 118.

13. Vernon K. Dibble, "The Garrison Society," in *Radical Perspectives on Social Problems: Readings in Critical Sociology*, ed., Frank Lindenfeld (London, Macmillan, 1968), 273.

14. Daniel Deudney, "Nuclear Weapons and the Waning of the Real-State," *Daedalus* 124, no. 2 (Spring 1995): 209–31.

15. Kenneth N. Waltz, *Theory of International Politics* (Reading, MA: Addison-Wesley, 1979), 112–113.

16. For an elaboration of the national security state, see Norrin M. Ripsman and T. V. Paul, *Globalization and the National Security State* (New York: Oxford University Press, 2010), 10–1.

17. Aaron L. Friedberg, "Why Didn't the United States become a Garrison State?" *International Security* 16, no. 4 (Spring 1992), 109–42.

18. An example of such a state is the pre-war Germany where the state was heavily militarized and the bourgeoisie was socialized into militaristic conceptions of national interests. Michael Mann, *The Sources of Social Power*, vol. 2 (Cambridge: Cambridge University Press, 1993), 322.

19. Mohammed Ayub Khan, *Friends Not Masters: A Political Autobiography* (Oxford University Press, 1967), 227.

20. Robert LaPorte Jr., "Succession in Pakistan: Continuity and Change in a Garrison State," *Asian Survey* 9, no. 11 (November 1969): 851.

21. Mazhar Aziz, *Military Control in Pakistan: The Parallel State* (London: Routledge, 2008), 94.

22. Ibid., 100.

23. Quoted in Praveen Swami, "God's Soldiers: Pakistan Army's Ideology," *The Hindu*, October 7, 2011, accessed November 30, 2012, http://www.thehindu.com/opinion/lead/article2515374.ece.

24. On this and other perversions in history textbooks, see Ayesha Jalal, "Conjuring Pakistan: History as Official Imagining," *International Journal of Middle East Studies* 27, no. 1 (February 1995): 73–89.

25. A.H. Nayyar and Ahmad Salim, *The Subtle Subversion: The State of Curricula and Textbooks in Pakistan* (Islamabad: Sustainable Policy Institute, 2003), especially chapter 5.

26. On this see, "Memogate and Its Aftermath," *The Dawn*, accessed August 9, 2012, http://dawn.com/memogate-and-the-aftermath/; Rob Crilly, "Memogate: Pakistani probe concludes ex-US envoy Husain Haqqani Drafted Memo" *The Telegraph*, June 12, 2012, accessed November 30, 2012, http://www.telegraph.co.uk/news/worldnews/asia/pakistan/9326351/Memogate-Pakistani-probe-concludes-ex-US-envoy-Husain-Haqqani-drafted-memo.html.

27. "Kayani not on Board with Zardari's 'no-first-use' N-policy: WikiLeaks," accessed May 30, 2013, http://www.defence.pk/forums/pakistan-strategic-forces/107215-kayani-not-board-zardaris-no-first-use-n-policy-wikileaks.html#ixzz2UKyL9wKd.

28. Juan J. Linz and Alfred C. Stepan, *Problems of Democratic Transition and Consolidation* (Baltimore: Johns Hopkins University Press, 1996), 3.

29. Ibid., 4.
30. See Alfred C. Stepan, *Rethinking Military Politics* (Princeton, NJ: Princeton University Press, 1988).
31. Hasan Askari Rizvi, *The Military and Politics in Pakistan* (Lahore: Progressive Publishers, 1974), 59.
32. Anita Joshua, "Pakistan is not like Iraq or Afghanistan, Kayani Tells Washington," *The Hindu,* October 19, 2011, accessed November 30, 2012, http://www.thehindu.com/news/international/article2551586.ece.
33. Samuel P. Huntington, *Political Order in Changing Societies* (New Haven: Yale University Press, 1968), 221. According to Finer, armed forces have three major political advantages over civilian organizations: "a marked superiority in organization, a highly emotionalized symbolic status, and a monopoly of arms." S. E. Finer, *The Man on the Horseback: The Role of Military in Politics* (New York: Praeger, 1962), 6.
34. Jack L. Snyder, *The Ideology of the Offensive: Military Decision Making and the Disasters of 1914* (Ithaca: Cornell University Press, 1984), 24.
35. Zahid Hussain, *Frontline Pakistan* (New Delhi: Penguin Books, 2007), 12.
36. Frédéric Grare, *Reforming the Intelligence Agencies in Pakistan's Transitional Democracy* (Washington, DC: Carnegie Endowment for International Peace, 2009), 17–38.
37. Barney Henderson, "Mumbai 26/11 Plotter David Headley Sentenced to 35 years," *The Telegraph,* January 24, 2013 accessed May 30, 2013, http://www.telegraph.co.uk/news/worldnews/asia/india/9825243/Mumbai-2611-plotter-David-Headley-sentenced-to-35-years.html.
38. Steve Coll, "The Stand-off: How Jihadi Groups Helped Provoke the Twenty-first Century's First Nuclear Crisis," *The New Yorker* (February 13–20, 2006), 126, accessed May 30, 2013, http://www.newyorker.com/archive/2006/02/13/060213fa_fact_coll.
39. On this, see Nawaz, *Crossed Swords,* 11–13.
40. Tan Tai Yong, *The Garrison State: The Military, Government and Society in Colonial Punjab, 1849–1947* (New Delhi: Sage Publications, 2005), 17–18. See also Pradeep Barua, *The State at War in South Asia* (Lincoln, NE: University of Nebraska Press, 2005), chapters 7 and 8.
41. Yong, *The Garrison State,* 308–309.
42. Hasan-Askari Rizvi, "The Legacy of Military Rule in Pakistan," *Survival* 31, no. 3 (1989): 261.
43. C. Christine Fair and Shuja Nawaz, "The Changing Pakistan Army Officer Corps," *Journal of Strategic Studies* 34, no. 1 (February 2011): 63–94.
44. Rounaq Jahan, *Pakistan: Failure in National Integration* (New York: Columbia University Press, 1972), 24; Frédéric Grare, "Does Democracy have a Chance in Pakistan," in *Pakistan: the Struggle Within,* ed., Wilson John (Delhi: Pearson-Longman, 2009), 9; Kavita R. Khory, "National Integration and Politics of Identity in Pakistan," *Nationalism and Ethnic Politics* 1, no. 4 (Winter 1995): 23–43.
45. Huntington, *Political Order in Changing Societies,* 244.

46. Proclamation by the President of Pakistan, October 7, 1958 (No.F. 81/Pres/58, October 25, 1958, *Gazette*, 31st), accessed on November 30, 2011, http://www.therepublicofrumi.com/archives/58ml.htm.

47. Pamela Constable, "Pakistan's Predicament," *Journal of Democracy* 12, no. 1 (January 2001): 15–29.

48. Hasan-Askari Rizvi, "The Paradox of Military Rule in Pakistan," *Asian Survey* 24, no. 5 (May 1984): 536.

49. Rizvi, *The Military and Politics in Pakistan*, 63.

50. *The Statesman*, October 28, 1950, quoted in Rizvi, *The Military and Politics in Pakistan*, 63.

51. Maya Chadda, *Building Democracy in South Asia*, (Boulder, Co: Lynne Reinner, 2000), 61.

52. Ibid., 32–3.

53. On Bhutto, see Shahid Javed Burki, *Pakistan Under Bhutto, 1971–1977* (New York: St. Martin's Press, 1980).

54. Kavita Khory pointed this out to me.

55. Stephen P. Cohen, *Shooting for a Century: The India Pakistan Conundrum* (Washington, DC: Brookings Institution, forthcoming), 142.

56. Alavi, "Class and State", 66–7.

57. Baldev Raj Nayar, *The Geopolitics of Globalization: The Consequences for Development* (New Delhi: Oxford University Press, 2005), 240–1.

58. Babr Sattar, "Pakistan: Return to Praetorianism," in *Coercion and Governance: the Declining Political Role of the Military in Asia*, ed. Muthiah Alagappa (Palo Alto: Stanford University Press, 2001), 397–8.

59. Ayesha Siddiqa, *Military Inc: Inside Pakistan's Military Economy* (London: Pluto Press, 2007), 115.

60. Ibid., 119–28.

61. Ibid., 5.

62. *Interview with the Author*, Copenhagen, June 19, 2013.

63. Daron Acemoğlu and James A. Robinson, *Economic Origins of Dictatorship and Democracy* (Cambridge: Cambridge University Press, 2006), 15.

64. Barrington Moore Jr., *Social Origins of Dictatorship and Democracy* (Boston: Beacon Press, 1966), 418.

65. Dietrich Rueschemeyer, Evelyne Huber and John D. Stephens, *Capitalist Development and Democracy* (Chicago: University of Chicago Press, 1992), 8.

66. Eva Bellin, "Contingent Democrats: Industrialists, Labor, and Democratization in Late-Developing Countries," *World Politics* 52, no. 2 (January 2000), 177.

67. Acemoğlu and Robinson, *Economic Origins*, 39.

68. Khalid B. Sayeed, *Politics in Pakistan: The Nature and Direction of Change* (New York: Praeger, 1980), 57.

69. Jahan, *Pakistan: Failure in National Integration*, 57–58.

70. Acemoğlu and Robinson, *Economic Origins*, 32. Pakistan typifies the argument that "authoritarianism predominates in those countries in which both

the level of inequality and the lack of capital mobility are high." Charles Boix, *Democracy and Redistribution* (Cambridge: Cambridge University Press, 2003), 3.

71. Shuja Nawaz, "The Clash of Interests and Objectives" in *The Future of Pakistan*, ed., Stephen P. Cohen (Washington, DC: Brookings Institution Press, 2011), 150. The per capita income remained at $2.50 in ppp terms. Muddassar Mazhar Malik, "Boosting Competiveness," in *Pakistan: Beyond the "Crisis State,"* ed., Maleeha Lodhi (New York: Columbia University Press, 2011), 201.

72. For discussions of the growing extremism of middle-class Pakistanis see, Graeme Blair, C. Christine Fair, Neil Malhotra, and Jacob N. Shapiro, "Pakistan's Middle Class Extremists: Why Development Aid Won't Solve Radicalism," *Foreign Affairs*, July 11, 2011, accessed on November 30, 2012, http://www.foreignaffairs.com/articles/67976/ graeme-blair-c-christine-fair-neil-malhotra-jacob-n-shapiro/pakistans-middle-class-extremists?cid=soc-tumblr-snapshots-pakistans_middle_class_extremists-071211. Also see, Stephen P. Cohen, "The Jihadist Threat to Pakistan," *The Washington Quarterly* 26, no. 3 (Summer 2003): 7–25.

73. C. Christine Fair, "Who are Pakistan's Militants and their Families?," *Terrorism and Political Violence* 20, no. 1 (January 2008), 49–65.

74. Rizvi, *The Military and Politics*, 107.

75. More than half of the 5000 sample of 18–29-year-olds expressed the view that democracy was not good for Pakistan. "Pakistani Youth 'Cool on Democracy'," *BBC World News*, April 2, 2013, accessed May 30, 2013, http:// www.bbc.co.uk/news/world-22001263.

76. Asif Choudary, "Youth Brings Color and Energy to Election," *The Dawn*, May 12, 2013, accessed May 30, 2013, http://dawn.com/2013/05/12/ youth-brings-colour-and-energy-to-election/.

77. On this, see Snyder, *The Ideology of the Offensive*, chapter 1.

78. Julian Schofield, *Militarization and War* (New York: Palgrave-Macmillan, 2007), 15.

79. Robert Jervis, *Perception and Misperception in International Politics* (Princeton, NJ: Princeton University Press, 1976), 102; Schofield, *Militarization and War*, 20.

80. Stephen Van Evera, *More Causes of War: Misperception and the Roots of Conflict*, unpublished book manuscript (Cambridge, MA: MIT, November 2011), 39.

81. Russell J. Leng, *Bargaining and Learning in Recurring Crises* (Ann Arbor: University of Michigan Press, 2000), 260.

82. Russell J. Leng, "Realpolitik and Learning in the India-Pakistan Rivalry," in *The India Pakistan-Conflict*, ed., Paul, 112.

83. Cohen, *The Idea of Pakistan*, 77.

84. Howard B. Schaffer and Teresita C. Schaffer, *How Pakistan Negotiates with the United States* (Washington, DC: United States Institute of Peace, 2011), 37–38.

85. Cohen, *The Idea of Pakistan*, 103.

86. Rizvi, *The Military and Politics*, 59–60.

87. Ahmad Faruqui, *Rethinking the National Security of Pakistan* (Hampshire: Ashgate, 2003), 48.

88. Shaun Gregory and James Revill, "The Role of the Military in the Cohesion and Stability of Pakistan," *Contemporary South Asia* 16, no. 1 (March 2008): 53.

Chapter 5

1. Cited in Feroz Hassan Khan, *Eating Grass: The Making of the Pakistani Bomb* (Palo Alto: Stanford University Press, 2012), 87.

2. Zulfikar Ali Bhutto, *If I Am Assassinated* (New Delhi: Vikas Publishing House, 1979), 138.

3. John Ward Anderson and Kamran Khan, "Pakistan Sets Off Nuclear Blasts," *Washington Post*, May 29, 1998, A.01.

4. Deborah Welch Larson, T. V. Paul, and William C. Wohlforth, "Status and World Order," in *Status in World Politics*, eds. Paul, Larson, and Wohlforth, (Cambridge: Cambridge University Press, 2014), chapter 1.

5. The Bolan Pass that opens through the Toba Kakkar region of Baluchistan has been another route for invaders to the subcontinent.

6. See Larry P. Goodson, *Afghanistan's Endless War: State Failure, Regional Politics, and the Rise of the Taliban* (Seattle: University of Washington Press, 2001), 131–136. For a succinct discussion of the "great game" see David Fromkin, "The Great Game in Asia," *Foreign Affairs* 58, no. 4 (Spring 1980), 936–951.

7. Peter Hopkirk, *The Great Game: On Secret Service in High Asia* (London: John Murray, 1990), 4.

8. Hassan Abbas, *Pakistan's Drift Into Extremism* (Armonk: M.E. Sharpe, 2005), 3–40.

9. Stanley Wolpert, *India* (Berkeley, CA: University of California Press, 1999), 40–44. See also, Hermann Kulke and Dietmar Rothermund, *A History of India*, 3rd ed. (London: Routledge, 1986), 152–169.

10. See, Annemarie Schimmel *et al.*, *The Empire of the Great Mughals* (New Delhi: Oxford University Press, 2005); Kulke and Rothermund, *A History of India*, 184–197.

11. Ifran Habib, "The Coming of 1857," *Social Scientist* 26, no. 1/4 (January–April 1998): 6–15.

12. Anatol Lieven, *Pakistan: A Hard Country* (London: Allen Lane, 2011), 50.

13. On the reforms among Muslims, see Qamar Hasan, *Muslims in India* (New Delhi: Northern Book Centre, 1988), chapter 1. See also Masood Ashraf

Raja, *Constructing Pakistan: Foundational Texts and the Rise of Muslim National Identity, 1857–1947* (Karachi: Oxford University Press, 2010).

14. Meredith L. Runion, *A History of Afghanistan* (Westport, CT: Greenwood Press, 2007), 76–7; Hopkirk, *The Great Game*.

15. Diana Preston, *The Dark Defile: Britain's Catastrophic Invasion of Afghanistan 1838–1842* (New York: Walker & Company, 2012); Edgar O' Ballance, *Afghan Wars: Battles in a Hostile Land, 1839 to the Present* (London: Brassey's, 2002), 18–28; Seth G. Jones, *In the Graveyard of Empires: America's War in Afghanistan* (New York: W. W. Norton, 2009).

16. Asta Olesen, *Islam and Politics in Afghanistan* (Richmond: Curzon, 1995), 27–28; See also, O' Ballance, *Afghan Wars*, 29–49.

17. Runion, *The History of Afghanistan*, 88–90.

18. Lawrence Ziring, "Weak State, Failed State, Garrison State: The Pakistan Saga," in *South Asia's Weak States: Understanding the Regional Insecurity Predicament*, ed., T. V. Paul (Palo Alto: Stanford University Press, 2010), 176.

19. Askari, *The Military and Politics in Pakistan*, 52–53.

20. On this dispute, see Bijan Omrani, "The Durand Line: History and Problems of the Afghan-Pakistan Border," *Asian Affairs*, 40, no. 2 (July 2009), 177–195

21. Reunion, *The History of Afghanistan*, 105–125.

22. The notion of "strategic depth" assumes Afghanistan offers a "safe back yard" enabling "Pakistan to better absorb and Indian blitzkrieg." Vali Nasr, "National Identities and the India-Pakistan Conflict," in *The India-Pakistan Conflict: An Enduring Rivalry*, ed. T. V. Paul (Cambridge: Cambridge University Press, 2005), 188.

23. Hopkirk, *The Great Game*, 6.

24. Ahmed Rashid, *Descent into Chaos* (New York: Viking, 2008), 25.

25. Ayesha Siddiqa, "Can Non-Provocative Defence Work for Pakistan?," in *International Relations in South Asia: Search for an Alternative Paradigm*, ed. Navnita Chadha Behera (New Delhi: Sage Publications, 2008), 240.

26. See Hasan-Askari Rizvi, "Pakistan's Strategic Culture," in *South Asia in 2020: Future Strategic Balances and Alliances*, ed. Michael R. Chambers (Carlisle, PA: Strategic Studies Institute, U.S. Army War College, 2002), 305–328.

27. Jean-Luc Racine, "Pakistan and the 'India Syndrome': Between Kashmir and the Nuclear Predicament," in *Pakistan: Nationalism without a Nation,* ed. Christophe Jaffrelot (London: Zed Books, 2002), 198–199.

28. Arun Shourie, "Arch Enemy or 'Naya dil,'" three-part series in *www.indianexpress.com*, May 11–13, 2005. On India's search for great power status, see, Baldev Raj Nayar and T. V. Paul, *India in the World Order: Searching for Major Power Status* (Cambridge: Cambridge University Press, 2002); Stephen P. Cohen, *India: Emerging Power* (Washington, DC: Brookings Institution Press, 2001); David M. Malone, *Does the Elephant Dance: Contemporary Indian Foreign Policy* (New York: Oxford University Press, 2011).

29. Ahmed Rashid, "The Anarchic Republic of Pakistan," *National Interest* 109 (September-October 2010): 23.

30. Ayesha Jalal, *The Sole Spokesman: Jinnah, the Muslim League and the Demand for Pakistan* (Cambridge, UK: Cambridge University Press, 1994), 276.

31. Penderel Moon, *Divide and Quit* (Berkeley: University of California Press, 1962), 52.

32. M.J. Akbar, *Tinderbox: The Past and Future of Pakistan* (New Delhi: Harper Collins, 2011), xi.

33. Farzana Shaikh, *Making Sense of Pakistan* (New York: Columbia University Press, 2009), 44.

34. Iqbal Akhund, *Trial and Error: The Advent and Eclipse of Benazir Bhutto* (Karachi: Oxford University Press, 2000), 116.

35. White Paper on Jammu Kashmir (Government of India, 85), cited in Hasan Askari Rizvi, *The Military and Politics in Pakistan* (Lahore: Progressive Publishers, 1974), 49.

36. Navnita Chadha Behera, *Demystifying Kashmir* (New Delhi: Dorling Kindersley, 2007), 69.

37. This section draws from T. V. Paul, "Why Has the India-Pakistan Rivalry Been So Enduring? Power Asymmetry and an Intractable Conflict," *Security Studies* 15, no. 4 (October-December 2006): 600–30.

38. On this, see P.R. Chari and Pervez Iqbal Cheema, *The Simla Agreement 1972: Its Wasted Promise* (New Delhi: Manohar, 2001).

39. Raju G.C. Thomas, *Indian Security Policy* (Princeton: Princeton University Press, 1986), 22–23.

40. On the role of limited probes in deterrence relationships, see Alexander George and Richard Smoke, *Deterrence in American Foreign Policy* (New York: Columbia University Press, 1974).

41. The Indian Parliamentary Standing Committee on Defense acknowledged in April 2002 that India's conventional superiority vis-à-vis Pakistan's military was barely 1:1.2 and at the time of Kargil conflict it stood at 1:1.1. Cited in Lt. Gen. (Retd.) V. K. Sood and Pravin Sawhney, *Operation Parakram: The War Unfinished* (New Delhi: Sage Publications, 2003), 158–9.

42. Ibid., 76–7.

43. Khalid Hasan, "Pakistan's Nuclear Assets Safe and Secure: Gen. Aslam Beg," *Daily Times*, August 2, 2003, accessed November 30, 2012, http://www.dailytimes.com.pk/default.asp?page=story_2-8-2003_pg7_13.

44. On this see Peter R. Lavoy, "Pakistan's Nuclear Doctrine," in *Prospects for Peace in South Asia*, ed. by Rafiq Dossani and Henry S. Rowen (Palo Alto: Stanford University Press, 2005), 280–300; Rajesh M. Basrur, *Minimum Deterrence and India's Nuclear Security* (Palo Alto: Stanford University Press, 2006); Rajesh Rajagopalan, *Second Strike: Arguments about Nuclear War in South Asia* (New Delhi: Penguin-Viking, 2005), chapters 3 and 4; Tim D. Hoytt, "Pakistani Nuclear Doctrine and The Dangers of Strategic Myopia," *Asian Survey* 41, no. 6 (November/December 2001), 956–77; Scott D. Sagan, "The Evolution of Pakistani and Indian Nuclear Doctrine," in *Inside Nuclear South Asia*, ed., Sagan (Palo Alto: Stanford University Press, 2009), 219–63.

45. See Jonathan Marcus, "India-Pakistan Military Balance," *BBC*, accessed November 30, 2012, http://newsvote.bbc.co.uk/mpapps/pagetools/print/

news.bbc.co.uk/2/hi/south_asia/17359. For the progress in arms purchases, see International Institute for Strategic Studies, *Military Balance 2005–06* (London: IISS, 2005), 254–6.

46. Sam Pearlo-Freeman, Julian Cooper, Olawale Ismail, Elisabeth Skons, and Carina Solmirano, "Military Expenditure: India," *SIPRI Yearbook 2011: Armaments Disarmament and International Security* (Oxford: Oxford University Press, 2011), 166–70.

47. Sunil Dasgupta and Stephen P. Cohen, "Is India Ending its Strategic Restraint Doctrine?" *The Washington Quarterly* 34, no. 2 (Spring 2011): 163–77.

48. Vipin Narang, "Posturing for Peace? Pakistan's Nuclear Postures and South Asian Stability," *International Security* 34, no. 3 (Winter 2009/10): 76.

49. International Crisis Group, "The State of Sectarianism in Pakistan," Asia Report 95 (April 18, 2005). See also Cohen, *The Idea of Pakistan*, chapter 5.

50. Siddiqa, "Can Non-Provocative Defense Work," 244.

51. For this assessment, see Anthony H. Cordesman, "The India-Pakistan Military Balance," (Washington, DC: Center for Strategic and International Studies, 2002), 3, accessed November 30, 2012, http://csis.org/files/media/csis/pubs/india_pak_mb%5B1%5D.pdf.

52. Jean-Luc Racine, "Pakistan and the 'India Syndrome': Between Kashmir and the Nuclear Predicament," in *Pakistan: Nationalism without a Nation*, ed. Christophe Jaffrelot (London: Zed Books, 2002), 198–199.

53. General V. P. Malik, "Kargil: Where Defence Met Diplomacy," *The Indian Express*, July 25, 2002.

54. Strobe Talbott, *Engaging India: Diplomacy, Democracy and the Bomb* (Washington, DC: Brookings Institution Press, 2004), chapter 8; Bruce Riedel, "American Diplomacy and the 1999 Kargil Summit at Blair House."

55. On this see General V. P. Malik, *Kargil: From Surprise to Victory* (New Delhi: Harper Collins, 2006). See also "World: South Asia—Clinton Urges India-Pakistan Talks," *BBC News*, July 5, 1999, accessed on November 30, 2012, http://news.bbc.co.uk/2/hi/south_asia/385534.stm.

56. Racine, "Pakistan and the 'India Syndrome,' " 199.

57. Hans M. Kristensen and Robert S. Norris, "Pakistan's Nuclear Forces, 2011," *Bulletin of the Atomic Scientists* 67, no. 4 (July 2011): 96–104.

58. See T. V. Paul, *The Tradition of Non-Use of Nuclear Weapons* (Palo Alto: Stanford University Press, 2009).

59. On this see, Subhash Kapila, "India's New 'Cold Start' War Doctrine Strategically Reviewed," *South Asia Analysis Group*, paper no. 991 (May 4, 2004).

60. Hussain Haqqani, *Pakistan: Between Mosque and Military* (Washington, DC: Brookings Institution Press, 2005), 323.

61. On the US policy toward Pakistan and India in the 1950s, see Robert J. McMahon, *Cold War in the Periphery: The United States, India and Pakistan* (New York: Columbia University Press, 1994).

62. Cohen argues that Pakistani leaders presented to the United States as a "Muslim Israel: loyal to Western values, committed to the same God as

Christians and Jews," and they portrayed themselves "as the Muslim David facing a Hindu Goliath—perhaps a smaller state, but one that was much tougher." This argument was used by Pakistani leaders "with considerable success until the fall of the Soviet Union." Stephen P. Cohen, *Shooting for a Century: The India Pakistan Conundrum* (Washington, DC: Brookings Institution, forthcoming), 96.

63. See McMahon, *Cold War in the Periphery*, 209–10; Dennis Kux, *The United States and Pakistan 1947–2000* (Washington, DC: Woodrow Wilson Center Press, 2002).

64. Ayub Khan, *Friends Not Masters*, 154.

65. For more on this, see Nayar and Paul, *India in the World Order*, 70–78.

66. For these, see Shirin Tahir-Kheli, *The United States and Pakistan: The Evolution of an Influence Relationship* (New York: Praeger, 1982), 2–10.

67. Ibid., 21.

68. McMahon, *The Cold War on the Periphery*.

69. On this, see Gary J. Bass, *The Blood Telegram* (New York: Knopf, 2013).

70. Marvin G. Weinbaum, "Pakistan and Afghanistan: the Strategic Relationship," *Asian Survey* 31, no. 6 (June 1991): 498. See also A. Z. Hilali, *US-Pakistan Relationship: Soviet Invasion of Afghanistan* (Aldershopt, Hants: Ashgate, 2005), 139–86.

71. Mark Hibbs, "Pakistan's Bomb," *The Nonproliferation Review* 15, no. 2 (2008): 381–91.

72. Douglas Frantz and Catherine Collins, *The Nuclear Jihadist* (New York: Twelve, 2007), 364.

73. See David Armstrong and Joseph Trento, *America and the Islamic Bomb: The Deadly Compromise* (Hanover, NH: Steerforth Press, 2007); Douglas Frantz and Catherine Collins, *Nuclear Jihadists* (New York: Twelve, 2007); Adrian Levy and Catherine Scott-Clark, *Deception: Pakistan, The United States and Secret Trade in Nuclear Weapons* (London: Atlantic Books, 2007).

74. Rasul Bakhsh Rais, *Recovering the Frontier State: War, Ethnicity, and State in Afghanistan* (Lanham, MD: Lexington Books, 2008), 70.

75. Rais, *Recovering the Frontier State*, 71.

76. For more see, Talbott, *Engaging India*; C. Raja Mohan, *Crossing the Rubicon: Shaping of India's New Foreign Policy* (New York: Palgrave-Macmillan, 2003).

77. Condoleezza Rice, *No Higher Honor: A Memoir of My Years in Washington* (New York: Crown, 2011), 128–30, 696–700.

78. Howard B. Schaffer and Teresita C. Schaffer, *How Pakistan Negotiates with the United States* (Washington, DC: US Institute of Peace Press, 2011), 24.

79. On this, see T. V. Paul, "Chinese/Pakistani Nuclear/Missile Ties and Balance of Power Politics," *The Nonproliferation Review*, 10, no. 2 (Summer 2003): 1–9. On the China-Pakistan-India strategic triangle, see Mohan Malik, *China and India: Great Power Rivals* (Boulder, CO: Lynne Rienner, 2011), chapter 6.

80. See Richard Sisson and Leo E. Rose, *War and Secession: Pakistan, India and the Creation of Bangladesh* (Berkeley, CA: University of California Press, 1990), 247–253.

81. On this, see Daniel L. Byman and Roger Cliff, *China's Arms Sales: Motivations and Implications* (Santa Monica: Rand, 1999), 14–16.

82. See Paul, "Chinese/Pakistani Nuclear/Missile Ties."

83. J. Mohan Malik, "South Asia in China's Foreign Relations," *Pacifica Review* 13, no. 1 (February 2001), 74.

84. However, the economic ties, especially in terms of exports and imports, still remain low and balance of payments remains in China's favor, partially because of the lack of products that Pakistan can export to China. Mohan Guruswami, "The China Factor," in *The Future of Pakistan*, ed. Stephen P. Cohen (Washington, DC: Brookings Institution Press, 2011), 129.

85. "China Poised to Control Strategic Pakistani Port," *The Dawn*, February 2, 2013, accessed February 3, 2013, http://dawn.com/2013/02/02/china-poised-to-control-strategic-pakistani-port/.

86. William T. Tow, "China and the International Strategic System," in *Chinese Foreign Policy: Theory and Practice*, ed. Thomas W. Robinson and David Shambaugh (Oxford: Oxford University Press, 1995), 152.

87. Robert S. Ross, "Engagement in US., China Policy," in *Engaging China: The Management of an Emerging Power*, ed. Alastair Iain Johnston and Robert S. Ross (London and New York: Routledge, 1999), 193.

88. John W. Garver, "China and South Asia," *Annals of the American Academy of Political and Social Science*, 519 (January 1992): 79–83.

89. Estimates are for 2011 and come from IISS, *The Military Balance 2012* (London: Routledge, 2012) and from the CIA *World Factbook*. See also Veena Kukreja, *Contemporary Pakistan* (New Delhi: Sage Publications, 2003), 62.

Chapter 6

1. Quoted in Ian Talbot, *Pakistan: A Modern History* (New York: St. Martin's Press, 1998), 1.

2. Kable Ali, "Islam Should Serve as Unifying Force: Kayani," *Dawn*, April 21, 2013, accessed May 30, 2013, http://dawn.com/2013/04/21/islam-should-serve-as-unifying-force-kayani/.

3. Seyyed Vali Reza Nasr, "State, Society, and the Crisis of National Identity in Pakistan," in *State, Society, and Democratic Change in Pakistan*, ed., Rasul B. Rais (New York: Oxford University Press, 1997), 106–7.

4. Graeme Blair, C. Christine Fair, Neil Malhotra, and Jacob N. Shapiro, "Pakistan's Middle Class Extremists: Why Development Aid Won't Solve Radicalism," *Foreign Affairs Online Edition*, July 2011, accessed November 30, 2012, http://www.foreignaffairs.com/articles/67976/graeme-blair-c-christine-fair-neil-malhotra-jacob-n-shapiro/pakistans-middle-class-extremists.

5. "Muslims Believe US Seeks to Undermine Islam," April 24, 2007, accessed November 30, 2012, http://www.worldpublicopinion.org/pipa/articles/

brmiddleeastnafricara/346.php. See also Pervez Hoodbhoy, "Jinnah and the Islamic State: Setting the Record Straight," *Economic and Political Weekly*, August 11, 2007: 3300.

6. Owen Bennett Jones, *Pakistan: Eye of the Storm* (New Haven: Yale University Press, 2002), 14. On the consequences of this attitude, see Wilson John, *Coming Blowback: How Pakistan is Endangering the World* (New Delhi: Rupa, 2009).

7. Muhammad Qasim Zaman, "Pluralism, Democracy, and the 'Ulama,' " in *Remaking Muslim Politics: Pluralism, Contestation and Democratization*, ed., Robert W. Hefner (Princeton: Princeton University Press, 2005), 71.

8. Anwar H. Syed, "The Sunni-Shia Conflict in Pakistan," in *Founder's Aspirations and Today's Realities*, ed., Hafeez Malik (Karachi: Oxford University Press, 2001), 245.

9. Jones, *Eye of the Storm*, 9.

10. Ibid., 10.

11. Muhammad Qasim Zaman, "Sectarianism in Pakistan: The Radicalization of Shi'i and Sunni Identities," *Modern Asian Studies* 32, no. 3 (July 1998): 689–716.

12. Vali Nasr, The *Shia Revival* (New York: W.W. Norton, 2007), 89–90.

13. Ibid., 88.

14. John L. Esposito, *Islam: The Straight Path*, 3rd ed. (New York: Oxford University Press, 2005), 102.

15. Ibid., 101.

16. Ayesha Jalal, *The Sole Spokesman: Jinnah, the Muslim League and the Demand for Pakistan* (Cambridge: Cambridge University Press, 1985), 3.

17. Maya Chadda, *Building Democracy in South Asia* (Boulder, CO: Lynne Reinner, 2000), 27.

18. Jones, *Eye of the Storm*, 109.

19. Ibid., 111.

20. Ambreen Agha, "Karachi Murder Hub," *South Asia Intelligence Review* 10, no. 1, July 11, 2011, accessed November 30, 2012, http://www.satp.org/satporgtp/sair/Archives/sair10/10_1.htm.

21. Jones, *Eye of the Storm,* 113.

22. On these see, Theodore P. Wright. Jr., "Center-Periphery Relations and Ethnic Conflict in Pakistan: Sindhis, Muhajirs, and Punjabis," *Comparative Politics* 23, no. 3 (April 1991): 299–312.

23. For a succinct summary of these grievances, see Alok Bansal, *Balochistan in Turmoil* (New Delhi: Manas Publications, 2010), 219–249.

24. Paul Titus and Nina Swidler, "Knights, Not Pawns: Ethno-Nationalism and Regional Dynamics in Post-Colonial Balochistan," *International Journal of Middle East Studies* 32 (February 2000), 64.

25. Malik Siraj Akbar, *The Redefined Dimensions of Baloch Nationalist Movement* (New York: Xlibris Corporation, 2011), 221–223; Declan Walsh, "Pakistan's Secret Dirty War," *The Guardian*, March 29, 2011, accessed November 30, 2012, http://www.guardian.co.uk/world/2011/mar/29/balochistan-pakistans-secret-dirty-war.

26. Carlotta Gall, "Pakistan's Bitter, Little-known Ethnic Rebellion," *The New York Times*, August 23, 2011, accessed November 30, 2012, http://www.nytimes.com/2011/08/24/world/asia/24baluch.html?pagewanted=all.

27. S. Akbar Zaidi, "Religious Minorities in Pakistan Today," *Journal of Contemporary Asia* 18, no. 4 (1988): 453.

28. See the full report, *A Question of Faith: A Report on the Status of Religious Minorities in Pakistan*, Jinnah Institute, 2011, accessed November 30, 2012, http://www.humanrights.asia/opinions/columns/pdf/AHRC-ETC-022-2011-01.pdf.

29. Stanley Wolpert, *Jinnah of Pakistan* (New York: Oxford University Press, 1984), 4.

30. Mohammed Ayoob, *The Many Faces of Political Islam: Religion and Politics in the Muslim World* (Ann Arbor: University of Michigan Press, 2008), 66.

31. Peter Mandaville, *Global Political Islam* (London: Routledge, 2007), 64–5. See also, Khalid B. Sayeed, "The Jama'at—Islami Movement in Pakistan," *Pacific Affairs* 30, no. 1 (March 1957): 59–68; Aziz Ahmad, "Mawdudi and Orthodox Fundamentalism in Pakistan," *Middle East Journal* 21, no. 3 (Summer 1967): 369–80.

32. Mandaville, *Global Political Islam*, 169.

33. Ibid., 170.

34. Khalid Bin Sayeed, "Religion and Nation Building in Pakistan," *Middle East Journal* 17, no. 3 (Summer 1963): 290.

35. Jones, *Eye of the Storm*, 14–15.

36. Mandaville, *Global Political Islam*, 170; Haqqani, *Between Mosque and Military*, 47–50.

37. Mandaville, *Global Political Islam*, 172.

38. Sadia Saeed, "Pakistani Nationalism and the State Marginalization of the Ahmadiyya Community in Pakistan," *Studies in Ethnicity and Nationalism* 7, no. 3 (2007): 135.

39. Zaman, "Pluralism, Democracy, and the 'Ulama,'" 72.

40. Jones, *Eye of the Storm*, 15–16.

41. Hussain, *Frontline Pakistan*, 14.

42. Anatol Lieven, *Pakistan: A Hard Country* (London: Allan Lane, 2011), 76.

43. Zaman, "Pluralism, Democracy, and the 'Ulama,'" 72.

44. Mandaville, *Global Political Islam*, 173.

45. Jones, *Eye of the Storm*, 17.

46. Saeed, "Pakistani nationalism . . . ," 140; Naveeda Khan, *Muslim Becoming: Aspiration and Skepticism in Pakistan* (Durham, NC: Duke University Press, 2012), 108–9.

47. Zaman "Pluralism, Democracy, and the 'Ulama,'" 72–3.

48. Jones, *Eye of the Storm*, 16.

49. Mandaville, *Global Political Islam*, 173.

50. Charles H. Kennedy, "Islamization in Pakistan: Implementation of the Hudood Ordinances," *Asian Survey* 28, no. 3 (March 1988): 308.

51. Jones, *Eye of the Storm*, 17.

52. Ibid.

53. Zahid Hussain, *Frontline Pakistan: The Struggle with Militant Islam* (New York: Columbia University Press, 2007), 19–21.

54. Veena Kukreja, *Contemporary Pakistan* (New Delhi: Sage Publications, 2003), 68–71.

55. A.R. Siddiqi, "Army Chickens are Coming home to Roost," *The Nation*, October 23, 1995, Cited in Kukreja, *Contemporary Pakistan*.

56. For the training and the numbers, see Bruce Riedel, *Deadly Embrace: Pakistan, America and the Future of the Global Jihad* (Washington, DC: Brookings Institution Press, 2011), 28–33.

57. Jones, *Eye of the Storm*, 17–18. See also, Vali R. Nasr, "Islam, the State and the Rise of Sectarian Militancy in Pakistan," in *Pakistan: Nationalism without a Nation?*, ed., Christophe Jaffrelot (New Delhi: Manohar Publishers, 2002), 102–109; Vali R. Nasr, "International Politics, Domestic Imperatives, and Identity Mobilization: Sectarianism in Pakistan, 1979–1998," *Comparative Politics* 32, no. 2 (January 2000), 171–90.

58. Jones, *Eye of the Storm*, 18.

59. Zaman, "Pluralism, Democracy, and the 'Ulama,' " 73.

60. Hussain, *Frontline Pakistan*, 8.

61. Husain Haqqani, "The Role of Islam in Pakistan's Future," *The Washington Quarterly* 28, no. 1 (Winter 2004–05): 91–93; Vali Nasr, "Military Rule, Islamism, and Democracy in Pakistan," *Middle East Journal* 58, no. 2 (Spring 2004): 202–209.

62. Mandeville, *Global Political Islam, 176*. See also, Haroon K. Ullah, *Vying for Allah's Vote: Understanding Islamic Political Parties, Political Violence, and Extremism in Pakistan* (Washington DC:, Georgetown University Press, 2013).

63. Karin Brullard, "In Pakistan even Anti-violence Islamic Sect Lauds Assassination of Liberal Governor," *Washington Post*, January 29, 2011.

64. Sarah A. Topol, "Pakistan Confronts Deepening Radicalism in Wake of Assassination," aolnews.com, January 14, 2011, accessed on November 30, 2012, http://www.aolnews.com/2011/01/14/pakistan-confronts-deepening-radicalism-in-wake-of-governors-as/.

65. "Pakistan Dismisses Blasphemy Case against Christian Girl after Global Uproar," Reuters, November 20, 2012, accessed November 30, 2012, http://blogs.reuters.com/faithworld/2012/11/20/pakistan-dismisses-blasphemy-case-against-christian-girl-after-global-uproar/.

66. John L. Esposito, *Islam: The Straight Path* (New York: Oxford University Press, 1988), 120.

67. For the Wahhabi teachings, see David Commins, *The Wahhabi Mission and Saudi Arabia* (London: I. B. Tauris, 2006).

68. Benazir Bhutto, *Reconciliation: Islam, Democracy and the West* (New York: Harper Collins, 2008), 51.

69. For a discussion on the origins of Wahhabism see, Michael Cook, "On the Origins of Wahhabism," *Journal of the Royal Asiatic Society of Great Britain and Ireland* 2, no. 2 (July 1992), 191–202. See also, Mushtaq K. Lodi, *Islam and the West: The Clash Between Islamism and Secularism* (Durham, CT: Strategic Book Club, 2011), 65–83.

70. John L. Esposito, *What Everyone Needs to Know About Islam* (Oxford: Oxford University Press, 2011), 53–5. See also Dale F. Eickelman and James Piscatori, *Muslim Politics* (Princeton: Princeton University Press, 1996), 60–3.

71. Ahmed Rashid, *Jihad: The Rise of Militant Islam in Central Asia* (New York: Penguin, 2002), 224.

72. C. Christine Fair, *The Madrassah Challenge* (Washington, DC: United States Institute of Peace Press, 2008), 56.

73. S. V. R. Nasr, "The Rise of Sunni Militancy in Pakistan: The Changing Role of Islamism and the Ulama in Society and Politics," *Modern Asian Studies* 34, no. 1 (February 2000), 142.

74. Mumtaz Ahmad, "Madrassa Education in Pakistan and Bangladesh," *Religious Radicalism and Security In South Asia*, ed. Satu P. Limaye, Mohan Malik, Robert G. Wirsing (Honolulu: Asia-Pacific Center for Security Studies, 2004), 103. For a contrary perspective, see Jaddon Park and Sarfaroz Niyozov, "Madrasa Education in South Asia and Southeast Asia: Current Issues and Debates," *Asia Pacific Journal of Education*, 28, no. 4 (December 2008): 323–351.

75. See, Husain Haqqani, "Islam's Medieval Outposts," *Foreign Policy*, no. 133 (November/December 2002), 58–64.

76. Zaman, "Pluralism, Democracy, and the 'Ulama,'" 76; See Riaz Ahmed Shaikh, "Developing Extremists: Madrasah Education in Pakistan," in *Development in Asia: Interdisciplinary, Post-Neoliberal, and Transnational Perspectives*, ed. Derrick M. Nault (Boca Raton, FL: Brown Walker Press, 2009).

77. "Pakistan Schools teach Hindu Hatred," *The Dawn*, November 9, 2011, accessed November 30, 2012, http://dawn.com/2011/11/09/pakistan-schools-teach-hindu-hatred/.

78. Hassan Abbas, *Pakistan can Defy the Odds: How to Rescue a Failing State* (Michigan: Institute for Social Policy and Understanding, May 2009), 20.

79. Sanchita Bhattacharya, "Pakistan: Destroying the Future," *South Asia Intelligence Review* 11, no. 47 (May 27, 2013), 4.

80. United Nations Children's Fund, *Situational Analysis of Children and Women in Pakistan* (Islamabad) (June 12, 2012), 74, accessed May 30, 2013, http://www.unicef.org/pakistan/National_Report.pdf.

81. Kanchan Lakshman, "An Education in Failure," *South Asia Intelligence Review* 8 no. 12 (September 28, 2009), 2.

82. Blair *et al.*, "Pakistan's Middle Class Extremists."

83. Fair, *The Madrassah Challenge*, 68–9.

84. Umer Faroog, "Islam in the Garrison," *Herald Beta*, August 16, 2011, accessed December 13, 2012, http://herald.dawn.com/2011/08/16/islam-in-the-garrison.html.

85. Hussain, *Frontline Pakistan*, 9.

86. Ibid., 13.

87. Mark Mazetti, Scott Shane, and Alissa J. Rubin, "A Brutal Haqqani Crime Clan Bedevils the U.S.," *The New York Times,* September 14, 2011, accessed November 30, 2012, http://www.nytimes.com/2011/09/25/world/asia/brutal-haqqani-clan-bedevils-united-states-in-afghanistan.html?pagewanted=all.

88. M. J. Akbar, *Tinderbox: The Past and Future of Pakistan* (New Delhi: Harper Collins, 2011), xv.

Chapter 7

1. Margaret Bourke-White, *Halfway to Freedom; A Report on the New India in the Words and Photographs of Margaret Bourke-White* (New York: Simon & Schuster, 1949), 92–3.

2. Dennis Kux, *The United States and Pakistan 1947–2000: Disenchanted Allies* (Washington, DC: Woodrow Wilson Center Press, 2001), 112–3.

3. Walter Isaacson, *Kissinger: A Biography* (New York: Simon & Schuster, 1992), 343–4.

4. There are obvious differences between Pakistan and these countries. It can be argued that their structural conditions or regional contexts have been somewhat different from Pakistan. For instance, Indonesia does not have a major military conflict with any of its neighbors. Similarly, Turkey's rivalry with Greece is somewhat muted. Egypt was more similar to Pakistan until 1975 as it had an intense rivalry with Israel, although the conflict over Sinai was not similar to Kashmir. However, all these states have one thing is common with Pakistan: overwhelmingly Muslim majority middle-sized states, where the military controlled politics for a long period of their existence claiming they only could offer security, national unity and prosperity. They all had considerable internal security threats and in Turkey and Indonesia's case, it had been the chief rationale for military control over politics, something the Pakistani military also used, although the conflict with India is dominant in the latter case. Both South Korea and Taiwan too have intense rivalries, but the difference is that they receive US security protection much more than Pakistan does or did. As no two countries are similar in all attributes, the comparison is made in the sense that military dominance has not produced the same results in these countries and that most of them have transformed over the years to become democratic and placing the military under civilian control. Turkey and Egypt are the latest cases of civilian assertion, with the latter looking more like Pakistan with the Muslim Brotherhood attempting to turn it into an Islamic state and the military overthrowing the Mohamed Morsi regime in July 2013. The puzzle is why Pakistan has such difficulty

fully taming its military and getting out of the hybrid system. The chapter addresses the similarities and differences between Pakistan and these cases in detail.

5. Andrew Mango, *Atatürk* (London: John Murray, 1999); Stephen Kinzer, *Crescent and Star: Turkey between Two Worlds* (New York: Farrar, Straus and Giroux, 2001).

6. Gerassimos Karabelias, "The Military Institution, Atatürk's Principles, and Turkey's Sisyphean Quest for Democracy," *Middle Eastern Studies* 45, no. 1 (January 2009): 57–69.

7. Ellen Kay Trimberger, *Revolution from Above: Military Bureaucrats and Development in Japan, Turkey, Egypt and Peru* (New Brunswick, NJ: Transaction Books, 1978).

8. Yilmaz Colak, "Nationalism and the State in Turkey: Drawing the Boundaries of 'Turkish Culture' in the 1930s," *Studies in Ethnicity and Nationalism* 3, no. 1 (March 2003): 14; 2–20.

9. Assistance data are in historical dollars, and including loans. Compiled from United States Agency for International Development, "Foreign Assistance Data," accessed August 14, 2012, http://gbk.eads.usaidallnet.gov/data/. Arms transfers are in SIPRI's "Trend Indicator Value," in 1990 US dollars. Compiled from Stockholm International Peace Research Institute, "Arms Transfer Database," accessed August 14, 2012, http://www.sipri.org/research/armaments/transfers/databases/armstransfers.

10. Jim Zanotti, "Turkey-U.S. Defense Cooperation: Prospects and Challenges," *Congressional Research Service Report to Congress* R41761, April 8, 2011, 4.

11. Ali Güngör Işıklar, "An Analysis of Turkish American Relations: Improvement or Deterioration?" (MA Thesis, Naval Postgraduate School, 2008), 80.

12. Aylin Güney, "Anti-Americanism in Turkey: Past and Present," *Middle Eastern Studies* 44, no. 3 (May 2008), 477.

13. Zanotti, "Turkey-U.S. Defense Cooperation," 3.

14. Güney, "Anti-Americanism in Turkey"; Zanotti, "Turkey-U.S. Defense Cooperation," 3.

15. Mustafa Aydın, "Securitization of History and Geography: Understanding of Security in Turkey," *Southeast European and Black Sea Studies* 3, no. 2 (May 2003): 164, 163–84.

16. Gabriella Blum, *Islands of Agreement: Managing Enduring Armed Rivalries* (Cambridge: Harvard University Press, 2007), 137.

17. Meltem Müftüler-Bac and Lauren M. McLaren, "Enlargement Preferences and Policy-Making in the European Union: Impacts on Turkey," *Journal of European Integration* 25, no. 1 (2003), 27; Neill Nugent, "EU Enlargement and 'the Cyprus Problem,'" *Journal of Common Market Studies* 38, no. 1 (March 2000), 142.

18. On this, see Panayotis J. Tsakōnas, *The Incomplete Breakthrough in Greek-Turkish Relations: Grasping Greece's Socialization Strategy* (London: Palgrave-Macmillan, 2010).

19. David McDowall, *A Modern History of the Kurds*, Third ed. (London: I.B. Tauris, 2004), 3; this estimate is confirmed in Central Intelligence Agency, *World Factbook* (Langley, VA: Central Intelligence Agency, 2012).

20. Sabri Sayari, "Turkey and the Middle East in the 1990s," *Journal of Palestine Studies* 26, no. 3 (Spring 1997): 47.

21. David Romano, *The Kurdish Nationalist Movement: Opportunity, Mobilization and Identity* (Cambridge: Cambridge University Press, 2006), 58.

22. McDowall, *Modern History of the Kurds*, 442–3.

23. Umit Cizre, "Demythologizing the National Security Concept: the Case of Turkey," *The Middle East Journal* 57, no. 2 (Spring 2003): 216.

24. Gareth Jenkins, "Context and Circumstance: The Turkish Military and Politics," *Adelphi Paper* 337 (London: International Institute of Strategic Studies, 2001), 33.

25. Dankwart A. Rustow, "Ataturk as Founder of a State," *Daedalus* 97, no. 3 (Summer 1968): 800.

26. Ali L. Karaosmanoğlu, "The Evolution of the National Security Culture and the Military in Turkey," *Journal of International Affairs* 54, no. 1 (Fall 2000): 200.

27. Ibid., 216.

28. Kemal Kirişci, "The Transformation of Turkish Foreign Policy: The Rise of the Trading State," *New Perspectives on Turkey* 40 (2009): 40.

29. World Bank, *World Development Indicators* 2012.

30. M. Asim Karaömerlioğlu, "Elite Perceptions of Land Reforms in Early Republican Turkey," *Journal of Peasant Studies* 27, no. 3 (2000): 115–41.

31. Reşat Aktan, "Problems of Land Reform in Turkey," *Middle East Journal* 20, no. 3 (Summer 1966): 320–2.

32. Ali H. Bayar, "The Developmental State and Economic Policy in Turkey," *Third World Quarterly* 17, no. 4 (1996): 773–86.

33. özay Mehmet, "Turkey in Crisis: Some Contradictions in the Kemalist Development Strategy," *International Journal of Middle East Studies* 15, no. 1 (February 1983): 47–66; David Waldner, *State Building and Late Development* (Ithaca: Cornell University Press, 1999).

34. Kemal Kirişci, "The Transformation of Turkish Foreign Policy," 40.

35. Pinar Tank, "Political Islam in Turkey: A State of Controlled Secularity," *Turkish Studies* 6, no. 1 (March 2005): 6.

36. Ümit Cizre Sakallıoğlu, "Parameters and Strategies of Islamic-State Interaction in Republican Turkey," *International Journal of Middle East Studies* 28, no. 2 (May 1996): 231.

37. Ibid., 238–9.

38. Niyazi Öktem "Religion in Turkey," *Brigham Young University Law Review*, 2 (2002): 371–403.

39. Talip Küçükcan, "State, Islam, and Religious Liberty in Modern Turkey: Reconfiguration of Religion in the Public Sphere," *Brigham Young University Law Review* 2 (2003): 475–506.

40. Malcolm Cooper, "The Legacy of Ataturk: Turkish Political Structures and Policy-making," *International Affairs* 78, no. 1 (January 2002): 118–9.

41. Nilüfer Narlı, "Civil-Military Relations in Turkey," *Turkish Studies* 1, no. 1 (2000), 120.

42. Mustafa Aydın, "Securitization of History and Geography: Understanding of Security in Turkey," *Southeast European and Black Sea Studies* 3, no. 20 (May 2003): 174.

43. On the merits and problems with Turkey's EU membership, see Tarik Oguzlu and Mustafa Kibaroğlu, "Incompatibilities in Turkish and European Security Cultures Diminish Turkey's Prospects for EU Membership," *Middle Eastern Studies* 44, no. 6 (November 2008): 945–62.

44. Anthony Shadid, "Leader Transcends Complex Politics of Turkey," *The New York Times*, May 31, 2011, accessed November 30, 2012. http://www.nytimes.com/2011/06/01/world/europe/01turkey.html?pagewanted=all.

45. William Hale and Ergun Özbudun, *Islamism, Democracy and Liberalism in Turkey: The Case of the AKP* (London: Routledge, 2010), 155.

46. Mehmet Ozkan, "The Ghost of September 12 in Turkey," IDSA Comment, October 7, 2010, accessed November 30, 2012, http://www.idsa.in/idsacomments/TheGhostofSeptember12inTurkey_mozkan_071010.

47. Karabekir Akkoyunlu, "Turkey: the Country of Contrasts," *The Hindu*, October 5, 2010, accessed November 30, 2012, http://www.thehindu.com/opinion/lead/article813038.ece?homepage=true.

48. Gul Tuysuz and Sabrina Tavernise, "Top Generals Quit in Group, Stunning Turks," *The New York Times*, July 29, 2011, accessed November 30, 2012, http://www.nytimes.com/2011/07/30/world/europe/30turkey.html?pagewanted=all.

49. Ivan Watson and Yesim Comert, "Turkish Court Issues Sentences in Coup-plot Case," CNN, September 21, 2012. http://www.cnn.com/2012/09/21/world/europe/turkey-coup-trial/index.html.

50. On this, see Mohammed Ayoob, *The Many Faces of Political Islam* (Ann Arbor: The University of Michigan Press, 2010), chapter 5.

51. Tim Arango, Sebnem Arsu and Ceylan Yeginsu, "Turkish Police and Protesters Clash in Square," *New York Times*, June 11, 2013, accessed July 24, 2013, http://www.nytimes.com/2013/06/12/world/europe/disputed-square-in-istanbul-turkey.html?pagewanted=all

52. Figures are in historical US$ and include $1.8 billion in loans in the Cold War and $3 billion in loans since. Compiled from United States Agency for International Development, "Foreign Assistance Data," accessed August 16, 2012, http://gbk.eads.usaidallnet.gov/data/.

53. The "mild secularism" contains three themes: "separation of state and religion, privatization of religion, and differentiation between religious and non-religious spheres," although religion is present in some fashion all spheres. Moch Nur Ichwan, "Secularism, Islam and Pancasila: Political Debates on the Basis of the State in Indonesia," 3, accessed December 13, 2012, http://www.ic.nanzan-u.ac.jp/ASIAPACIFIC/documents/110228-0301_Ichwan.pdf.

54. Michael Morfit, "Pancasila: The Indonesian State Ideology According to the New Order Government," *Asian Survey* 21, no. 8 (August 1981): 840–1.

55. Harold A. Crouch, *The Army and Politics in Indonesia*, rev. ed., (Ithaca: Cornell University Press, 1978), 22.

56. Geoffrey Robinson, "Indonesia: On a New Course?," in *Coercion and Governance: The Declining Political Role of the Military in Asia*, ed., Muthiah Alagappa (Palo Alto: Stanford University Press, 2001), 227.

57. Ibid., 227.

58. M.C. Ricklefs, *A History of Modern Indonesia since c.* 1200, Third ed. (Palo Alto: Stanford University Press, 2001), 405–7, 417.

59. Freedom House, *Freedom in the World* (New York: Greenwood Press, 2007).

60. Kikue Hamayotsu, "Islam and Nation Building in Southeast Asia: Malaysia and Indonesia in Comparative Perspective," *Pacific Affairs* 75, no. 3 (Autumn 2002): 374.

61. Howard M. Federspiel, "The Military and Islam in Sukarno's Indonesia," *Pacific Affairs* 46, no. 3 (Autumn 1973): 407–20.

62. Allan A. Samson, "Army and Islam in Indonesia," *Pacific Affairs* 44, no. 4 (Winter 1971–1972), 545.

63. Ricklefs, *A History of Modern Indonesia*, 1–17.

64. Robert H. Hefner, "Muslim Democrats and Islamist Violence in Post-Suharto Indonesia," in *Remaking Muslim Politics*, ed. Hefner (Princeton, NJ: Princeton University Press, 2005), 277.

65. Edward Aspinall and Mark T. Berger, "The Break-up of Indonesia? Nationalism after Decolonisation and the Limits of the Nation-State in Post-Cold War Southeast Asia," *Third World Quarterly* 22, no. 6 (December 2001): 1003–24.

66. Jusuf Wanandi, "Indonesia: a Failed State?," *The Washington Quarterly* 25, no. 3 (Summer 2002): 135–46.

67. Stephen McCloskey, "Introduction: East Timor—From European to Third World Colonialism," in *The East Timor Question: The Struggle for Independence from Indonesia*, ed. Paul Hainsworth and Stephen McCloskey (London: I. B. Tauris, 2000), 1–16; Benetech Human Rights Data Analysis Group, "The Profile of Human Rights Violations in Timor-Leste, 1974–1999," report to the Commission on Reception, Truth and Reconciliation of Timor-Leste, February 9, 2006, accessed August 16, 2012, https://www.hrdag.org/resources/timor_chapter_graphs/timor_chapter_page_01.shtml.

68. Geoffrey Robinson, "*Rawan* Is as *Rawan* Does: The Origins of Disorder in New Order Aceh," *Indonesia* no. 66 (October 1998): 126–157; Tim Kell, *The Roots of Acehnese Rebellion* (Ithaca: Cornell Modern Indonesia Project, 1995).

69. Wanandi, "Indonesia."

70. See Justin V. Hastings, *No Man's Land: Globalization, Territory, and Clandestine Groups in Southeast Asia* (Ithaca: Cornell University Press, 2010), chapter 6.

71. For this, see Ibid., chapters 3–5.

72. Andrew MacIntyre, "Indonesia as a Poorly Performing State?" in *Short of the Goal: U.S. Policy and Poorly Performing States*, ed., Nancy Birdsall, Milan

Vaishnav and Robert Ayers (Washington, DC: Center for Global Development, 2006), 124.

73. Andrew Rosser, "Escaping the Resource Curse: The Case of Indonesia," *Journal of Contemporary Asia* 37, no. 1 (February 2007), 38.

74. Crouch, *The Army and Politics in Indonesia,* 23.

75. MacIntyre, "Indonesia as a Poorly Performing State?," 124.

76. Robinson, "Indonesia: On a New Course?," 226.

77. Steven A. Cook, *The Struggle for Egypt: From Nasser to Tahrir Square* (New York: Oxford University Press, 2012), 63.

78. Derek Hopwood, *Egypt: Politics and Society 1945–1981* (London: George Allen & Unwin, 1982), 76–8.

79. Tarek Osman, *Egypt on the Brink: From Nasser to Mubarak* (New Haven: Yale University Press, 2010), 45–6.

80. Hopwood, *Egypt,* 96–7.

81. On this see Christina Phelps Harris, *Nationalism and Revolution in Egypt: the Role of the Muslim Brotherhood* (The Hague: Mouton, 1964).

82. Afaf Lutfi Al-Sayyid Marsot, *A History of Egypt: From the Arab Conquest to the Present* (Cambridge: Cambridge University Press, 2007), 154.

83. Osman, *Egypt on the Brink,* 243.

84. Hopwood, *Egypt,* 105–6.

85. William B. Quandt, *Camp David: Peacemaking and Politics* (Washington, DC: Brookings Institution Press, 1986).

86. Figures are in historical US$ and include $344 million in loans. Compiled from United States Agency for International Development, "Foreign Assistance Data," accessed August 16, 2012, http://gbk.eads.usaidallnet.gov/data/.

87. Dilip Ratha, "Workers' Remittances: An Important and Stable Source of External Development Finance," in *Global Development Finance 2003: Striving for Stability in Development Finance,* vol. 1 (Washington, DC: World Bank, 2003), 159.

88. Marsot, *A History of Egypt,* 163–5.

89. Saad Eddin Ibrahim, *Egypt: Islam and Democracy* (Cairo: American University Press, 2002), 37.

90. Maye Kassem, *Egyptian Politics: The Dynamics of Authoritarian Rule* (Boulder: Lynne Rienner, 2004); Kevin Koehler, "Authoritarian Elections in Egypt: Formal Institutions and Informal Mechanisms of Rule," *Democratization* 15, no. 5 (2008): 974–90; Joshua Stacher, *Adaptable Autocrats: Regime Power in Egypt and Syria* (Palo Alto: Stanford University Press, 2012).

91. Kassem, *Egyptian Politics,* 30–6.

92. David D. Kirkpatrick, "On Eve of Vote, Egypt's Military Extends Its Power," *New York Times,* June 15, 2012; Ernesto Londoño and Leila Fadel, "Egypt's Generals Vow to Transfer Authority, but U.S. Officials Concerned About Power Grab," *The Washington Post,* June 18, 2012.

93. Ernesto Londoño, "Egypt's Morsi Replaces Military Chiefs in Bid to Consolidate Power," *The Washington Post,* August 12, 2012; "Crowds in Cairo praise

Morsi's army overhaul," *Al-Jazeera*, August 13, 2012; "English Text of President Morsi's New Egypt Constitutional Declaration," *Ahram Online*, August 12, 2012, accessed August 16, 2012, http://english.ahram.org.eg/NewsContent/1/64/50248/Egypt/Politics-/English-text-of-President-Morsis-new-Egypt-Constit.aspx.

94. Edmund Blair, "Egypt's Army Shows No Sign of Challenging Mohammed Morsi After He Dismisses Top Generals," *Reuters*, August 13, 2012; Henry Shull and Ingy Hassieb, "Egypt's Morsi Decorates Generals He Dismissed," *The Washington Post,* August 14, 2012; "President Consulted Army over Changes—General," *Reuters*, August 12, 2012.

95. Youssef Rakha, "Egypt Shows How Political Islam is at Odds with Democracy," *The New York Times* July 15, 2013, accessed July 24, 2013, http://www.nytimes.com/2013/07/16/opinion/global/egypt-shows-how-political-islam-is-at-odds-with-democracy.html?pagewanted=all&_r=0

96. Adnan R. Khan, "Egypt, Like Pakistan Before, is Making its Constitution a Work of Fiction," *The Globe and Mail*, November 28, 2012, accessed on December 13, 2012, http://www.theglobeandmail.com/commentary/egypt-like-pakistan-before-is-making-its-constitution-a-work-of-fiction/article5750498/; Thomas L. Friedman, "Egypt: The Next India or the Next Pakistan?," *New York Times*, December 15, 2012, accessed, December 18, 2012, http://www.nytimes.com/2012/12/16/opinion/sunday/friedman-egypt-the-next-india-or-the-next-pakista-.html?ref=thomaslfriedman&_r=1&.

97. "India, Bangladesh Ink Landmark Border Pact," *Deccan Herald*, September 6, 2011.

98. Richard F. Doner, Brian K. Ritchie and Dan Slater, "Systemic Vulnerability and the Origins of Developmental States; Northeast and Southeast Asia in Comparative Perspective," *International Organization* 59, no. 2 (April 2005), 328. See also Richard Stubbs, "Whatever Happened to the East Asian Developmental State? The Unfolding Debate," *The Pacific Review* 22, no. 1 (2009), 5–6; Adrian Leftwich, "Bringing Politics Back in: Towards a Model of the Developmental State," *The Journal of Development Studies* 31, no. 3 (February 1995): 405.

99. Doner *et al*, "Systemic Vulnerability," 328.

100. Hagen Koo, "The Interplay of State, Social Class, and World System in East Asian Development: The Cases of South Korea and Taiwan," in *The Political Economy of the New Asian Industrialism*, ed., Frederic C. Deyo (Ithaca: Cornell University Press, 1987), 172.

101. Sunhyuk Kim, "State and Civil Society in South Korea's Democratic Consolidation: Is the Battle Really Over?," *Asian Survey* 37, no. 12 (December 1997): 1135–44.

102. David Kuehn, "Democratization and Civilian Control of the Military in Taiwan," *Democratization* 15, no. 5 (December 2008): 870–890.

103. Lin Chen-Wei, "State Reformation and the Formation of a Newly Emerging Welfare State in Taiwan," *The Developing Economies* 42, no. 2 (June 2004): 176–97.

104. Doner *et al*, "Systemic Vulnerability," 341.
105. Young-Kwan Yoon, "South Korea in 1999: Overcoming Cold War Legacies," *Asian Survey* 40, no. 1 (January–February 2000), 166.
106. Yakub Halabi, "Protracted Conflict, Existential Threat and Economic Development," *International Studies* 46, no. 3 (July 2009), 319–48.
107. Nick Cullather, "'Fuel for the Good Dragon': The United States and Industrial Policy in Taiwan, 1950–1965," *Diplomatic History* 20, no. 1 (January 1996): 1.
108. Koo, "Interplay," 107–108.
109. Omar Noman, *Economic and Social Progress in Asia: Why Pakistan did not Become a Tiger* (Karachi: Oxford University Press, 1997), 176–7.
110. Atul Kohli, *State-Directed Development* (Cambridge: Cambridge University Press, 2004), 18; Stephan Haggard, *Pathways from the Periphery* (Ithaca: Cornell University Press, 1990), chapter 3; Bruce Cumings "The Origins and Development of the Northeast Asian Political Economy: Industrial Sectors, Product Cycles, and Political Consequences," *International Organization* 38, no. 1 (Winter 1984): 1–40.
111. Kohli, *State-Directed Development*, 27–36.
112. Tun-Jen Cheng, Stephan Haggard, and David Kang, "Institutions and Growth in Korea and Taiwan: The Bureaucracy," in *East Asian Development: New Perspectives*, ed. Yilmaz Akyuz (London: Frank Cass, 1999), 87.
113. Koo, "Interplay," 172.
114. Linda Weiss, "Governed Interdependence: Rethinking the Government-Business Relationship in East Asia," *The Pacific Review* 8, no. 4 (1995): 612.
115. Anne Booth, "Initial Conditions and Miraculous Growth: Why is South East Asia Different From Taiwan and South Korea?" *World Development* 27, no. 2 (February 1999): 301–21." Another study in a similar vein argues that the "successful developmental states in Korea and Taiwan were fundamentally based on relative income equality, and the equalization of income was radically achieved in the form of land reforms. In contrast, most Southeast Asian countries inherited colonial rule and, as a consequence, income inequality was perpetuated." Wonik Kim, "Rethinking Colonialism and the Origins of the Developmental State in East Asia," *Journal of Contemporary Asia* 39, no. 3 (August 2009): 396.
116. Alice H. Amsden, "Taiwan's Economic History: A Case for Etatisme and a Challenge to Dependency Theory," in *Toward a Political Economy of Development*, ed., Robert H. Bates (Berkeley: University of California Press, 1988), 142–175.
117. Koo, "Interplay," 171.
118. Booth, "Initial Conditions," South Korea had less than a thousand graduates under the Japanese occupation, but by 1959, this number reached 70,000 and by 1991 some 1.5 million Koreans were studying at higher education institutions. Education expenditures consumed some 10% of the GDP, a far cry from Pakistan's meager spending on education. Frank Gibney, *Korea's Quiet Revolution: From Garrison State to Democracy* (New York: Walker and Company, 1992), 4–5.

119. David Kang qualifies this judgment, arguing that moneyed interests did have an important influence on Korean politics in the Park era; it was just that the coherent state kept the influence of money in politics in check. After the shift to less coherent multi-party democracy, he argues, corruption was able to gain in strength. David C. Kang, "Bad Loans to Good Friends: Money Politics and the Developmental State in South Korea," *International Organization* 56, no. 1 (February 2002): 177–207. More generally, scholars do argue that the close relationship between the state and industrial conglomerates contributed to the Korean financial crisis of 1997: the belief that the state would protect them led Korea's banks and industrial conglomerates to make excessively risky moves. Stephan Haggard and Jongryn Mo, "The Political Economy of the Korean Financial Crisis," *Review of International Political Economy* 7, no. 2 (Summer 2000): 197–218. But this does not undermine the crucial role that the developmental state played in the previous 35 years of rapid growth.

120. Peter Evans, *Embedded Autonomy: States & Industrial Transformation* (Princeton: Princeton University Press, 1995), 52–3.

121. John Minns, "Of Miracles and Models: The Rise and Decline of the Developmental State in South Korea," *Third World Quarterly* 22, no. 6 (December 2001): 1025–43.

122. For an early assessment, see James Cotton, "From Authoritarianism to Democracy in South Korea," *Political Studies* 37, no. 2 (June 1989): 244–59. On Roh see Su-Hoon Lee, "Transitional Politics of Korea, 1987–1992: Activation of Civil Society," *Pacific Affairs* 66, no. 3 (Autumn 1993): 351–67. On Kim Young-sam see Sunhyuk Kim, "State and Civil Society in South Korea's Democratic Transition: Is the Battle Really Over?" *Asian Survey* 37, no. 12 (December 1997): 1135–44.

Chapter 8

1. Krishnadev Calamur, "Socks are Optional as Pakistan Grapples with Power Cuts," *National Public Radio*, May 21, 2013, accessed May 30, 2013, http://www.npr.org/blogs/parallels/2013/05/20/185664019/socks-are-optional-as-pakistan-grapples-with-power-cuts; Zafar Bhutta, "Fuel Shortage: Petroleum Ministry Warns of More Power Cuts in Summer Months," *The Express Tribune*, May 19, 2013, accessed May 30, 2013, http://tribune.com.pk/story/551207/fuel-shortages-petroleum-ministry-warns-of-more-power-cuts-in-summer-months/?print=true.

2. Mark Memmott, "In Pakistan, Sharif Turns to Unstable Nation's Dire Problems," *National Public Radio*, May 13, 2013, accessed May 30, 2013, http://www.npr.org/blogs/thetwo-way/2013/05/13/183558930/in-pakistan-sharif-turns-to-unstable-nations-dire-problems.

3. Charles Tilly, "War Making and State Making as Organized Crime," in *Bringing the State Back In*, ed. Peter B. Evans, Dietrich Rueschemeyer, and Theda Skocpol (Cambridge: Cambridge University Press, 1985), 171.

4. Kalevi J. Holsti, *The State, War, and the State of War* (Cambridge: Cambridge University Press, 1996), 117.

5. Victoria Tin-bor Hui, *War and State Formation in Ancient China and Early Modern Europe* (Cambridge: Cambridge University Press, 2005), 168.

6. Charles Tilly, *Coercion, Capital and European State* (Oxford: Blackwell, 1992), 195. See also, Charles Tilly, "Reflections on the History of European State-Making," in *The Formation of National States in Western Europe*, ed., Tilly (Princeton: Princeton University Press, 1975), 81.

7. Tilly, "War Making," 186; Anna Leander, "Wars and the Un-making of States: Taking Tilly Seriously in the Contemporary World," in *Contemporary Security Analysis and Copenhagen Peace Research*, ed. Stefano Guzzini and Dietrich Jung (London: Routledge, 2004), 78.

8. Peter Halden, "Unpacking the Warfare Thesis through the Holy Roman Empire," Paper Presented at the Post-Tilly Workshop, Center for Business and Politics, University of Copenhagen, October 2–4, 2009, 4–5.

9. John A. Hall, "The Tilly Thesis: Qualifications and Additions," Paper Presented at the Post-Tilly Workshop, Center for Business and Politics, University of Copenhagen, October 2–4, 2009, 1. Michael Mann sees three principal reasons for British decline, and these are common to other similar cases as well: (1) Competitors learn the techniques of power pioneered by the dominant state; (2) others gang up and finish it off; and (3) internal constraints make it difficult within the social structure that constrains further development. Michael Mann, *States, War and Capitalism: Studies in Political Sociology* (Oxford: Basil Blackwell, 1988), 211.

10. Michael Mann, Comments Made at the Conference on "Nationalism and War," McGill University, March 26, 2011; See also, Mann, *The Sources of Social Power*, vol. II (Cambridge: Cambridge University Press, 1993), 395.

11. Miguel Centeno, Comments Made at the Conference on "Nationalism and War," McGill University, March 26, 2011. See also, Barry R. Posen, "Nationalism, the Mass Army, and Military Power," *International Security* 18, no. 2 (Fall 1993): 80–124.

12. Leander, "Wars and the Un-making of States," 79.

13. World Economic Forum, *The Global Competitiveness Report, 2012–13*, 284, accessed November 30, 2012, http://www3.weforum.org/docs/WEF_GlobalCompetitivenessReport_2012-13.pdf.

14. *World Population to 2300* (New York; United Nations, 2004), accessed November 30, 2012, http://www.un.org/esa/population/publications/longrange2/WorldPop2300final.pdf.

15. Moeed W. Yusuf, "Youth and the Future," in *The Future of Pakistan*, ed., Stephen P. Cohen (Washington, DC: Brookings Institution Press, 2011), 264–265.

16. On this see, John E. Mueller, *Retreat from Doomsday: the Obsolescence of Major Wars* (New York: Basic Books, 1989).

17. Karen Rassler and William R. Thompson, "Rivalry, War and State-making in Less Developed Contexts" Paper Presented at the Annual Meeting of the International Studies Association, New York, February 2009, 13.

18. Interview, Nasir Jamal, "India Enjoys Veto Power over Pakistan's Progress," *The Dawn*, August 15, 2010.

19. Fareed Zakaria, *The Future of Freedom* (New York: W.W. Norton, 2003), 53.

20. For this, see Daron Acemoğlu and James Robinson, *Why Nations Fail* (New York: Crown, 2012).

INDEX

Aceh, 152, 164, 166, 167, 168
Afghanistan, 5, 11, 22, 23, 27
    Anglo-Afghan Wars (1839–42; 1878–81; 1919), 100
    civil conflict in, 58
    as "graveyard of empires," 100–101
    International Security Assistance Force mission in, 154
    Pakistan's policy toward, 64–65, 95, 103, 148, 185, 192, 193
    relations with Pakistan, 101–2
    resistance in, to direct rule, 100
    Soviet invasion of, 55–57, 119
    US offensive in, (2001), 61–62
Africa, 8
Afro-Asian movement, 46
Ahl-I Hadith, 144
Ahmad, Mirza Ghulam, 130, 138
Ahmadiyya (Ahmadis), 130, 131, 138, 139
Ahmed, Aziz, 48
Akbar, Jalal ud-din, 55, 97–98
Akbar, M. J., 106, 149
Akhund, Iqbal, 25, 106
AKP. *See* Justice and Development Party
Alavi, Hamza, 42–43, 88
Aligarh Muslim University, 99
alliance politics, 116

All-India Muslim League, 36, 37, 38–40, 42–43
All Pakistan Muslim League, 66
al-Qaeda, 14, 57, 58, 59, 61, 103, 120, 122, 141
al-Sisi, Abdul, 173
al-Wahhab, Muhammad ibn Abd, 143
Amnesty International, 134
ANP. *See* Awami National Party
A. Q. Khan network, 14–15, 17, 59, 120
Arab Spring, 172
arbitrator type, of praetorian state, 72
Argentina, 78, 196
Armitage, Richard, 61, 212fn.86
Army Welfare Trust, 87
Ashraf, Raja Pervez, 66, 77
Association of Southeast Asian Nations (ASEAN), 167
asymmetric warfare, 12, 44, 57, 89, 104, 110, 113
Atatürk, Mustafa Kemal, 32, 37, 137, 142, 153, 157, 159
Aurangzeb, 55, 98, 141
Aurora, Jagjit Singh, 51
Austria-Hungary, 7, 187
Awami League, 84
Awami National Party, 66
Aydin, Mustafa, 155
Azad Kashmir, 43–44

Babar, Nasirullah, 120
Babar, Zahir ud-din, 97
Baghdad Pact, 45
Bahadur Shah II, 98
Baharia Foundation, 87
Balkan states, 187
Baloch, 66, 132, 133–34
Balochistan, 133–34
Balochistan Liberation Army, 134
Balochistan Republican Army, 134
Baloch National Front, 134
Bangladesh, 51–52, 174–75, 180, 181,
    190. See also East Pakistan
Barelvis, 130, 143, 144
Barlow, Richard, 120
Basic Democracy, 75, 89
Beg, Mirza Aslam, 111
Bengal, 40
Bengal Army, 98
Benin, 19
Bhatia, Shyam, 60
Bhatti, Shahbaz, 63
Bhutto, Benazir, 66, 90, 143
    advancing Pakistan's Islamic
        character, 141
    assassination of, 63, 71
    becoming prime minister, 58
    contributing to Sunni dominance,
        130–31
    helping create terrorist
        organizations, 59
    hybrid government of, 77
    nuclear program under, 59–60
    placating the military, 85
    refusing to act on Kashmir, 69
    siding with the Taliban against, 59,
        120, 148
Bhutto, Zulfikar Ali, 48, 55, 63, 108
    assuming power, 84–85
    contributing to Islamization
        of Pakistan, 25, 27–28, 137–38
    contributing to Sunni dominance,
        130–31
    hanging of, 34, 71

hybrid government of, 77
jailing of, 54
on Kashmir, 69–70
launching nuclear weapons
    program, 52–53, 94
socialist ideology of, 53–54, 119
Bibi, Aaasia, 135
bin Laden, Osama, 1, 61, 64, 119, 121,
    122, 141, 144
bin Qasim, Mohammad, 97
Bismarck, Otto van, 187
blasphemy laws, 90, 135, 139, 142–43,
    147
Bogra, Muhammad Ali, 45, 46
border security, principles of, 58
Bourke-White, Margaret, 150
Brazil, 78, 177, 189, 196
Brezhnev, Leonid, 55
BRIC countries, 177
Britain, 8, 20, 21, 187
    in Egypt, 168
    India strategy of, principles of,
        99–100
    Pakistan's emergence and, 39–40
    ruling the Indian subcontinent,
        98–100
    wars with Afghanistan, 100
British East India Company, 98, 99
Bugti, Bugti Brahumdagh, 134
Bugti, Nawab Akbar, 134
Bulgaria, 187
Burgundy, 8, 187
Bush (George H. W.) administration,
    120
Bush (George W.) administration, 17,
    121

Camp David Agreements (1978–79),
    170, 171
Carter, Jimmy, 56
Carter administration, 119
Centeno, Miguel, 8
CENTO. See Central Treaty
    Organization

Central Asian republics, 192
Central Intelligence Agency, 17, 56, 57, 102, 147
Central Treaty Organization, 45, 117, 118
Chaudhry, Iftikhar Muhammad, 63
Chauhan, Prithvi Raj, 97
Chiang Kai-shek, 178
Chile, 78, 196
China, 44, 76, 176, 177, 180, 186, 188, 194
    aiding Pakistan's nuclear program, 59
    Bangladesh and, 175
    economic progress of, 33, 74
    and the Kashmir dispute, 47
    relations with India, 122, 123–24
    relations with Pakistan, 28, 30, 31, 71, 116, 122–25, 193
    relations with the US, 118, 151
    string of pearls strategy in the Indian Ocean, 124
China-India war (1962), 47, 122
CHP. *See* Republican People's Party
Churchill, Winston, 208n17
CIA. *See* Central Intelligence Agency
Clinton, Bill, 60–61, 114, 121
Clinton administration, 121
coercion, 35, 185
Cohen, Stephen P., 24, 71, 204n.30; 206n.47, 222n.62
Cold Start doctrine, 115
Cold War, 5, 57, 58, 116, 118, 176, 187
    Pakistan's role in, 18, 46, 56, 79, 117, 150–51
    Turkey in, 154
colonialism, Japanese, 178–79
Congress Party, 37–40, 88, 99, 105
conquest, wars of, 8
consociationalism, 35
Cripps, Stafford, 40
Cripps Mission, 40
CTO. *See* Central Treaty Organization
Cyprus, 152, 155

Dalai Lama, 123
Darul Islam, 166
Davutoğlu, Ahmet, 157
Delhi Sultanate, 97
Deng Xiaoping, 188
Deobandis, 129, 130, 131, 140, 144
development, 2–3, 6, 7, 9, 10, 11, 12, 14, 19, 20, 22, 32, 33, 34, 64, 81, 95, 153, 177, 179, 180, 186, 189, 193, 194–95; 196, 197; 202n.34
    rapidity of, 32–33
    war and, 7, 15
developmentalism, 189
developmental state, 3, 11, 15, 18, 23, 35, 55, 79, 158, 167, 173, 175, 178, 180, 181, 186, 188, 197, 201, n.26, 236, n.115, 237, n.119
developmental state strategy, 11, 16, 175, 181, 187, 188
Din-Ilahi, 98
drones, 90, 122
Dulles, John Foster, 117
Durand, Mortimer, 102
Durand Line, 100, 102
Durrani, Mahmud Ali, 210n49

East Pakistan, 12, 13, 22, 26, 49–50, 84, 108
    independence of, 51–52
    liberation movement in, US response to, 118
East Timor, 164, 166, 168
economics, as explanation for garrison state, 85–88
Egypt, 76, 151–52, 177, 180–81, 196, 229n4
    Pakistan compared to, 31, 168–74
    rentier economy of, 6
    sharia law in, attitude toward, 128–29
    US foreign aid to, 56, 119
Eisenhower, Dwight, 117
Eisenhower administration, 117
electoralist fallacy, 78

Enan, Sami, 173
Erdoğan, Recep Tayyip, 161–62
Eritrea, 189
Ethiopia, 189
EU. *See* European Union
Europe
    constant war in, and nation
        strength, 187
    formation of nation-states in, war
        and, 6–9
European Union, 155, 157, 161, 162

Failed State Index, 13
Fauji Foundation, 87
Federal Shariat Court, 140
foreign aid curse, 19
France, 8, 20, 168
Freedom House, 164
Free Officers Movement, 168
Fretilin independence movement, 166
Frontier Gandhi. *See* Khan, Khan
    Abdul Ghaffar
Frontier Works, 87

Gaddafi, Moammar, 18
Gandhi, Indira, 51, 118
Gandhi, Mohandas, 37, 99, 105
garrison state, 72–74, 78–79, 80, 81, 85,
    90–93, 175
Garver, John, 124
geostrategic curse, 126, 152
    in Egypt, 170–71
    in Pakistan, 5, 18, 19–22, 57, 117–18,
        126, 151, 180, 182, 196
Gerakan Aceh Merdeka, 166
Germany, 8, 20, 21, 161, 187, 199n1
Ghauri, Mohammad, 97
Ghazi, Tariq Waseem, 87
Ghazi, Waseem, 211n61
ghost schools, 146
Gilani, Yousaf Raza, 63, 65, 77
Global Competitiveness Index, 190
globalization, 189, 190
governance, liberal-democratic model
    of, 10

Government of India Act (1935), 38
Great Britain. *See* Britain
Great Game, 96
Greece, 150, 155, 187, 229n4
Green Book, 65, 76
Guatemala, 78
Guided Democracy, 164
Gül, Abdullah, 161
Gul, Hamid, 27
Gulf War, (1990–91), 154
Gürsel, Cemal, 159

Hamayotsu, Kikue, 164
Haqqani, Hussain, 26, 27, 77, 116
Haqqani, Jalaluddin, 147
Haqqani family, 62
Haqqani Network, 147
Hassan, Javed, 26
Headley, David, 81
Herbst, Jeffrey, 8
Hinduism, 135
Hindus, in Pakistan, 134–35
historical-cultural explanation, for
    garrison states, 81–82
Hobbesian worldview, 24, 35, 196
Holsti, Kal, 186
Hudood ordinance, 140
Human Rights Watch, 134
Huntington, Samuel, 83

IAEA. *See* International Atomic
    Energy Agency
ICS. *See* Indian Civil Service
IDA. *See* International Development
    Association
ideas, role of, in Pakistan, 23–31
IMF. *See* International Monetary
    Fund
import substitution policy, 42
inclusive capitalism, 178
India, 5, 11, 12–13, 177, 192, 194
    aggregate indicators in, compared to
        Pakistan, 108, 109
    Bangladesh and, 175
    corruption in, 189

defense modernization program in, 111–12
defense policy toward Pakistan, 110
defensive strategy of, toward Pakistan and Kashmir, 112
invasion of, through present Pakistan, 96
involved with East Pakistani independence, 51
Kargil Heights occupation and, 60–61
military capabilities of, 110–11, 124
military strategies of, 115
mindset in, 26
no-first-use policy of, 111
not becoming a garrison state, 82
Pakistan's peace process with, 65
Pakistan's relations with, 193
Pakistan's rivalry with, 5, 24, 26–27, 40–41, 94–95, 103–16, 185, 193
relations with China, 122, 123–24
relations with the US, 116–17, 121–22
responding to Pakistan's actions, 91
separatist movements in, 53
war with China, 47
War of Independence (1857), 98–99
wars with Pakistan, 12, 48–49, 108
Indian Civil Service, 42
Indonesia, 31, 76, 129, 151–52, 163–68, 180–81, 190, 196, 229n4
institutionalist explanation, for garrison states, 79–81
International Atomic Energy Agency, 17
International Development Association, 20
International Monetary Fund, 1, 20, 21, 31, 33, 71, 183, 186
Iqbal, Muhammad, 37–38, 127
Iran, 15, 17, 56, 59, 117, 120, 156
Iraq, 17, 59, 117, 156
Iraq war (2003), 154
ISI (Inter-Services Intelligence), 60, 70, 102, 120
and radicalization of Pakistan, 147
strategy of, for weakening India, 107, 125

supporting the mujahedeen, 57, 102
supporting the Taliban, 62, 64–65
training jihadists, 141
weakening democracy, 35, 80–81
Islam, 4. See also political Islam
invading India, 96–97
nationalism incompatible with, 136
national military strategy and, 141
in Pakistan, 14, 24, 25–26, 76. See also Pakistan, Islam-related subentries
populist interpretation of, 85
radical, effect on Pakistan's military
socialism and, 169
in Turkey, 159
war in, 27
Islamic Council, 139
Ismailis, 130
Israel, 11, 56, 74, 76, 119, 151, 157, 168–69, 170, 171, 229n4

Jadoon, Khalid, 143
Jahan, Rounaq, 49–50
Jahan, Shah, 98
Jahangir, Nurud-din, 98
Jaish-e-Mohammed (JeM), 59, 81, 147
Jalal, Ayesha, 131–32
Jamaat-e-Islami (JI), 136, 137, 139, 141, 167
Jamiat Ulema-e-Islam (JUI), 63
Jammu, 28
Japan, 20, 21, 32, 153, 178–79, 187
Javanese culture, 165
JeM. See Jaish-e-Mohammed
Jervis, Robert, 91
JI. See Jamaat-e-Islami
Jinnah, Muhammad Ali, 25, 37–41, 42–43, 105, 106, 127
on Pakistan's geostrategic importance, 150
using Islam to build Pakistan, 135–37
views on secularism, 41, 135–36
Jinnah Institute, 135
Jizya, 97, 98

Johnson (Lyndon B.) administration, 118
Joseph, John, 142
JUI. See Jamiat Ulema-e-Islam
Junejo, Mohammed Khan, 54
Justice and Development Party, 153, 158, 161

Kang, David, 237n119
Kant, Immanuel, 10
Kantian worldview, 24
Karaosmanoğlu, Ali, 157
Kargil Heights, 60–61, 69, 113–14, 121
Karmal, Babrak, 56
Karzai, Hamid, 61
Kashmir, 59, 108
    China as party to dispute over, 47
    Indian and Pakistani strategies toward, 112–13
    insurgency in, 119
    Pakistan's involvement in, 11, 12, 22, 28, 69, 89, 193–94
Kashmir War, first (1947–48), 43–44
Kayani, Ashfaq Parvez, 65, 79, 127
Kemalists, 136, 153, 157, 159
Kennedy, John F., 47, 118
Kennedy administration, 118
Khaja community, 136
Khalistan movement, 53
Khan, Abdul Qadeer, 17, 59–60. See also A. Q. Khan network
Khan, Agha, 130
Khan, Dost Mohammed, 100
Khan, Imran, 62, 90
Khan, Khan Abdul Ghaffar, 101
Khan, Khan Abdul Wali, 101, 127
Khan, Liaquat Ali, 45, 84, 106
Khan, Mohammad Ayub, 28, 49, 83
    alienating the Baloch, 134
    Basic Democracy program of, 75, 89
    dismissing President Mirza, 34, 46–47
    economic progress in era of, 50
    and the Turkish model, 163
    on joining alliances, 117
    launching offensive in Kashmir, 69–70
    resignation of, 51
    secular turn of, 137
Khan, Muhammad Zarfrullah, 138
Khan, Syed Ahmed, 99
Khan, Yahya, 51, 84
Khan Research Laboratories, 59. See also A. Q. Khan network
Khilafat movement (1919–24), 37
Khomeini, Ruhollah, 56
Khoso, Mir Hazar Khan, 183
Khyber Pass, 96
Kim Young-sam, 181
Kirişci, Kemal, 158
Kissinger, Henry, 118, 151
Kohli, Atul, 32
Koo, Hagen, 176
Kurdistan Workers' Party, 156
Kurds, 155–56

Lahore peace process, 60
Lashkar e-Taiba (LeT), 59, 81, 147
Latin America, 8
Legal Framework Order of 1970, 51
Leghari, Farooq, 60
legitimacy, for a state, 10, 11
Leng, Russell, 91
LeT. See Lashkar e-Taiba
LFO. See Legal Framework Order of 1970
Libya, 5–6, 15, 18, 59, 120, 170
Linz, Juan, 77–78
Lockean worldview, 24

Madagascar, 19
madrassas, 55, 89, 90, 130, 139, 144–47
Mahmud of Ghazni, 97
Majid, Tariq, 76
Makarios III, 155
Malaysia, 59, 190
Maldives, 26
Mali, 19

Malik, Akhtar, 48
Malik, S. K., 27
Manekshaw, Sam, 51
Mann, Michael, 187, 238n9
Mansour, Adli, 173
Masih, Rimsha, 143
Mawdudi, Abdul Ala, 136
McMahon Line, 123
Mead, Walter Russell, 193
Meiji restoration, 153, 178
middle class, role of, in democracy,
    87–88
militarism, 73, 81, 106
militarization, 91
millet system, 160
Mirza, Iskander, 34, 45, 46, 50, 83
MMA. *See* Mutahhidah Majlis
    Amal
Mohajirs, 132–33
Muhammad, Malik Ghulam, 45
Montenegro, 187
Moore, Barrington, 87–88
Morocco, 129
Morsi, Mohamed, 173, 229n4
Mountbatten, Louis, 41
MQM. *See* Muttahida Qaumi
    Movement
Mubarak, Hosni, 172, 173, 174
Mughal Empire, 25, 97–98, 105–6,
    204n30
mujahedeen, 57–58, 102, 120
Musharraf, Pervez, 90, 121, 125
    abdicating power, 168
    as Ataturk of Pakistan, 142, 163
    intending to make Pakistan a
        moderate Islamic country, 142
    planning operations in Kashmir, 69
    placed under house arrest, 66–67
    placing civilian positions under
        military control, 75
    protecting A. Q. Khan, 17, 60
    staging coup against Sharif, 34, 61
    suspending the constitution,
        62–63

Muslim Brotherhood, 169, 171, 172,
    173, 174, 229n4
Muslim League, 84, 99, 105, 191
Muslim rule, 25
Mutahhidah Majlis Amal, 142
Mutiny, the, 98–99
Muttahida Qaumi Movement, 66, 132
Mutual Aid Assistance agreement, 45

Naqvi, Saifi Ahmad, 76
Nasr, Vali, 128, 130–31
Nasser, Gamal Abdel, 117, 168–69, 173,
    174
National Defense College, 76
national integration, 35
National Logistics Cell, 86
national security explanation, for
    garrison states, 78–79
national security state, 73–74
nation-building, 35
NATO. *See* North Atlantic Treaty
    Organization
Nazimuddin, Khawaja, 45, 50
Nehru, Jawaharlal, 46, 47, 82, 105, 117
Netherlands, the, 7
Nigeria Gabon, 19
Nixon, Richard, 118, 151
Nixon administration, 52, 118
NLC. *See* National Logistics Cell
nonaligned movement, 46, 117, 118
North Atlantic Treaty Organization,
    62, 154, 155, 157
North Korea, 15, 17, 59–60, 120, 176, 189
Northern Alliance, 59, 65, 193
Northern Tier of Defense project, 117
Northwest Frontier Province,
    significance of, 100
Nuclear Non-Proliferation Treaty, 123
nuclear weapons, and India-Pakistan
    relations, 111. *See also* Pakistan,
    nuclear weapons program of

Obama, Barack, 64
Obama administration, 90, 121–22

Objectives Resolution (1949), 129, 136, 139
Öcalan, Abdullah, 156
Operation Gibraltar, 48, 70
Operation Parakram, 115
Osman, Tarek, 170
Ottoman Empire, 157, 160
Ozel, Necdet, 162

Pakhtunistan, 101
Pakistan
    Afghanistan policy of, 55–57, 95, 148, 192, 193
    aggregate indicators in, compared to India, 108
    alliance support for, 116, 117
    ambitions of, unrealistic, 104–5
    antidemocratic tendencies in, 44–45
    asymmetric strategy of, 44, 112–13, 119
    blasphemy laws in, 90, 135, 139, 142–43, 147
    challenging India's deterrent capabilities, 110
    civilian departments in, under military control, 75–76
    civilian weakness in, 13, 45–46, 82–85
    civil-military relations in, 1, 75, 122,
    civil society in, 30, 62, 63, 88–89, 128, 141, 180, 196
    coercion in, use of, 185–86
    colonial legacy of, 81–82
    compensation in, for military, 86
    conflicts in, 1–2, 3, 21–22, 23, 127–28, 130
    corruption in, 90
    coup threat in, 77, 78
    defense spending in, 46, 124
    democracy in, 71, 74–75, 83–85
    demographic challenges in, 190
    development in, 3, 9, 193
    development of, 12–15
    discrimination in, against minorities, 134–35
    domestic instability in, 1–2, 3
    double games, 21, 62, 119, 154, 192, 195, 197
    economic activities in, controlled by military, 86–88
    economic condition of, 1
    economic progress in, 50, 180
    economic reforms in, 140
    education system in, 76–77, 145–47, 189–90
    Egypt compared to, 168–74
    elites in, 3, 5, 11, 18–19, 21–24, 30, 53, 81
    emergence of, 36–44
    entitlement to power in, 106
    establishment of, core ideas of, 24–28
    ethnic cleavages in, 131–35
    evolution of, as nation-state, 36
    extremism in, 103
    extremist groups in, 35
    fearing Indian hegemony in the subcontinent, 104
    first constitution of, 136–37
    foreign aid to, 1, 6, 20–21
    foreign policy of, 147, 152
    as garrison state, 71–74, 75, 78–93
    geostrategic curse of, 57, 117–18, 182, 186, 195
    geostrategic significance of, 3, 5–6, 18, 19, 54, 61, 94–95, 117, 119, 125
    Global Competitiveness Index ranking of, 190
    goals of, in Afghanistan, 64–65
    Hobbesian worldview of, 196
    hyper-realpolitik worldview of, 3–4, 22, 28, 58, 91, 102–3, 152, 167
    Indonesia compared to, 163, 165–68
    internal conflicts in, 103, 133, 135
    Islamic extremism in, 128–29, 152
        See also Pakistan, religious divisions in
    Islamic identity of, 4, 14, 127–29, 131
    Islamization of, 55, 57, 120, 137–49

and Kargil Heights, occupation of,
    60–61, 69, 113–14, 121
lacking plans for long-term regional
    stabilization, 103
lacking public educational system,
    145–46
land reform in, 53, 88
legal reforms in, 140
media in, 66
middle class in, 63, 88–90, 142–43,
    146–47
militarism in, 106
military in, 22–23, 29, 30, 34–35,
    54–55, 70–73, 91, 160–61
military capabilities of, 110–11, 112,
    123, 124
military rule in, 34–35, 46–47
military's Islamization in, 140–41
modernization in, unevenness of,
    133
nationalization in, 53
national unity in, 12–13, 95
nationhood and identity of, 4
nostalgia in, 204n28
nuclear first-use policy of, 111
nuclear proliferation and, 14–15
nuclear weapons program of, 2,
    52–53, 55, 57, 59–60, 94, 107,
    111, 114–15, 120, 123
offensive-defensive strategy of, 112
peace process with India, 65
political parties in, antipathy
    toward, 89
power supply in, 67, 183
preoccupied with military security,
    2–5
protecting Muslim interests, 25–26,
    125, 127
provincial autonomy in, demands
    for, 132
relations with Afghanistan, 5, 101–2.
    See also Pakistan, Afghanistan
    policy of
relations with China, 122–25, 193

relations with India, 5, 11, 12–13,
    193. See also Pakistan, rivalry
    with India; Pakistan, wars with
    India
relations with the Taliban, 61–62,
    64–65, 102–3
relations with the US, 46, 64,
    117–20, 121
religious factions in, 128, 129–35
remittances to, 20
as rentier state, 18, 22, 116, 186
response of, to East Pakistan
    independence, 51–52
rivalry with India, 40–41, 94–95,
    103–16, 193
schools in, 146
sectarianism in, 103
sharia law in, 90, 128–29
social divisions in, 14
social indicators, 20
socialism in, 53–54
soldiers in, unrealistic view of, 92
South Korea compared to, 175–80
structural constraints on, 180
structural weakness of, 41–42
Sunni domination of, 129–30
supporting Indian separatist
    movements, 53
supporting the mujahedeen, 57–58
Taliban control in, 63–64
Taliban-inflicted violence in, 183
Talibanization of, 65
tax collections in, 20
transformation of, 191–97
transnational terrorism in, 14
treatment of non-Muslim minorities
    in, 134–35
Turkey compared to, 153–63
undermining Indian unity, 107
Wahhabi influence in, 143–46
war-making in, 2, 186
as warrior state, 2, 3–4, 28, 43,
    47–48, 57, 59, 70, 95, 104, 181,
    184, 194

Pakistan (*cont.*)
  wars with India, 12, 48–49, 108
  youth in, 90, 189–90
  zero sum perspective in, related to
      India, 125
  Zia coup in, 54–55
Pakistan Muslim League, 58, 142
Pakistan Muslim League-Nawaz, 66,
    67, 183
Pakistan National Alliance, 54, 137
Pakistan People's Party, 51, 54, 55,
    58–59, 66, 84, 142, 191
Pakistan's Dirty War, 134
Pakistani Taliban, 66, 67, 147, 192
Pancasila (five principles) (Indonesia),
    163–64, 165
Park Chung-hee, 177, 179
Pashtuns, 101–2, 132
Perlmutter, Amos, 72
Philippines, the, 6, 181
PKK. *See* Kurdistan Workers' Party
PML. *See* Pakistan Muslim League
PML-N. *See* Pakistan Muslim
    League-Nawaz
PNA. *See* Pakistan National Alliance
Point Four program, 117
Poland, 187
political Islam, 128, 129, 141–48, 159,
    180
Portugal, 7, 187
power, as Muslim birth right, myth
    of, 106
Powers, Gary, 151
PPP. *See* Pakistan People's Party
praetorian state, 72
princely states, 99–100
PTI. *See* Tehreek-i-Insaf
Punjab, 40, 81–82
  and military culture, 81–82

Qadri, Mumtaz, 143
Qadri, Tahirul, 66
Quit India Movement (1942), 40, 99
Quranic Concept of War, The (Malik), 27

Rahman, Sheikh Mujibur, 51
Rais, Rasul, 120
Rann of Kutch conflict (1965), 91
Rashid, Ahmed, 59, 104
Rashytriya Swayamsevak Sangh (RSS),
    107
Rasler, Karen, 191
Reagan, Ronald, 56
Reagan administration, 119, 120
realpolitik, 3–4. *See also* hyper-
    realpolitik worldview
Rehman, Hamoodur, 51
religious education, 160. *See also*
    madrassas
rentier state, 18, 186
Republican People's Party, 161
resource curse, 5–6, 19, 167, 186
revenge, 53, 92
Rhee, Syngman, 178, 179
Rice, Condoleezza, 121
rivalry, 191. *See also* Pakistan, rivalry
    with India
Rizvi, Hasan-Askari, 92
Roh Tae-woo, 181
Ross, Robert, 124
Rosser, Andrew, 167
RSS. *See* Rashytriya Swayamsevak
    Sangh
Rueschemeyer, Dietrich, 88
ruler type, of praetorian state, 72
Russia, 96, 100, 177, 192
Rustow, Dankwart, 157

Sabri, Ali, 170
Sadat, Anwar, 169–74
Saudi Arabia
  providing aid to Egypt, 170
  providing aid to Pakistan, 1, 30, 31,
      71, 119, 186
  resource curse of, 5–6
  supporting the mujahedeen, 57
  supporting Wahhabism, 55,
      144
Sayeed, Khalid Bin, 35

SCAF. *See* Supreme Council for the Armed Forces
Schofield, Julian, 91
SEATO. *See* Southeast Asia Treaty Organization
sectarianism, militant, 145
secularism, evolution to, in Turkey, 153
security dilemma, 28, 205–6n46
September 11, 2001, attacks of, 61–62, 121
Serbia, 187
Shaheen Foundation, 87
Shaikh, Farzana, 106
sharia law, 55, 90, 128–29, 142, 166
Sharif, Nawaz, 63, 66, 183, 191, 192
  coup against, 34, 61
  exile of, 71
  hybrid government of, 77
  introducing sharia law amendment, 142
  Kargil Heights occupation and, 60–61, 69, 114
  Lahore peace process and, 60, 125
  ordering nuclear tests, 60, 94
  peace initiatives with India, 67
Shastri, Lal Bahadur, 47, 49
Shias, 130, 131
Shuja, Shah, 100
Siddiqa, Ayesha, 86–87
Sierra Leone, 20
Sinai, 170
Sindh, 132–33
Sindhis, 132, 133
Singh, Hari, 43
Singh, Jaswant, 121
Singh, Manmohan, 125, 175
single-resource economies, 19
Sino-Indian War (1962), 47, 122
social revolution, 29–30
Somalia, 189
South Africa, 59, 189
South Asia
  China's policy in, 124
  conflict in, inevitability of, 126

extreme Islamic ideas introduced to, 55
history of, before Muslim invasions, 76
invasions of, 97
Islam's spread to, 135
Muslim rule in, 25
Pakistan's emergence in, 36
US policy toward, 122
Southeast Asia Treaty Organization, 45, 117, 118
South Korea, 11, 151, 181, 196
  economic development in, 33, 74, 152, 188, 189, 190–91
  Pakistan compared to, 31–32, 175–80, 181, 229n4
  US policy in, 31
Soviet Union, 7, 8–9, 55–58, 117, 123, 150–51, 170
Spain, 7, 187
Special Communications Organization, 87
Sri Lanka, 26
state authority, bureaucratic conception of, 80
state strength, 8–11, 33
state-strength dilemma, 10, 186
State of the Taliban (NATO), 62
status, importance of, for Pakistan, 95–96
Stepan, Alfred, 77–78
Stephens, Evelyne Huber, 88
Stephens, John D., 88
strategic depth, 23, 27, 102–3, 115
strategic parity, 103–4, 105, 107–8, 114, 116, 118, 122
Suez Canal, 168
Sufism, 131, 143
Suharto, 163, 164, 165, 166, 167
suicide terrorists, 62, 145, 147
Sukarno, 117, 163, 164
Sunnis, 129, 130
Supreme Council for the Armed Forces, 172–73

Sweden, 7
Syria, 156, 157, 170, 177

Taiwan, 151, 188, 196
    economic development of, 11, 33, 74,
        152, 189, 190–91
    Pakistan compared to, 11, 31, 175–80,
        181, 229n4
Talbott, Strobe, 121
Talib, Ali ibn Abu, 130
Taliban, 14, 148
    control of, 121
    controlling regions of Afghanistan,
        64
    creation of, 58
    fighting Soviet invasion of
        Afghanistan, 119
    mujahedeen at core of, 57, 120
    occupying Pakistani territory, 13
    Pakistani, 66, 67, 147, 192
    Pakistan's relations with, 5, 59,
        61–65, 102–3
    Pakistan taking on, 191
    Saudi relations with, 144
    US attacks on, 122
Tantawi, Mohamed Hussein, 173
Tanzeemaat Madaris Deeniya, 146
Tanzim-ul-Madaris Ahle Sunnat, 146
Taseer, Salmaan, 63, 90, 142
Tashkent Declaration, 49
Tehreek-i-Insaf, 66
Tehreek-i-Taliban. See Taliban,
    Pakistani
Thompson, William, 191
Tibet, 123
Tilly, Charles, 7, 184–85, 186–87
Timur, 97
trading state strategy, 74, 175, 188,
    189
Treaty of Gandamak, 100
Treaty of Lausanne, 155
Truman administration, 117
truncated asymmetry, in India-Pakistan
    relations, 108, 116, 126

Turkey, 76, 117, 150, 151, 196
    foreign policy of, 152
    Pakistan compared to, 31–32, 153–63,
        180–81, 229n4
    US foreign aid to, 56

Ulama-i-Hind, 136
United Arab Emirates, 59, 144
United Kingdom. See Britain
United Nations, 101, 104, 155
United States, 44, 74
    drone campaign by, 90, 122
    entering Afghanistan after 9/11,
        61–62
    foreign aid of, 1, 6, 20–21, 56, 118,
        152, 154, 163, 170, 176, 177–78
    foreign policy of, 30–31
    Indonesia's cooperation with, 167
    navy of, 1, 64
    relations with China, 118, 151
    relations with Egypt, 170
    relations with India, 116–17, 121–22
    relations with Pakistan, 1, 6, 17–18,
        30–31, 46, 49, 61–62, 64, 71,
        116, 117–20, 121, 171
    responding to East Pakistan
        liberation movement, 118
    responding to Soviet invasion of
        Afghanistan, 56–57
United States Agency for International
    Development (USAID), 31, 178
US Commission on International
    Religious Freedom, 145

Vajpayee, Atal Bihari, 60, 69, 125
Vietnam War (1959–75) 181

Wafq-ul-Madaris, 146
Wahhabism, 55, 143–46
Wahid, Adburrahman, 164, 167–68
war
    asymmetric, 44
    constant, effects of, 187, 188
    degenerative effects of, on states, 7–8

development and, 15
nation-building and, 6–9, 151–52
preparation for, 6–7, 15, 73
racketeering aspect of, 184–85
state strength and, 8–11
"War Directive No. 5," 113
warrior states, 5, 9, 28, 104, 151, 176,
    181, 197
    pathologies of, 29
    trap of, 184
    self-destruction of, 188–89
Warsaw Pact, 57
WB. *See* World Bank
Weiner, Myron, 35
Wikileaks, 62
Wiranto, 164
World Bank, 1, 20, 21, 31, 71, 186

Yousafzai, Malala, 64

Zaidi, Akbar, 134
Zakat tax, 140
Zardari, Asif Ali, 63, 66, 67, 77, 90,
    125, 135, 191
Zardari, Bilwal Bhutto, 66
Zia-ul-Haq, Muhammad, 121, 128
    bargaining with the US, 56–57
    death of, 58
    elections under, 75
    and the Islamization of Pakistan, 25,
        26, 138–41, 159
    military takeover of, 34, 85, 119, 131,
        137–38
    staging coup over Zia, 54–55
Zina ordinance, 140